ASIA'

MW01077198

The Drivers Behind the World's Most Exciting Growth Story

Brook Taylor and **Sam Korsmoe**

Foreword by

Carlyle A. Thayer

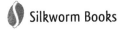

Silkworm Books

ISBN 978-616-215-201-6 (Paperback)
ISBN 978-616-215-202-3 (e-book)

© 2023 by Silkworm Books
All rights reserved

No part of this publication may be reproduced, stored in a retrieval system, or transmitted, in any form or by any means, electronic, mechanical, photocopying, recording or otherwise, without the prior permission in writing of the publisher.

First edition published in 2023 by
Silkworm Books
430/58 M. 7, T. Mae Hia, Chiang Mai 50100, Thailand
info@silkwormbooks.com
www.silkwormbooks.com

Cover Design and Art Direction: A. Salisbury

Typeset in Minion Pro 10.5 pt. by Silk Type
Printed and bound in the United States by Lightning Source

*For updated information and discussion on Vietnam's economy, please check
www.AsiasRisingStar.com*

DEDICATIONS

For Vietnam.
The country that has given me and my family so much.
Brook Taylor

To the legions of people who have made and are making
a difference for Vietnam.
Sam Korsmoe

ACKNOWLEDGMENTS

First, my heartfelt thanks to Sam, my co-author, who turned my original ideas into a coherent and compelling narrative and contributed many of his personal experiences and observations that enriched the discussion. I also want to thank Rebecca, my wife and unofficial editor, who patiently read the manuscript multiple times and constantly challenged me to ensure our manuscript was concise and comprehensible to a broad audience. I also want to thank my VinaCapital colleagues for creating a stimulating work and research environment and for the source of many ideas in this book. Thanks also to the many people I have met and worked with in Vietnam who have shared their knowledge and perspectives with me.

Finally, I want to thank my friends and acquaintances who have patiently listened to me, at dinner or over a beer, espouse my ideas about Vietnam. Their positive feedback encouraged me to write this book so that the stories could be shared with everyone.

Brook Taylor

For over 30 years, I have had a front-row seat to Vietnam's development and have met many people who have positively impacted this country. They are too numerous to name and thank individually, but I could have never completed this book without them. I also want to thank my teachers at the University of Washington and Vietnam Language Studies, my business colleagues, my son Colter who was born in Vietnam, my Vietnam friends, my Montana family, and most especially those like Thao H. and the Cungs who have become part of my family in Vietnam. Thank you all.

Three years ago, Brook Taylor shared that he had "an idea for a book" and asked if I was interested in working on it with him. The book put us on a three-year journey of discovery that I probably would have never had the opportunity to take. I thank Brook for his confidence and support on this incredible journey to help people better understand this amazing country.

Sam Korsmoe

CONTENTS

FOREWORD

by

Carlyle A. Thayer

From the moment I finished reading the initial proposal by co-authors Brook Taylor and Sam Korsmoe for a book on Vietnam as Asia's next Tiger Economy, I became an ardent supporter of this initiative. I have been visiting, researching, and writing about Vietnam for the past fifty-five years. My focus was on the recent past and present in Vietnam and rarely did I venture to forecast developments a few years into the future.

As I read various drafts of *Vietnam: Asia's Rising Star*, I was prompted to reassess how I had framed my knowledge and experience about contemporary Vietnam and compare it with theirs. I was then led to engage intellectually with the co-author's central concern: Does Vietnam have what it takes to become Asia's next Tiger Economy, and, if so, what factors will enable it to do so?

Taylor and Korsmoe bring together more than fifty-seven years of experience living and working in Vietnam. On this basis that they explore what Vietnam's future will be. *Vietnam: Asia's Rising Star* is a riveting and stimulating treatise on the drivers behind Asia's next Tiger Economy.

The approach that the authors employ transcends normal academic discourse and disciplinary methodologies. They opt to look beyond economic models and take an interdisciplinary overview based on rigorous deductive reasoning. They extrapolate key themes from Vietnam's geography, history, culture, and government to mould this overview. They then incorporate into their analysis the views of ordinary Vietnamese men and women they interviewed. This expanded interdisciplinary and eclectic approach provides a stimulating prologue to the main part of *Vietnam: Asia's Rising Star*.

Taylor and Korsmoe apply a rigorous methodology by developing, evaluating, and testing the metrics for their two-part central hypothesis:

(1) Vietnam is the next Tiger Economy of Asia, and (2) it will grow and develop in a similar way to how South Korea and Taiwan grew as the Tiger Economies of their era. For the first part of their analysis, the co-authors identified key metrics associated with South Korea and Taiwan that defined them as Tiger Economies. Vietnam is measured against these metrics.

For the second part of their analysis, Taylor and Korsmoe introduce additional metrics to select pertinent case studies. Six wide-ranging case studies make the final cut, ranging from education; leapfrog technology; the role of women; tourism, cuisine, art, and Olympic Dreams; to value-added agriculture and public works.

The case studies draw on data from Taiwan, South Korea, and elsewhere for comparative purposes. The analysis of each case study is evaluated through a series of testing tools. The result is a finely crafted qualitative assessment. The reader is literally invited to add their perspective to this process and decide whether the co-authors have made their case. *Vietnam: Asia's Rising Star* concludes with a chapter entitled Vietnam in 2050 with a positive, forward-looking, and compelling account of the factors that will influence Vietnam's rise.

Vietnam: Asia's Rising Star will fill a lacuna in the literature on Vietnam because it is interdisciplinary, contemporary, and forward-looking. There is no book on the market that fills this gap. This book will appeal to an extremely wide audience because it is original and rigorous in its approach and superbly well-written. *Vietnam: Asia's Rising Star* should be read by anyone with interest in Vietnam—students at all levels, academics of whatever discipline, diplomats in or about to be posted to Vietnam, government aid workers and NGOs, tourists, investors and financial analysts, overseas Vietnamese, and anyone else with an interest in the future of Asia.

Carlyle A. Thayer
Emeritus Professor
University of New South Wales,
Canberra
August 2023

PREFACE

In the months prior to the COVID-19 pandemic, we (Brook Taylor from New Zealand and Sam Korsmoe from the United States) launched a research project about the future of Vietnam. Collectively, we have been living, working in, and studying Vietnam for more than fifty-seven years. We have read about and, more importantly, participated in the 'Vietnam Growth Story' that has spanned the past three decades. Despite this long-term growth trend, there are few published works that explains how and why Vietnam has grown and developed. As a result, the 'Vietnam Growth Story' is not easily understood even by those who live and work in the country. We believed the time was right for a new and comprehensive look at Vietnam and where it is heading. We had a basic question we wanted to answer: 'Is Vietnam undergoing a flash of development that will eventually die out or are the foundations for long-term, equitable growth now being poured?' This is an exceptionally difficult question, but the results of our research into it are within the pages of this book.

We began our research journey at about the same time that the COVID-19 virus began its deadly journey across the world. This meant we were forced to adjust our research methods several times as travel restrictions and lockdowns impacted our ability to schedule interviews and conduct other types of field research. The first adjustment began in March 2020 due to what we call 'COVID I,' which Vietnam handled well compared to most countries worldwide. The second adjustment started about a year later, in May 2021, and by mid-2022 had largely played itself out. We call this 'COVID II' and it featured the much more contagious Delta variant of COVID-19. It also included the Omicron variant, which was less deadly but spread more rapidly despite many people having already been vaccinated. These two variants hit Vietnam as viciously as COVID I hit the rest of the world. Although tragic and for the most part over, COVID I and COVID II provided additional insight into how equipped Vietnam was to overcome a new and major challenge of the modern world. It also showed Vietnamese leaders' pragmatic nature, which was most clearly revealed with the government's decision to 'live with COVID' rather than to try and pursue a zero COVID strategy.[1] The pandemic became another means to test the hypothesis, and we have included that analysis in this book.

We have extensive experience of living and working in Vietnam, but we are not epidemiologists adept at understanding diseases, nor are we economists working for multilateral institutions or journalists working for any media organization. Part of the challenge when writing a book about Vietnam's economic and social development is the plethora of pundits who throw out sound-bite theories and models of what Vietnam is doing. Vietnam, say the pundits, is following 'the China model,' 'the authoritarian model,' 'the free trade and investment model,' 'the preserve-the-Party model,' and 'the Poster Boy for the World Bank model,' among others. We feel these explanations are often agenda-driven and do not adequately explain what has happened and what is happening in the country. We had no agenda other than to try and explain what we thought had been happening over the past 25–30 years that we have been living and working in Vietnam. More importantly, we wanted to try and understand the future. Above all, we wanted to get a sense of what Vietnam will be like in the decades from 2020 to 2050.

How can such a research goal be obtained amid a global pandemic, especially as it is not only about COVID-19? Geopolitics, climate change, new technologies, growing nationalist movements in many countries, the Russian invasion of Ukraine, and potentially a Cold War between China and the United States in which Vietnam might be asked to choose sides, has complicated this research quest. Although we had no agenda, we did have to create a road map to study and then report on the future of Vietnam.

Our means of doing this was to test a hypothesis. The hypothesis had two parts. Part 1 asked whether Vietnam is, was, or will be a 'Tiger Economy.' We developed specific metrics to define, measure, and then test this question. Part 2 then asked whether Vietnam will grow and develop in the same way that

---

1. Government Resolution No. 128/NQ-CP, October 11, 2021.

South Korea and Taiwan did when they were 'Tiger Economies' in the 1980s and 1990s. Both countries survived and thrived in their respective postwar, postcolonial environments, and within a period of fifty years became rich and joined the list of wealthy nations.

We recognize that the environment of South Korea and Taiwan in the 1980s and 1990s is not entirely comparable to Vietnam in the twenty-first century. There are many differences and making a direct comparison is foolhardy. We did not attempt to, and never could, make an apples-to-apples comparison, but we felt it was appropriate that our hypothesis contain a basic and compelling question: 'Can Vietnam do the same thing? Can it grow and develop from 2020 to 2050 in a similar way to how South Korea and Taiwan grew from 1980 to 2000?'

Why not compare Vietnam to its Southeast Asian neighbors, or perhaps to some other emerging market country in the world, such as contemporary China which is also transitioning from a command economy to a market economy, or to Japan of the 1950s and 1960s which offers a good example of a postwar, rags-to-riches success story? There are two main reasons we selected South Korea and Taiwan as the comparative case study countries for this book. The first is a cultural argument and the second a historical argument based on the 1980s and 1990s successes of these Tiger Economy countries and how they have become high-income nations today. We expand on these two issues in Chapter 1.

This book comprises twelve chapters, and within one of those chapters are six case studies. We begin with our hypothesis and defend the merits of this approach. We then cover some of the key events from Vietnamese history, followed by an analysis of the cultural roots of this history. We focus on the Doi Moi ('renovation') policies of the late 1980s and 1990s, which set the stage for the first steps of Vietnam's opening to the world and established the foundation for what we call 'the point of no return' in the mid-2000s. This was when Vietnam committed itself to free trade as its primary means to grow and develop its economy. This step culminated with Vietnam's entry into the World Trade Organization, on January 1, 2007.

Chapters 1–6 serve as the foundation for our research. We then explore the core questions involved with the hypothesis. First is the definition of a 'Tiger Economy' and whether Vietnam is one. We then introduce some of the key reasons why South Korea and Taiwan were Tiger Economies in the 1980s and 1990s and how they were able to leverage those advantages to break out of the

Middle-Income Trap and join the ranks of high-income nations by 2000. The leaders of those countries had several 'tools' that they effectively leveraged to help their countries achieve success. In Chapter 9 we examine the additional 'tools' (we call them 'cards' in this book) that Vietnam has and assess how they will contribute to Vietnam's growth from 2020 to 2050. The six case studies that follow in Chapter 10 offer evidence of the Vietnamese cards in action: education, technology, public works, agriculture, sports, tourism, cuisine, and social issues like the role of women. Each topic is part of a trend in Vietnam that *might facilitate* Vietnam's replication of the success of South Korea and Taiwan of the 1980s and 1990s.

In Chapters 11 and 12 we look to the future. We project Vietnam's growth from 2020 to 2050. We consider what can go wrong and what kinds of issues Vietnam's leaders, investors, partners, and citizens should be aware of in the 2020s and 2030s that might alter, prevent, or delay current growth trends.

We wrote this book with a broad readership in mind, initially with a focus on students, foreign investors, NGOs, government workers, and overseas Vietnamese. As the book and its themes matured, we realized that it would also be an important resource for local Vietnamese who wanted to better understand their own country's long-term potential. Whether Vietnam replicates the South Korea and Taiwan experience or not, coming close will still provide a compelling story that is worth documenting.

The Vietnam of today is a young country. The median age of Vietnamese is around thirty-two years. The country has only experienced peace and independence since 1990, even though it was unified after the end of the American War in April 1975. Due to the hardship and poverty that many Vietnamese had to endure during the French and American war years, the first decade after liberation, and before Doi Moi, it is not surprising that they do not often contemplate the country's long-term path. For this reason, we hope this book gives Vietnamese, and anyone else seeking to understand Vietnam, a greater appreciation of the country's potential and the key drivers contributing to its growth story and its success.

MY EXTENDED O.E.

My very first memory of television was watching the North Vietnamese Army enter Saigon in 1975. It was on my parents' black-and-white Phillips television. I was too young to understand what was really happening, but it amuses me now that I have spent half my life in a country whose most defining day of the twentieth century was so implanted in my mind.

My first real engagement with Vietnam came twenty years later, in 1995. I had been working for the accounting firm Arthur Andersen in New Zealand for five years and had just returned from the New Manager School in Chicago. My supervisor asked if I wanted to go to Vietnam for two weeks to teach a new batch of recruits for Arthur Andersen's latest office. Many of my friends were heading to Australia or the United Kingdom for their O.E. (Overseas Experience, a rite of passage for New Zealanders), but he knew that I wanted a move to Asia and thought a short sojourn in Vietnam might satisfy my passion to get some first-hand working experience there.

I did not really know what to expect upon arrival in Vietnam. I did not have time to do any research on the country. I had only traveled outside New Zealand a few times, so I was very naive about the world. My brief knowledge of Vietnam came from two young refugees who had arrived in my high school class one day, as well as the steady stream of Hollywood movies that portrayed Americans soldiers as heroes (or victims) and the Viet Cong as the enemy. But while I was naïve, I was also open-minded and prepared to make sense of this foreign country that was so very different from my home in New Zealand. At the time, I had no idea that those few short weeks would spark my interest in Vietnam and set the scene for much of the rest of my life.

I remember vividly my first week at the newly opened Equatorial Hotel in District 5 of Ho Chi Minh City (formerly Saigon). This was the site for teaching Arthur Andersen's newly hired Vietnamese team. Their commitment and enthusiasm for learning was beyond anything I had experienced, as were their academic achievements. At the end of the two weeks, all eighteen new staff, including the receptionists who had joined the training, passed the final exams despite none of them having any prior knowledge of the subjects. One person, who is now a partner with an international law firm, achieved a score in the top few percentiles in the world. It was at that point that I realized that Vietnam would not lack the commitment, energy, and intellectual capital needed to move the country forward.

I remember visiting the War Remnants Museum—at that time officially referred to as the Exhibition House for Crimes of War and Aggression—in Ho Chi Minh City and seeing for the first time the Vietnam-American War from the other side. The museum contained blatant propaganda intended to villainize the successive colonial powers that had occupied the country for 150 years. However, I also saw it as a small voice trying to rebalance the West's ingrained perceptions of the country. More importantly, it sought to humanize the war and show the true horrors of what had happened. The museum, as one might expect, was full of haunting black-and-white images of events during the war. But it was the jars, now since gone, containing unborn fetuses that were deformed by the effects of Agent Orange that best highlighted the atrocities that had occurred. North Vietnam may have been the victor, but the entire country paid a very high price for that victory.

After another visit to Vietnam in 1996, to again teach Arthur Andersen's latest batch of new graduates, I was offered a full-time position with the company in 1997. My wife Rebecca and I relocated to Vietnam in May of that year. I often admit that my first two weeks in Vietnam were among the most challenging of my life. The work was not difficult, but everything else was so different to what I had been used to. I seriously considered moving home after the first week.

The posting was only supposed to be a two-year stint, but as so often happens plans change. I found that my career moved forward faster, and I enjoyed what I was doing so much more than what I would have been doing somewhere else. Rebecca and I agreed that we would stay until we had children. That later changed to staying until our children started primary school, which then became the start of middle school, and then obviously the start of high school. Now my eldest children are at university in Australia and the UK, and there is no longer any need for us to really think about moving on.

I would prefer not to start a book by writing about war but mention the word 'Vietnam' to most people in the West and that is immediately what comes to mind. As a proper noun 'Vietnam' is often considered a war, not a country. Why? More recent conflicts in the Middle East and Africa have not tarnished those countries with the same stigma that surrounds Vietnam. Is it because the United States lost? Is it because international media (both fact and fiction) have only focused on the stigma and have only presented one side of the story? Is it because the war left what is today one of the few surviving communist regimes in the world? Perhaps defining the reason for such thoughts matters less than understanding that the West's preoccupation with the war has created biases and preconceptions about the country that are often unjustified and wrong. As a result, Vietnam today is probably one of the most misunderstood countries in the world.

We all need to remember that the Vietnam War (or 'the American War' as it is referred to in Vietnam) concluded nearly fifty years ago. A lot can happen in that time, and indeed it has. Vietnam is no longer a war-ravaged country struggling to rebuild from its ashes. Nor do its people harbor deep animosity towards the United States and its allies for what happened in the past. The reality today is that Vietnam is a fast-growing dynamic nation of almost a hundred million highly motivated and hardworking people whose lives and successes are improving by the day.

For those people who do not get a chance to experience Vietnam first-hand, these preconceptions make it hard for them to appreciate Vietnam for what it is today. It was the first reason I wanted to write this book. There is a desperate need for someone to explain to people outside Vietnam what Vietnam is today and where it is heading.

My second reason for writing developed as I began to discuss with Vietnamese colleagues and friends some of the ideas presented in our narrative. It was clear during these conversations that young Vietnamese had very little understanding of their country's potential and the direction in which it was going. Discussions about the country's future were usually short-term in nature and led by individuals who, rightly or wrongly, lacked credibility for not having appropriate international experience or, more significantly, were not viewed as objective. Ironically, this meant that such a book had to be written by foreigners with experience in the country if it was to be considered credible to a local audience.

I am not an economist, anthropologist, sociologist, historian, or an expert in any of the other fields covered in this book. My Vietnamese language skills are not very good either. But I have the knowledge and experience that come from more than twenty-six years of living and working in Vietnam. For this book, that is enough. Almost everything that has been written about Vietnam is researched from a particular angle, whether it be economics, history, or some other field. As a result, those books often fail to look at 'the big picture' and draw conclusions that might be contradicted by research in other fields. They can also be very technical.

In writing this book, Sam and I have attempted to set out very simply what Vietnam is today and where it is heading. Much of what we are presenting is supported by well-documented academic theories, but the approach we have taken is to present ideas based on anecdotal evidence and observations. Some might not consider this an authoritative reference tool, but we hope that our conclusions make sense, and that the reader will see these conclusions come true.

We started writing this book before the COVID-19 pandemic outbreak and finished it after the worst of it was over. While internationally other countries' successes handling COVID-19 have received more media attention, Vietnam's ability to overcome the worst of the virus is a testament to the actions of the government and the willingness of the people to work together for the common good. If anything, the actions taken by the nation over those two years and the results that have been achieved clearly illustrate exactly what we, the authors, want you to understand. Vietnam is ready to be called the next Asian Tiger.

Brook Taylor
Ho Chi Minh City
Vietnam
August 2023

MY THIRTY-YEAR JOURNEY

In 1990, a mere fifteen years after the end of the American War, Vietnam hosted its first ever official Year of Tourism. The previous year, a friend and I had cycled in China and had an amazing experience. When we learned about Vietnam's new tourism campaign, we immediately made plans to cycle from Saigon to Hanoi.

It was early days for Vietnamese tourism. There were not many flights into the country, and it was not at all clear if you could freely travel within Vietnam upon arrival. There were rumors that you had to join a tour group, needed travel papers to go between cities, and could not stay in most hotels. Despite this, a Thai tourist agency obtained visas for us and booked us on the one and only Vietnam Airlines flight from Bangkok to Ho Chi Minh City (Saigon). We checked in, boarded a shuttle bus, and started driving towards an old Russian-made Tupolev airplane that was parked at the edge of the airport complex. There were about fifteen people onboard, mostly Taiwanese businesspeople.

With passport and boarding pass in hand, we got off the bus and walked to the stairs leading to the plane's door where a Vietnamese woman in an unkempt ao dai stood with a defiant look on her face. She refused to make eye contact with anyone and said nothing. She just stared ahead, stone-faced, and ignored us all. The Taiwanese guys who apparently had taken the flight before, told us, "Just go. Sit anywhere. It doesn't matter."

This was good since there were no seat numbers on our boarding passes. We entered the plane, and I peered down the aisle but could not see a thing. It was filled with what looked like smoke but was, in fact, steam. We could not see more than a few feet ahead as we slowly walked down the aisle in a thick fog. The pilots had apparently just turned on the air-conditioning and steam roared out from the vents. We found some seats and nervously sat and waited to see what would happen. No pilot announcements. No inflight safety demonstration. No sign of a flight attendant. Nothing.

The Taiwanese gentlemen settled in, lit up their cigarettes, and with legs draped over the armrests casually started chatting with each other. The doors closed and the plane started to taxi towards the runway and eventually took off. A few minutes later, the flight attendant appeared. She was pushing a shopping cart down the aisle which contained small boxes. As she passed us, she grabbed a box and threw it towards us without a word of warning. Whether it landed in our laps, the seat, the floor, whatever.... I don't think she cared. It was our box lunch. She then returned with another shopping cart with cans of soda. These, too, were just thrown at us without aiming or warning. Then she disappeared again. So began Day 1 of my thirty-two-year relationship with Vietnam.

My 1990 cycling trip to Vietnam was as amazing as my 1989 trip to China. There were lots of challenges, but there were some great stories too. There were enough of these to compel me to return in November 1990 and enroll at the University of Hanoi to study the Vietnamese language. Learning Vietnamese and trying to understand contemporary Vietnam of the early 1990s was my strategy to gain admission to a good graduate school in the United States. I knew, or at least I hoped, that Vietnam and the United States would eventually have to shake hands and move forward from the war years and there would be a dearth of Americans who knew anything about contemporary Vietnam since few had lived there after 1975. There would be a demand for people who understood Vietnam and I intended to be one of those Americans who could meet this demand. I would be one of the bridge-builders. This would get me into a high-quality graduate program and hopefully win me some scholarships.

The strategy worked. I studied in Hanoi for eight months, and in the Fall of 1991 was accepted into the Jackson School for International Studies at the University of Washington (UW) in Seattle. Of the seven quarters I attended, five were paid for by scholarship because I was 'the Vietnam guy.' At UW, I studied two more years of Vietnamese language and wrote my MA thesis on Doi Moi, the economic renovation policies that set Vietnam on its current trajectory.

After my graduate work, I moved to Vietnam in 1993 with a plan to study for a couple more years and then return to academia for a Ph.D. in international economics. I was hugely curious to learn more about how very closed countries like Vietnam, China, the Soviet Union, and Eastern European countries open and begin to join the global world. How do they take those first steps? The Iron Curtain was history, and what was to come next was the unanswered question of the era. I wanted to refine my question on this issue and then return to the United States and try to find the answer within an academic setting.

The plan worked again. I was accepted into two Ph.D. programs, but I declined. I rationalized that if I really wanted to learn how countries move from being totally closed to being active nation states in a globalized world, I should remain on the frontlines of the country that was doing this. I was in the right place at the right time in Vietnam and I did not need a Ph.D. to learn how to be a good observer. I ended up staying in Vietnam for eleven years working as a journalist, entrepreneur, and finally a last effort as a writer, which resulted in the publication in 2006 of an oral history titled *Saigon Stories*.

I have returned to Vietnam and have put my writer's hat back on for this book. My co-author Brook Taylor and I wanted to learn and then share some things about Vietnam by comparing it to how South Korea and Taiwan grew and developed in the 1980s and 1990s.

There have been numerous books written about Vietnam. I read many of them during my graduate studies. These are often categorized as books on the economy, the country's history, the country's trade, the country's culture, and so on. There is a tendency for them to be written for specific audiences and often with specific agendas. For example, a book on Vietnam's economy is written by an economist for economists.

The American War (Vietnam War) probably produced the longest list of books on Vietnam, each with its own agenda. One of the best is *Dispatches* by Michael Herr, published in 1977. Assigned to Vietnam in the late 1960s, Herr's journalistic method was to talk with regular soldiers about their experiences and to deliberately avoid talking to politicians, military officers, or any kind of government leader who inevitably had an agenda to support. The regular army soldiers had no agenda other than to stay alive. Herr's collection of stories and narratives was novel for its time. In 2016 *The Guardian* newspaper published a list of the Top 100 Nonfiction books of all time and *Dispatches* was ranked ninth.

For this project, we replicated Herr's research methodology and spoke to 'regular people' as often as possible. These are the people who have no agenda other than to make money for their families and to make sure Vietnam keeps growing and developing and never returns to the poverty of its past. This was likely the very same agenda held by many 'regular' South Koreans and Taiwanese from the 1950s onwards. While their government leaders were engaged with Cold War issues, reunification dilemmas, what the Americans were doing in South Vietnam, or any of a myriad of issues of that era, they were working hard to improve their families lives and in doing so created 'Tiger Economies.'

Like Herr did with his book, we used a 'man on the street' approach and spoke with a variety of people about culture, policy, current trends, outdated trends, demographics, family, education, art, sports, investment, the internet, the environment, and many other topics. We believed that these interviewees would be less concerned with what 'model' Vietnam was following and more interested in figuring out what works so they can obtain some success for their families, community and, for many, their private businesses. We wanted to know what they thought because it was bound to be more relevant than what commentators think.

Brook and I became good at asking questions. We became even better listeners. We did not have any model or agenda in mind, although we did have a hypothesis involving the success of South Korea and Taiwan. Like so many others, we want to know and be ready if Vietnam *really is* the next Tiger Economy of Asia, and if it is, how far can the country go?

We have spent the past three years testing a hypothesis. Here are the results as we learned them. In the spirit of pure science, we look forward to hearing your thoughts and reviews so that testing can continue.

Sam Korsmoe
Ho Chi Minh City
Vietnam
August 2023

Chapter 1

THE HYPOTHESIS

Vietnam is the next Tiger Economy of Asia, and it will grow and develop in a similar way to how South Korea and Taiwan grew as Tiger Economies of Asia.

When Nostradamus sat down to write *The Prophecies* in 1555, he was probably not trying to predict the future. More likely, he was simply on a mission to earn a living. He had already published several almanacs which were quite popular and this set the stage for his seminal work, a collection of major, long-term predictions told through quatrains (four-line poems). As it turned out, history was kind to Nostradamus. But even Nostradamus would probably agree that the future cannot be predicted. Sometimes things just happen. But other times, things happen for a reason or because a series of events has been set up so that something can happen in a particular way. In the case of Vietnam and as noted in this book's preface, there is a long line of people offering theories and models of what Vietnam is doing, why, and what it will become. The authors believe that none of these models is individually correct and that the true path forward can only be understood by looking beyond the economic models and at the nation's history, culture, government, religion, and geography, among other factors. Any serious analysis of a country like Vietnam must look at the past and the present, and only then can it look into the future. This is what we have done in this book.

Like every country on earth, Vietnam was tested during 2020 and 2021. The test was how well or how poorly the country managed the COVID-19 pandemic. Everyone, it seemed, was curious about the country's growth and development. And for good reason.

The country's GDP, trade, foreign direct investment (FDI), stock market, property market, and other economic and business metrics have grown consistently for more than two decades. For more than twenty consecutive years, Vietnam has exported commodities such as coffee, cashews, rice, crude oil, and a range of manufactured products to ports around the world. There are numerous bilateral trade agreements in place to provide the needed transparency in trade. As the extreme poverty rate declined significantly, the makings of a Vietnamese middle class emerged. Since at least the year 2000, the economy has been doing extremely well. It has also been fairly equitable. The country has been on a positive trend in terms of household income, living standards, and other metrics that measure the well-being of average Vietnamese citizens as opposed to a select elite. How this was happening and whether it would continue was unclear. As described in the preface, this was a key reason for writing this book. We wanted to learn how and why Vietnam will grow and for how much longer these growth trends might continue.

In *Vietnam: Asia's Rising Star*, we are attempting to predict the future of Vietnam. We want to know what could happen from 2020 to 2050. We know the future cannot be reliably predicted, but we believe that ideas about the future can be identified and tested. If enough of our ideas are proven correct, they provide compelling evidence to answer the core hypothesis of this book which is: 'Vietnam is the next Tiger Economy of Asia, and it will grow and develop in a similar way to how South Korea and Taiwan grew as Tiger Economies of Asia.'

There are two questions embedded within the hypothesis. The first is whether Vietnam is, or will, be a Tiger Economy. The second is whether Vietnam as a Tiger Economy can grow and develop in the same way that South Korea and Taiwan grew and developed when they were the Tiger Economies of Asia in the 1980s and 1990s. We cover the first question in detail in Chapter 7, and the second in Chapters 8–10. In brief, we employed two steps to address our hypothesis.

Step 1 was to define a set of metrics to measure whether Vietnam is a Tiger Economy. This would help us address the first part of the hypothesis. Step 2 was to propose a set of lenses that we use to measure how well or how poorly Vietnam as a Tiger Economy could replicate the South Korea and Taiwan growth model, assuming the first part of our hypothesis proved correct. We then applied these lenses to a series of ongoing themes related to Vietnam's future. These themes are presented as case studies in Chapter 10.

Step 1: The Tiger Economy Metrics

We selected six criteria to measure whether Vietnam can credibly call itself a 'Tiger Economy.' Vietnam had to meet all or most of these metrics to be considered as such:

1. **Numbers**. Net growth for at least ten consecutive years (e.g., measurable outcomes such as GDP, FDI, trade, and foreign exchange reserves, have consistently grown for many years in a row).

2. **Exports**. Consistent movement up the value chain of manufactured products for export (e.g., the country's factories consistently invest in and improve their operations to produce more sophisticated, higher margin, and more technical products for export and local consumption).

3. **Industrialization**. The foundations for the current and future industrial development and growth of the country are in place in terms of policy (e.g., an outward-looking free trade business environment, international competition rather than import substitution, openness to FDI, restructuring SOEs, a downward trend of agriculture's share of GDP replaced by an upward trend of industry's share of GDP, and other issues) and the country's physical infrastructure is being built (e.g., roads, bridges, seaports, airports, and power generation) to facilitate industrial expansion.

4. **Expertise**. An expanding educated and highly skilled workforce (e.g., newly educated government workers and senior managers in the private sector are developing and implementing new management techniques while the workers who used to toil away on assembly lines to make shoes and garments are being trained to operate robotics and machinery with a much higher skill level).

5. **Markets**. Access to multiple global markets for Made-in-Vietnam products (e.g., locally made products are sold globally because the country has multiple free trade agreements with several countries in place as well as membership in global trading alliances).

6. **Leaders**. Strong leadership that is more a meritocracy than an oligarchy (e.g., while not always transparent, there are leadership changes that reflect a commitment to growth and development of the country rather than to an ideology or a dynasty).

Hong Kong, Singapore, Taiwan, and South Korea obtained and met most of these criteria from the 1970s onwards. Those countries' ability to accomplish these metrics were part of the reason they became Tiger Economies. The authors key question is whether Vietnam can also meet these criteria.

As noted in the preface, there were two primary reasons we selected South Korea and Taiwan as the comparative case study countries for this book as opposed to one of the other two Tigers or a different country, such as China or Japan. The first reason is a cultural argument, and the second a historical argument based on the success of the Tiger Economy countries in the 1980s and 1990s.

The cultural reason lies in our belief that all three countries—Vietnam, Taiwan, and South Korea—share Northeast Asian cultural traits. These cultural traits include a commitment to education, respect for authority, a mostly single ethnicity among its population, postwar grit, and a work ethic that not too many countries possess. We argue that Vietnam, on these issues and others, leans more towards the culture of China, Japan, and Korea than towards Indonesia, Malaysia, and Thailand. China was ruled out due to its size (among other issues) and Japan was ruled out because its development, although similar to that of South Korea and Taiwan, happened a much longer time ago.

This left us with the four Tiger Economies of Asia. Hong Kong and Singapore were immediately ruled out because they were city-states and thus not useful comparatives, so only South Korea and Taiwan remained. This made sense because these two countries were prime examples of how to execute the East Asian Development Model of development,[1] which led to both countries becoming high-income countries by the year 2000. They were poor and undeveloped in the 1950s and 1960s, just like Vietnam was up to the 1990s, but they achieved remarkable success over the four decades from 1960 to 2000.

Vietnam's growth from 2000 to 2020 has told a similar story in terms of the growth of various metrics essential to the East Asian Development Model. This includes trade, foreign direct investment, local investment, foreign currency reserves, official development aid, and other measurable metrics. Vietnam achieved these metrics in a similar way to how South Korea and Taiwan met those same metrics in the 1960s, 1970s, and 1980s. Moreover, Vietnam has several advantages that South Korea and Taiwan did not have, such as

---

1. This is discussed in more detail in Chapter 8, pp. 107–122.

agricultural wealth, oil and gas resources, advantageous geography, and a much larger population and thus workforce.

With this cultural and historical backdrop established, we then proposed a comparison of a twenty-year period of significant economic development for South Korea and Taiwan (1980–2000) against a thirty-year period for Vietnam's future (2020–2050). These were the reasons we selected these two former Asian Tiger Economies as our benchmarks and as part of our hypothesis for this book.

Step 2: The Testing Lenses for Replicating the South Korea and Taiwan Model

We researched and wrote six case studies on economic and social sectors, such as education, technology, the role of women, sports, tourism, cuisine, agriculture, and public works. These are presented in Chapter 10. By reviewing each case study through five lenses, we were able to determine whether the observations in the case studies either nudge Vietnam closer to or further away from affirming our hypothesis is correct. The lenses through which we viewed each of these case studies are briefly described below.

1. **Culture**. Vietnam lies in a unique position in Asia. It borders China, a predominantly Confucian Northeast Asian country, as well as Cambodia and Laos, two distinct Southeast Asian Buddhist nations. Thailand is quite close, as is the Philippines, two more distinct Southeast Asian nations. These neighbors are relevant when considering which types of economic development and strategy Vietnam might follow, but they are less comparable when culture characteristics are considered. Our hypothesis states that Vietnam will shape its growth and development like South Korea and Taiwan, two Northeast Asian countries, and therefore not along the lines of Southeast Asian nations. Will Vietnam follow an authoritarian Confucian model or an often-chaotic Buddhist model? Where does its culture lie and how does it support our hypothesis?

2. **Technology**. Technology can be transformative for any country. This has been the case since ideas and knowledge could be shared across borders. The greatest invention of the twentieth century, the internet, has connected the world in an unprecedented way, but not

all countries have approached the internet in the same way. Some countries, such as China, have set up firewalls and other barriers to the internet while others have opened their doors wide. How receptive a country is to new technology and the flow of new ideas is sure to impact how that country will grow.

Vietnam has been relatively open to these types of IT and internet developments. In the 1980s and 1990s, South Korea and Taiwan did not have the internet, but they were quite open to whatever technology existed and imported it into their country. Is Vietnam's openness to the internet and other technologies a good trend that will lead to positive outcomes? Will it attract the type of IT talent and entrepreneurship that so many countries in the world desire as the world gets increasingly more connected online? The test within each case study is to identify whether the path Vietnam has taken in respect to accessing and adopting technology significantly supports its future growth.

3. **Environment**. Environmental changes are affecting the future of every country in the world. In the past, significant economic development has been achieved most often through the exploitation of natural resources rather than preservation, and there was little regard given to the negative impacts to the environment. This is no longer an option. Increasingly, people around the world are waking up to the fact that continuing down this development path is no longer sustainable if humans are to remain on this planet.

    As a fast-developing, low-lying coastal country, Vietnam is much more vulnerable to environmental issues than many countries. In some cases, such as waste management and power generation, Vietnam can tackle the causes head on. In other cases, such as rising sea levels due to global warming, it is on the defensive and paying the price for the past actions of other countries. A recent climate report published by Climate Central, an American science organization that researches climate change and its impact on the public, revealed that most of the Mekong Delta, the country's 'rice basket,' will be under water by 2050 due to rising sea levels.[2]

---

2. *Flooded Future: Global vulnerability to sea level rise worse than previously understood,* Climate Central, October 29, 2019.

It is hard to be optimistic on this issue. Whatever the tangible impacts, all countries must prepare for an uncertain world due to climate change, not to mention keeping their environment clean and safe for its citizens. Forty years ago, South Korea and Taiwan could choose to deal with or ignore much of the environmental impact of growing their economies. Vietnam does not have the same choice, but will it solve its environmental challenges? Can it adopt or find new environmental technologies better than other countries? Will it become a victim or a strong survivor of climate change? The real challenge this lens explores is not whether environmental factors will help Vietnam grow but whether they will hinder its growth.

4. **Policy.** Since the introduction of Doi Moi at the 6th National Congress of the Communist Party of Vietnam in 1986, the Party has seemed willing to endorse policies that keep opening Vietnam's doors and windows ever wider. Vietnam is already one of the 'most globalized' countries in the world.[3] It relies heavily on free trade and investment from outside to drive its economy. This is unlike China or Japan, which consider themselves large enough or strong enough to have their own markets. Perhaps for this and other reasons, import barriers are set up. They need less from outside markets.

   Vietnam is different. For better or worse, it has fully embraced all that free trade and globalization have to offer and the government has put these intentions into policy. For example, this embrace is apparent in the foreign investment law and in the many free trade agreements and groups that the country has joined. Is this the right move? Can Vietnamese leaders reverse course if they need or want to, or have they passed the point of no return? What kind of policies were put in place by South Korean and Taiwanese leaders in the 1980s and 1990s? How much FDI did they allow in? This lens looks at whether there is evidence in the case studies that Vietnam will take advantage of the progressive policies that are already in place and whether similar new policies will continue to be adopted.

5. **Governance.** There are several reasons why countries get stuck at a certain economic and social level and/or remain poor. One of the most common is the inability of the government in power to govern

---

3. See Chapter 5, Free Trade Better Work, pp. 53–74.

effectively. This might be due to a weak legal infrastructure that leads to too many gray areas that result in corruption as the only means of getting something done. Sometimes there is an effort among elites to go slow on policies and projects that threaten their status quo—the status quo that has made them rich—and they want to maintain it even if it means the rest of the country remains poor. A small payoff to offload a container at the port is corruption, but it has a limited impact. A year-long delay in the development of a large infrastructure project because bureaucrats are intent on steering the construction contracts to certain individuals and companies is much more devastating for a country that wants to maintain its growth trends. We collectively label these issues as governance.

Governments create, pass, and implement policies, but they are not monolithic entities. They are composed of a large group or groups of individuals making hundreds of individual decisions, sometimes with limited resources or knowledge and often with numerous opportunities for self-interest. Reducing corruption and the application of laws for the good of all the people is particularly thorny as it relies on strong leadership that focuses on positive outcomes for the entire country rather than a chosen elite.

In less than fifty years South Korea and Taiwan achieved remarkable success. This is the reason we chose them as our comparative case study countries. The term 'Asian Economic Miracle' emerged from their success, as did the label 'Tiger Economy.' Thus, it is worth analyzing how South Korea and Taiwan achieved success because they offer viable development models.[4]

Would Nostradamus have approved of our approach? Comparing Vietnam's growth model today to the successful growth models of two countries in the 1980s and 1990s? Long essay-style case studies instead of quatrains? Who knows and who cares? The business of predicting the future is not for the faint of heart nor the thin of skin. The authors are neither of those things, nor are we clairvoyant. In the best way we could, we were simply trying to better understand this country as it moves through the 2020s and what it might look like by the year 2050.

---

4. As noted earlier, these steps are covered in Chapter 8, What the Asian Tigers Had, pp. 107–122.

The hypothesis made sense, and so that is how we began this research project. However, by the Tet holidays of 2020, we had to rethink our approach to describing what was happening in Vietnam. Everything had suddenly become much more complicated, and not just in Vietnam. The entire world had changed.

COVID I and COVID II

During the initial research and first draft writing stages of this book project (January–April 2020), the world changed. A coronavirus, more commonly known as COVID-19, started in Wuhan China at the end of 2019 and within three months exploded into a pandemic that circled the globe. In April and May 2020, most of the world was in some form of lockdown. It was as if the world had stopped spinning and stopped orbiting the sun. By the end of 2022, there were more than 655 million COVID-19 cases worldwide, which resulted in 6.7 million deaths according to the World Health Organization. More than three years later (2023), COVID can be written about in the past tense for most countries, including Vietnam. In the case of Vietnam, there were two sets of challenges, which we refer to as COVID I (February 2020 to April 2021) and COVID II (May 2021 to March 2022).

Vietnam's battle against COVID I was very successful. Despite the country's proximity to the epicenter in Wuhan China, there were only around 1,500 cases and just 35 deaths in Vietnam due to COVID-19 by the end of 2020. This happened because the Vietnamese government quickly put together a plan. At the beginning of February 2020, the border with China and all flights to and from China were shut down. Schools were closed and online classes for students started after the Tet holidays (Tet was on 25 January 2020). Taxi companies closed. Essential businesses (i.e., grocery stores, pharmacies, medical clinics, etc.), positioned guards at the door who checked your temperature and ensured that you were wearing a mask before allowing you in. Testing, aggressive contact tracing, and quarantining of specific locations—neighborhoods, apartment buildings, and even entire villages— were widespread anywhere there was a perceived threat. On around March 15, 2020, international commercial flights into Vietnam ceased and did not resume until two years later. Prime Minister Nguyen Xuan Phuc of Vietnam announced a national lockdown for the entire month of April 2020.

Vietnam has had to do this kind of mass mobilization before and is adept at it. The country showed its resolve while many other countries faltered and thousands of their citizens died. The government's quick and decisive response paid off and there was even optimism among the Vietnamese public. Between April 3 and April 19, 2021, the Singapore-based social research agency Blackbox Research and Toluna surveyed 12,500 people from twenty-three countries about their leaders' response to the pandemic. The survey measured four key indicators: national political leadership, corporate leadership, community, and the media. Out of a score of 100 points, the global average was 45. Only seven nations rated their leadership above 50 percent. China led the survey with a score of 86 followed by Vietnam with a score of 77. Taiwan's leadership earned a score of 50 while South Koreans gave their leaders a low score of 31.[5]

As the world began to rebound from COVID-19, Vietnam was considered one of the countries that was going to be ready to move forward quickly. Its citizens were healthy, its medical system had not collapsed, and manufacturers from China and other countries were lining up to move in and set up operations in the country that had proven itself against COVID-19. But then Vietnam's world changed again with the arrival of COVID II (the Delta and later the Omicron variants) in May 2021.

COVID II posed a more significant challenge. By August and September 2021, the daily death count was in the hundreds. Triage hospitals had to be set up and new policies—Directive 15 and Directive 16—called for strict lockdowns, even a total ban on people leaving their homes. The military was called in to help enforce the ban with roadblocks and assist with food deliveries and testing. In July 2021, the government launched a vaccination program and immediately faced two problems. First, it did not have an adequate supply of vaccines. The government initially sought to rely on COVAX, the World Health Organization's vaccine distribution program, but quickly recognized that this would take too long to get the supplies it needed. Instead, it worked with the private sector to sign deals with companies in other countries to get enough vaccines into the country. Second, the government had to set up a vaccination program from scratch. The various vaccines that were obtained were distributed in an ad hoc and often chaotic manner. However, in a brief period, order prevailed. Vietnam's first focus was to deliver vaccines to essential

---

5. *Toluna-Blackbox Index of Global Crisis Perceptions*, Singapore, May 2021.

services, factory workers, and businesses deemed essential to supporting the economy. For many Vietnamese, the impact of an economic crisis could have been worse than COVID itself. Over the previous thirty years, the country had worked hard to reduce its severe poverty rate and a return to that environment was not an option. By the end of March 2022, virtually everyone in the country over eighteen years old had been fully vaccinated and 50 percent of the population had received three vaccine shots.

In early October 2021 the government also announced Resolution 128 which called for a 'safe and flexible adaptation and effective control over the COVID-19 pandemic.' The more common reference to this resolution was that Vietnam had made the decision to 'live with COVID' rather than try to pursue a 'zero COVID' policy. To that end, the government announced that the country would begin to open in October. This was a mere four months after the vaccination program had started.

None of these government programs and campaigns were perfect, nor did they protect everyone or every community, but they showed the pragmatic nature of not just the government but also the people. There was never any groundswell of an antivaccination campaign as there had been in many other countries. There was a frank recognition that the country *could withstand* the kind of extended case counts and death tolls that so many other countries experienced. At the same time, the country *could not withstand* being closed for an extended period because too many people rely on a daily wage for survival. They were simply too poor to take so much time off work. They had to go back to work so the country had to learn to live with COVID. Thus, the citizens of the country agreed to the lockdowns, agreed to the gradual reopening, maintained social distance guidelines, wore masks, and most importantly got vaccinated.

COVID-19 provided an opportunity to analyze and report on a real-time crisis that Vietnam had to deal with. It was a perfect test of the hypothesis. Had the country failed to deliver during this time of crisis, our hypothesis might have been totally negated or at a minimum poorly chosen. However, the results achieved through COVID I and COVID II showed that our hypothesis remains valid. It is likely to strengthen our understanding of where Vietnam is heading. We have tested our hypothesis in multiple ways for this book and we begin, in the next chapter, with some historical evidence which shows that dealing with crises is something that Vietnam has been doing for centuries.

Chapter 2

THE FIRST TWO THOUSAND YEARS

Vietnam: Asia's Rising Star is not a history book. However, to understand what drives and motivates a society with a recorded history of more than two thousand years, there should be at least a short discussion of the country's history for readers not familiar with it because it is fundamental to understanding the country today. Rather than a standard historical narrative, we have decided to present an abridged history of the people and events who are commemorated on the streets of Vietnam's town and cities. We also provide oral history narratives from Vietnamese who experienced the most recent hardships—from a long line of hardships—that the country has endured.

Immortalized on Maps

Extending over 1,650 kilometers from north to south in an elongated S-shape, Vietnam could be considered the world's largest outdoor history museum. Although it is hardly the first nor the only country to name its streets and erect statues to commemorate its history, it arguably takes this to a higher level. There are few streets with generic names of trees, flowers, mountains, or rivers in Vietnam. Instead, the major and minor street names as well as the large statues erected at major intersections and roundabouts are named after the scores of people who fought in and endured Vietnam's numerous and seemingly constant wars for independence and freedom. Much of Vietnam's history has been described through the lens of its various wars against a range of 'others,' including China but also France, Japan, the United States, and even the Cham if one chooses to go back far enough.

Vietnam is a proud nation. When a country's fight for independence and freedom takes around a hundred and sixty years, from the first battles against the French to the last ones against the Americans and the Khmer Rouge, or even two thousand years if the first conflict with China is included, the list of people deserving of a street name, park, or intersection becomes lengthy. There are a lot of heroes in Vietnamese history, and they are remembered by their names on iconic sites and important locations. The most obvious is the renaming of Saigon as Ho Chi Minh City after unification in 1975. There have been a lot of newly named streets since 1975, but there are probably more streets named after Vietnam's heroes from two thousand years ago to 1975. Visitors who want to get a sense of Vietnamese history and to learn how Vietnam has made it so far need only to walk the streets of any city in the country with a guidebook or a travel app in hand. There lies a history story on every street and several more at the major intersections. Street names are not assigned at random; they must be earned. The list below, separated by eras, comprises the most common names that will inevitably be in any urban area of Vietnam.

Independence from China

Hai Ba Trung Street. This is probably the most common street name in Vietnam. It is the family name of two sisters who led the fight against Chinese rule in a successful though short-lived revolution at the turn of the first millennium. It was one of the very first and best-known rebellions against the Chinese. After their defeat, the Trung sisters committed suicide by drowning themselves rather than surrender to the Chinese.

Tran Hung Dao Street. Tran Hung Dao was a Vietnamese general during the Tran Dynasty (1228–1330). He is considered Vietnam's most brilliant military strategist. He defeated the Mongol army on two separate occasions at a time when the army was running rampant as far away as Europe.

Le Loi Street. Le Loi was the first emperor of the Later Le Dynasty (1428–1788). He successfully repelled the Ming Dynasty's armies from China. He is the source of several legends, the most famous of which is about a sword that was given to him by a tortoise in Hoan Kiem Lake in modern-day Hanoi. He used the sword to defeat the Chinese and then took the name Le Thai To upon becoming emperor from 1428 to 1443. After defeating the Chinese, legend has it that he ceremoniously threw the sword back into the lake.

Le Thanh Ton Street. Le Thanh Ton (also called Le Thanh Tong) was a Vietnamese emperor who was notable for his relatively peaceful reign (1442–97) and for his poetry. He was the fifth emperor of the Dai Viet Dynasty. He expanded a Chinese-style centralized administration into the southern part of Vietnam. This included new taxing authority as well as the construction of prisons. The southern region had been dominated by the Cham who formed the Champa Kingdom and traded with numerous nations in the region. Ton's armies defeated the Cham in 1471.

Nguyen Hue Street. Also known as Emperor Quang Trung, Nguyen Hue was the second emperor of the Tay Son Dynasty (1753–92). He reunited the whole of Vietnam through a military conquest of the divided factions. He is considered one of the country's greatest military commanders.

The French War

Nguyen Thai Hoc Street. Nguyen Thai Hoc (1902–30) was a revolutionary and founding leader of the Vietnamese Nationalist Party. He was captured and executed by French authorities.

Dong Du Street. Translated as 'Eastern Study,' this was a political movement started by Phan Boi Chau and Phan Chu Trinh, who also have streets named after them, that encouraged Vietnamese to study abroad. The goal was to train a new group of revolutionaries to oppose French rule and to begin to create a modern nation state. Sun Yat Sen, considered the Father of Modern China, launched a similar campaign around the same time in China.

Nam Ky Khoi Nghia Street. The term means 'Southern Uprising' and it represents a campaign against the French in the South. The movement took place in the early 1940s. The campaign ended with all the leaders being captured and executed. Nguyen Huu Tien, one of the leaders, is credited with creating and displaying for the first time the current Vietnamese flag during this campaign.

Cach Mang Thang Tam Street. This translates as the 'August Revolution,' the most important event in modern Vietnamese history aside from the liberation and unification of the country in April 1975. It was a series of events that began on August 19, 1945 in which the Viet Minh, led by Ho Chi Minh, began to establish authority throughout Vietnam. These events culminated in the country's Declaration of Independence, announced by Ho Chi Minh in Ba Dinh Square in Hanoi on September 2, 1945.

Vo Nguyen Giap. There are several streets, town centers, and statues dedicated to Vo Nguyen Giap, who is considered Vietnam's greatest military general and among the world's most respected and well-known military strategists of the twentieth century. There have been numerous books written about him and his military campaigns. He came onto the global stage most prominently as the architect of the French military defeat at Dien Bien Phu. He continued as Vietnam's military strategist and general during the American War. He died on October 4, 2013, at the age of 102.

Dien Bien Phu Street. Along with Hai Ba Trung, nearly every city and town in Vietnam has a Dien Bien Phu Street. Dien Bien Phu was the site of one of Vietnam's most famous battles against the French in 1954. General Vo Nguyen Giap defeated the French army at Dien Bien Phu by leading a group of Viet Minh soldiers and citizens, including many women, who carried artillery and ammunition miles up into the mountains surrounding the valley. From there they rained bombs on the French forces who had established their garrison in the valley. It was the beginning of the end of French colonialism in Indochina.

The American War and afterwards[1]

Dong Khoi Street. This name translates as 'General Uprising.' Formerly named Rue Catinat, it featured prominently in Graham Greene's novel, *The Quiet American*. The new name recognizes a revolutionary movement that took place in Ben Tre Province in 1959 and 1960, one of the first rebellions against the South Vietnamese government. Dong Khoi is one of the main streets in District 1 of Ho Chi Minh City.

Nguyen Van Troi Street. Nguyen Van Troi (1940–64) was a Viet Cong guerrilla. He attempted to plant bombs under the Cong Ly Bridge with plans to detonate them when United States Secretary of Defense Robert McNamara

---

1. Through-out this book, we refer to the conflict in Vietnam between 1965 and 1975 as 'the American War.' Outside Vietnam, it is usually referred to as 'the Vietnam War', but because this book is about Vietnam referring to it as the American War is appropriate to differentiate it from the many other conflicts Vietnam has engaged in during its long history.

drove over the bridge during his visit to Saigon. However, he was caught and executed by firing squad. The same bridge and road used by McNamara now bears his name.

Truong Son Street. The Truong Son Mountains form the range that extends between Vietnam and Laos. It is also the site of the Ho Chi Minh Trail which Northern forces used to deliver weapons and goods to fight in South Vietnam via a labyrinth of roads and trails. The expansive network of roads and trails was built and rebuilt in a remote jungle environment that was repeatedly bombed by the Americans during the American War.

Le Duan Street. Le Duan (1907–86) was a top policymaker and the number two person behind Ho Chi Minh for the Vietnamese government in North Vietnam and then as sole leader under a unified Vietnam. He served as the General Secretary of the Central Committee of the Vietnamese Communist Party from 1960 until his death in 1986. He was instrumental in setting policy during the American War. He was an active revolutionary leader in South Vietnam during the first Indo-China War in the late 1940s and early 1950s.

Truong Sa Street and Hoang Sa Street. These street names are the Vietnamese names for two groups of islands referred to in English as the Spratly Islands and Paracel Islands, respectively. The archipelagos sit within an area of the ocean that also has two names. These are the South China Sea, as it is called by China and many other countries, and the East Sea, as it is called by the Vietnamese. Much of the area is disputed due to multiple ownership claims by Vietnam, China, Taiwan, Malaysia, the Philippines, and Brunei. This dispute is one of the most serious geopolitical issues facing Vietnam today. The area is important because of the shipping routes that pass through it as well as potential oil and gas reserves the area may contain. In both the Truong Sa and the Hoang Sa islands, China has established military outposts which Vietnam strongly opposes.

A Nation at War

War against French Colonialism (1858–1941)
Japanese Occupation (1941–45)
August Revolution (August 14, 1945)
Declaration of Independence (September 2, 1945)
French War (1945–54)

American War (1965–75)
Liberation of Saigon and the Unification of Vietnam (April 30, 1975)
Border War with China (1979)
War in Cambodia (1978–89)

From the list of wars above and the preceding list of immortalized names, it is clear that Vietnam was at war for much of the nineteenth and twentieth centuries. Political and social historians within and from outside Vietnam debate at length the title of each war, the reasons for it, its starting date, its finishing date, the countries involved, the identity of the enemy, the winner, the loser, and a host of other issues. Vietnam has probably endured more fighting during this time than any other nation. It is logical, therefore, that these conflicts have had an enduring impact on the country and its people.

The American War has generated the most debate and remorse along with numerous articles, papers, books, documentaries, movies, and Ph.D. dissertations. But the title, 'the American War,' inappropriately omits the participation of an entire government's military forces, the Armed Forces of South Vietnam (ARVN), which lost an estimated 250,000 soldiers. In addition, Australian, South Korean, New Zealand, Laotian, Cambodian, Thai, and Filipino soldiers participated and were killed in the war.

There is little debate about the number of Vietnamese people, both civilians and military personnel, who were killed. Most history books round the figure off at roughly three million dead between 1945 and 1975. Even this figure ignores a devastating famine that hit northern Vietnam during World War II in which an estimated two million Vietnamese died of starvation. The main reason for the famine was the Japanese Army's occupation and its policies which forced farmers to grow industrial crops like cotton and jute instead of rice. Historians can also provide evidence that rice output steadily declined over the thirty years of French colonial rule prior to World War Two. The resulting millions of deaths can therefore be added the tally of deaths caused by the occupations and conflicts the country has endured for much of the 20th century.

For the younger generation of Vietnamese, the American War has become a part of their history in a way that World War II is a part of many European and American's history. It is rarely mentioned or thought about except when taught in school, visiting a museum, viewing a film, enjoying a national holiday, or sometimes noticing a war monument that has been up for so long that it has become part of the environment. For this generation, the brief but violent border war with China in 1979 is more relevant and concerning.

For the middle-age generation, those Vietnamese born in the mid- to late 1960s, the American War is in the past, and far enough in the past to be able to forget about it almost completely. Despite its viciousness and the fact that only about fifty years have passed, the war is not a part of daily life even though some memories remain. The ten-year-long guerrilla war in Cambodia against the Khmer Rouge, and the hardship experienced after liberation in 1975, is much more relevant to this generation.

For the older generation, there is no doubt that the American War, the Liberation, and the unification of the country on April 30, 1975, were the defining events of their generation. People have clear memories of where they were and what they did before and after Liberation Day and how it has impacted their lives since. Most of them no longer dwell on such memories, but it is an integral part of their personal history. Like the generation of people who lived through the Great Depression and World War II in the United States, Europe, and other countries, these events shaped their behavior and their lives. They can never forget it.

One of the reasons that the older generation of Vietnamese can never forget is that it was a civil war, so it was never completely obvious which side a friend, a neighbor, or a stranger was on. This was most evident in the South where a soldier might be an ARVN (Army of the Republic of Vietnam) by day and a Viet Cong by night. For many people, the situation was so confusing that the ideology being fought for became less relevant than the actual outcome. To make sure that they had someone who could eventually take care of them, many Vietnamese parents sent children to fight on different sides to ensure they had at least one child on the winning side.

An Oral History Project: The American War

The American War is distinct from other major wars in that the losing side went on to write most of the stories for the history books. Whether it was because the United States had a louder voice or because Vietnam became more internally focused and had more pressing things to attend to, the world knows very little about the feelings and experiences of the Vietnamese people during, and especially after, the American War. For this reason, co-author

Sam Korsmoe was compelled to write about the war and its aftermath from the Vietnamese perspective in an oral history of five separate families. Each family came from a different geographical and political background, which meant the same question posed to all the families often meant five different answers. The book is titled *Saigon Stories* and was published in 2006.

For *Vietnam: Asia's Rising Star*, we have drawn on excerpts from *Saigon Stories* to share with readers the hardships that people experienced around two important periods in Vietnamese history. These are the days leading up to April 30, 1975, and then the ten years after unification which led to the Doi Moi policies of 1986. For Vietnamese readers, our intention is to remind everyone of the challenges you, your parents, and/or your grandparents experienced and why the youth of Vietnam today owe a lot to the previous generations. For foreign readers, our intention is to show examples of the challenges and uncertainties ordinary people experienced during these difficult times. We have been living in Vietnam for a long time and are constantly humbled by the stories of hardship every Vietnamese person over the age of forty shares with us. These family stories provide context to the spirit of the Vietnamese people today, which might be used to propel Vietnam forward over the next three decades.

The Days Before April 30, 1975

For most of the Western world, the most vivid image of the end of the American War involves helicopters—huge Chinooks and smaller, nimbler Hueys dropping down and lifting off from the rooftops of Saigon's tallest buildings. In all its war movies, Hollywood has mastered the dull '*thump thump thump*' sound and the image of helicopters racing away to offshore ships. For the Vietnamese, helicopters were one of many images of the last days of the American War. For some, helicopters were a possible way out of the country. For others, they were a sad last moment of seeing family, friends, and compatriots fleeing. For still others, they were signs of victory. The enemy was fleeing by the very last means available. From the rooftops of Saigon's tallest buildings, they had been driven out.

One of the most enduring memories of the end of the war was not the flight of the defeated but the silent entry of the victors. There was no final bloodbath on the streets of Saigon. A few shots were fired. In fact, the streets were flooded with hastily discarded ARVN weapons and uniforms instead of locked and loaded South Vietnamese soldiers preparing to make a last stand. When the Viet Cong soldiers arrived, they did so calmly and without bravado. Vietnamese families from the southern tip of the Mekong Delta to the northern border with China were all tuned in to the same set of events during the month of April 1975. Each, of course, had very different ideas about what was going to happen and what they wanted to happen.

1. An Unforgettable Impression

The narrator grew up in Hanoi and became a schoolteacher in the North and after Liberation in Ho Chi Minh City in the South. She taught in various schools, often those built underground to escape the American bombing campaigns. Prior to the end of the war, she taught math in a provincial school 100 kilometers from Hanoi. Every weekend she would cycle from her school into Hanoi to be with her family. She frequently had to cycle during the night because of the bombing raids.

That period of my life is unforgettable and has left a lasting impression on my mind. After the Dien Bien Phu campaign, I thought that there would not be any more war or fighting. I thought that there would be peace and independence and how I would love it all. However, there was still all this fighting after Liberation, and it grew into an unforgettable impression. Secondly, because of the war, students ate very miserably. Russia provided aid. It was wheat flour which we would hold in our hands in lumps like this [makes gesture with her fists] and throw these lumps into the boiling water. Once cooked, we would take them out and give them to the students to eat. Their meal consisted of these lumps of wheat flour, some chili salt and boiled morning glory water as soup. That was it. There was a period when we were very hungry. So hungry that we had to go out looking for sweet potato buds. We would boil them and eat them to keep our stomachs full. We would also go to the villages where the people there would feed us sugar cane. They provided the students with good care and had a lot of sympathy for them.

I remember that time when there was no more fighting in Hanoi [after the 1973 Paris Peace talks]. There was no more bombing of the North and we were allowed to go to school. The government was preparing some forces to end all this fighting and to take over. We were teachers so we knew only teaching but upon hearing that the fighting had stopped everyone kind of expected news of unification of the entire country. South and North would become one. That was the only kind of news we expected to hear. Unification and peace.

We had to wait two years. It was in 1975 and I was in class when I heard "Liberation already, Unification already!" and the whole school came out. I was teaching in Vinh Phu when we heard the news. Back then there were no personal radios. We all had to listen to the one speaker attached to a tree in the school yard. We were all so happy. The whole country was happy. The whole of North Vietnam was happy. So happy because there was no more war. No more death.

2. Something Terrible Was Happening

In the final years of the American War, the narrator was a small child who grew up in the North and moved around constantly because her father was a senior official in the North Vietnam government. She recalls the war, but also remembers how much fun she had when she was young playing with other children while 'something else' was happening outside their homes. During the American bombing raids, she remembers hiding inside her father's coat until the bombing was over and then she would just continue playing with her friends. That was the case until one bombing run in particular hit her very hard and remains with her today.

I think I was about four years old. We were in La Vie and we moved down to Nhon [name of the villages] with my father's company and there were a lot of children in that village. I made friends with the new children and played with them. Then we received some information that they would bomb that village, so we left half an hour before the bombing.

It was a couple of days afterwards when we returned. We had to go back to that village because that was where my father's company put all its people. Because they [the villagers] couldn't go anywhere, they could just go deep underground. All the children and people and even buffaloes and cows were all lying down all over the village. When we went back there, we saw all that and it was terrifying. I remember I was crying, and I saw my friend who I used to play with and ... [pause] ... and that is ... [in a quivering voice] ... it really, really hit me. That was my first memory and now for years and years when I see bombings in movies I start crying. I can't watch the bombing scenes.

When that village was bombed, it was the first time I realized something terrible was happening. I knew that it was the Americans because before the bombing runs they always had [speaking as if on a loudspeaker in Vietnamese] "Attention, attention the American planes are 10 kilometers from Hanoi" or whatever so I knew that it was American planes. I knew it was Americans, but I had no idea who the Americans were ... just somebody.

3. Banana Flowers across the Moon

The narrator is the son of a revolutionary leader from the Mekong Delta who joined the Viet Minh in the 1940s and moved to Hanoi before the Geneva Convention in 1954. He was born in Hanoi in 1959 and grew up during the American War years. In early 1975 he lied about his age to try and get into the army to be part of the final campaign.

On the first day of the twelve days and nights bombing [the Christmas Bombings of Hanoi in 1972], I heard the alarm siren go off and then the roaring of the airplanes, so I jumped inside a bomb shelter. That was one of the unique aspects of Hanoi back then. Everyone would dig a shelter-pit about up to here [gestures to chin level] and two meters in diameter. It could hold say no more than one or two persons. It is kind of round like this, like a drainage pipe, and about two meters deep. I jumped down there because they were bombing very fiercely. Then they stopped for a while before doing another round. Taking the opportunity, I climbed out and ran home.

I later saw the American planes flying into Hanoi. They flew into the center to drop bombs. In the middle of the night when the moon rose, the airplanes were like banana flowers. Banana flowers that have not yet bloomed. They appeared one by one flying across the moon. There were so many of them, countless numbers of them. I had been through it for two days in Hanoi already and I thought to myself: "Wow! Hanoi is really being heavily attacked."

I was scared because I could see with my own eyes people hit by the bombs. They were cut into pieces. When the twelve days and nights of bombing were over and walking on Kham Thien Street you could still smell the stench. They dug up the bodies to be identified and put them all over the street. You passed by and thought, "Oh, My God!"

I was only conscious that all this blood was due to the American bombardment. People were losing their limbs. It was all these things that had a strong impact on me. I was a young kid after all. All this suffering and death created a sense of grudge in me.

After 1973 and the Paris Agreement, the fighting was the same except that there were no more bombardments. Life, however, was the same and I heard that fighting was still going on around the border area. Over here were the ARVN soldiers and over there the North Vietnamese soldiers. The two sides occasionally exchanged gunfire. By January or February 1975 [and the end of the war was apparent], we were very happy, so extremely happy. Honestly speaking, the happiness was rising in me so high that I even hid it from the family that I had registered to join the army. I was only sixteen, but I lied about my age to join the army because I saw that the final fighting had begun. I heard Pleiku in the highlands was liberated first. Then it was the takeover of the Southern Laos Road 9. After that the Ho Chi Minh Campaign was set into motion.

4. The End of the Patriotic War

The narrator was a member of parliament in the government of South Vietnam. At that time, he was known as a member of the 'Third Force.' These were South Vietnamese who did not align themselves with either the Americans or the Communists. They sought a peaceful conclusion to the war through negotiated peace. In the final days of the American War, the narrator was appointed to the rank of Minister of Communication for the South Vietnam government.

I went on television on April 28 to call on the people not to divide and I guaranteed them that there would not be a last battle in Saigon. Before then, the Americans and former President Thieu's people figured that there was going to be a bloody war when the Communists made it to Saigon. As a result, many people were scared and evacuated. I was on television to tell the Vietnamese people that they should remain here and should not abandon the country because it was their homeland. It was where their ancestors' graves were.

The truth was I really did not know what was going to happen, but I knew for sure that there was not going to be a [final] war with the Communists because I knew this war was a patriotic war. Thus, if standing before them were people who did not like war, then the Communists would have no reason to fire artillery shells into Saigon.

From where I was [inside the Presidential Palace on the evening of the April 29], I could see the American Embassy. I saw helicopters going up and down. It was about 9 or 10 p.m., and it went on like that until five the next morning. I felt very strange. There was something about such a scene, something fantastic about it. There was this high beam of light to help the helicopters come down and pick up people. If you went to Tan Son Nhat Airport, you could see people leaving and you felt puzzled. You would see that it is not a normal airport. The people there are your friends and relatives. So many of them. Seeing people leave like that and you start to wonder if it is right that you are staying back or if it is right that they are leaving.

[On the morning of the 30th] President Minh [Duong Van Minh had assumed the presidency on April 28] and I and about fifteen VIPs sat in Nguyen Van Thieu's workroom to wait for the South Vietnam Liberation Front to arrive. Around 11 a.m. or so, I saw a tank, a T35 or something, appearing at the Zoo gardens at the end of Le Duan Street (current name of street). President Minh, I, and all the others stood up before the steps to welcome them in.

When the tank and the soldiers entered the palace grounds, the soldiers in the corridors and hallways pointed their guns and ordered everyone inside Thieu's room to come out and surrender. President Minh, I, and some 15–20 people walked out of the room and at once we were told, "Weapons down! Hands up!" So, we all put up our hands. When I had my hands up, a strange thought hit my mind. I was someone who struggled for peace. Someone who struggled to overthrow Thieu and now I am the one to put my hands up like this? This ending was not logical.

But upon arriving at the main hall of the Presidential Palace, there were many friends that revealed themselves as Communists. They ran over to hug me because they knew how long I had struggled against Thieu. They hugged me and said, "We have won! We have won! We are the winners." My hands were up like this and yet I am the winner? Tears began to fall, and I was unable to express my emotions then.

Life before Doi Moi (1975–86)

The world changed for so many Vietnamese on the morning of April 30, 1975. The war was over. The Americans had fled. The last president of South Vietnam, Duong Van Minh, had ordered all ARVN troops to put down their weapons. The killing would stop. After three decades of war, peace had arrived. No one was ready.

From 1975 to 1985 life was worse than poor. It was desperate. It was this desperation which convinced people to board leaky boats to try to escape when the conventional wisdom, as well as some hard evidence, pointed to a phenomenally low success rate. It was believed that fewer than half of those who tried to leave by boat would physically survive the attempt. It was accepted that half would die a horrible death. Of those who survived, many would be robbed, raped, and nearly starved before finding land and eventually making it to a refugee camp somewhere in Southeast Asia. From those camps, some of them left within a year for their newly adopted countries in the West. Others lingered in refugee camps for years. These people, the ones who were living far from their native land in an alien culture and usually on government assistance, were considered the lucky ones.

Most of the elite of South Vietnam had already left by April 30, 1975. The people fleeing Vietnam in the late 1970s and early 1980s were not the elite. With some exceptions, most of them were not fleeing political persecution or the type of persecution faced by other refugees of the twentieth century. The country's Chinese population was forced out, either back across the border into China even though most had been living in Vietnam for generations or allowed to take their chances as 'Boat People.' Although the Chinese were a targeted ethnic group, there was no Cambodia-style 'Killing Fields' in Vietnam, nor were there any of the purges common to the Stalin era of the Soviet Union or during Mao Tse Tung's Cultural Revolution in China. Most of those fleeing were economic refugees who were living in a country that they believed had no future. Leaving was fraught with danger but they could not stay any longer.

The socioeconomic indicators were horrific. Annual inflation was in triple digits. The per capita gross domestic product (GDP) was less than US$150 per year. The country had to import food and fuel to survive. One of the biggest exports was scrap metal, the debris of thirty years of war. Vietnam was one of the poorest countries in the world and very few people in the West knew or seemed to care.

5. No Hope. None.

The narrator moved to the South from the North in May 1975. He was a veterinarian who followed his schoolteacher wife south. He was born in Hanoi, and although he had two uncles who were part of the revolution, he was not from a political family—not that having revolutionary credentials would have helped much.

In the late 1970s life for the whole of Vietnam was difficult. We all had to rely mainly on our salary and the family income was barely enough to live on. It was enough to put the children in schools, but my wife had to do other things to earn more to care for them. Life was at a subsistence level. The most miserable time was 1978 or 1979 or so. We had to eat sorghum and some kind of wheat during that period. It was aid from the former Soviet Union or some country. Back then, after the war and after Liberation, there were some changes in how we ran our economy. Our policies were not that open. There were no free trading activities. People in the countryside abandoned their fields. Since there was no free trade, there was no circulation of goods. Rice brought down from the North was not sold freely. Mekong Delta farmers abandoned their fields and even if they did produce goods, they could not bring their produce to the city.

Ideologically speaking, I didn't have any hope. None. We had to struggle to make a living. From 1980 to 1985 we had to do a lot of things. I was in the animal husbandry field, so I raised animals to earn extra income. At that time, people who raised animals could sell them so some extra income could be earned. People mainly raised pigs or chickens at home because there were no ranches or farmhouses, at least not big ones. They were not allowed by the government. I made some medicinal products for use in animal husbandry, and I visited animal farms to provide them with more support. I worked at my office job as well. Everyone had to work two jobs like that. We had no choice.

6. The Motivation to Leave

The narrator is the wife of an ARVN officer who was sent to a re-education camp in Tay Ninh after Liberation. She had family members on both sides. Three siblings moved north in 1954 to join the revolution while one brother joined the South Vietnamese Army and was killed in an artillery attack in 1972. She married young and already had four children by the time April 1975 arrived.

I was helpless. We were living some kind of life and suddenly it changed. We had to cut down on everything, put a limit on everything. There was nothing for sale. We ate whatever there was. Sometimes cassava, sweet potato, or sorghum. Meat? That was impossible [laughing]. There was no meat. We ate different kinds of vegetables and dried shrimp. Fish? My God! Very scarce. Partly because we did not have money and partly because there were so little fish back then. You could only buy half a kilogram of fish per month! There was no beef and pork to eat. We ate only the intestines of those animals.

I had changed my mind about escaping Vietnam by boat. We [husband and wife] both agreed that unless we went, we could not change our children's lives. We did not believe that it could be like today [2004]. We thought life would be the same forever. The thought "How could we live on like this" made me want him [my husband] to go and to take our only son. What would happen if they both died? If we had no food, we would all die anyway. No one could lift their heads. Thus, he must go. But they were caught and arrested.

I tell my children this. From small to big, from misery to better and better. I tell them what it was like then and what we ate then. What the rice was like. What the porridge was like. The different things I mixed in the porridge that would make it look very much like, excuse me, pig's mash. The kind of food people cook for pigs. Yet, the whole family would gather around the big porridge pot to eat it. Everyone would eat and eat and empty it anyway. Not only me, but my children will always remember that time.

7. What Was Happening?

The narrator was the first child of his large South Vietnamese family to travel to the United States for his university education. He was always a good student, but also very aware of the political situation in his country. His Saigon friends were split almost evenly between 'pro-South' and 'pro-North,' but he never really took sides because he was so set on preparing to study abroad in the United States. It was from the United States that he became more politically aware as he watched the end of the war in his country. He became, he said, 'more pro-VC' in the United States than he ever was in Vietnam.

When so many Vietnamese people started coming out in 1978, I knew something was wrong. My brother and his family were still in Vietnam. They would write us letters that had to go through France. Every time we got a letter from them, we would cry. They could not write directly in the letter. We had to use code words. My brother could never say how they suffered or that they didn't have any food.

Nothing like that, but we knew. I remember that whenever we got a letter the whole family, my father and mother, would cry.

When the boat people started coming, I began to change my mind about the North. Up to that time, I still admired the North Vietnamese leadership. I knew that something was wrong when so many people were trying to get out. You talk about Liberation? You talk about independence? So why were there so many people trying to leave the country?

8. The Sacrifice

The narrator is the wife of a member of parliament of the South Vietnamese government and the mother of several children. In the late 1960s and early 1970s, she played an active role as a politician's wife as well as working with several Saigon newspapers. After the war, she baked cakes and sold them on the street to make ends meet. Later, the family became one of the leading restaurant entrepreneurs in Ho Chi Minh City.

On the afternoon of April 30, I came home from the Presidential Palace. My God! How am I to describe such an emotion? I was very sad that I had to lose everything for independence. This was something I had expected. I lost all my career. I lost everything in return for freedom. I did not hear gunfire anymore. No more war. All of which was precious. The beginning was miserable, which was okay because a new change always entails such misery. What was sad about it was that such a long time passed but things did not get better. You felt sad even though you understood. You just had no right to criticize.

The very worse time, when I was financially most miserable, was in 1984 and 1985. Even more miserable than in 1978 and 1979 because I still had some assets [back then]. My house was robbed but I still had certain things left in the house. I sold all these things one by one until I had to sell even the glass doors and the glass in the windows. We had a house with no more doors. The piano! My family loved music very much. But that year, we were so poor that we had to sell the piano. What would you do if you had no rice to eat?

We tried doing different things to live. We would feel good in the case of success because we could make some money to care for the family. However, in the case of failure, we would not feel sad because we would learn. In my family, no one would feel sad due to losing money. Why? Because we have been so poor before [laughing].

What's Next?

This chapter describes Vietnam's long and documented history and that for so many of those two thousand years of history Vietnam has been fighting to escape successive adversaries. It began early on with the Chinese and continued the moment French colonialists stepped foot on Vietnamese soil. During World War II, there was a new enemy with the Japanese, and then the French returned followed by the Americans, the Chinese again, and finally the Khmer Rouge. Yet, by 1990 this state of war, as well as the economic chaos, was almost over. The post-Liberation mistakes were on the mend. The Doi Moi policies were beginning to bear fruit for the economy. It was all about what comes next for a country that had known nothing but war and poverty for generations. But, before pursuing this question, we need to understand how Vietnamese people were able to endure so much for so long.

Chapter 3

THIS IS WHO WE ARE

After endless reels of often one-sided, ill-informed, and agenda-driven movies about Vietnam, in September 2017 the documentary film directors Ken Burns and Lynn Novick premiered an objective ten-part eighteen-hour series called *The Vietnam War*. In our opinion, they got it closer to 'correct' than anyone else who has tried to explain on film what Vietnam is all about.

The series provides insights into what happened and who was involved in Vietnam from 1858 to 1975. The directors deliberately did not seek out politicians and army officers from either side. Instead, they interviewed some eighty people, including Americans who had fought in or opposed the war and Vietnamese soldiers and civilians from the North and South. They did what good documentarians should do. They asked what had happened and then they listened. Throughout the documentary, there is a slow dawning and realization among the Americans as to why 'the enemy' was fighting so hard despite enormous losses. As this became understood, a sense of respect developed among the American interviewees. They did not fully understand why they were there, but they knew why the Vietnamese were. One American soldier wrote home to his family, "If I were Vietnamese, I would be with them." An American commander said, "I would love to have two hundred of them under my command" when asked his opinion of the Vietnamese soldiers he was fighting against.

This motivation, a part of Vietnamese history that so few outsiders understand well, is the fight for independence and freedom. Ironically, independence and freedom are intrinsically American and French ideals that are enshrined in each country's declaration of independence. It was the reason for everything in Vietnam. Yet, the idea of independence and freedom got caught up in the politics of the era and was often forgotten. The reality is that few nations have had to fight for as long and as hard as the Vietnamese to achieve it.

The Misnomer of Labels

One of the challenges that Vietnamese have faced is to convince others who they are and who they are not. During colonial times, the French assumed, or at least convinced themselves, that they were on a civilizing mission in Vietnam. They were there to help and could point to the written language, government institutions, and other ideals such as education as evidence of the value of their presence. They viewed the Vietnamese fighting against them as 'agitators' and over time as 'communists' while they tried to cement their colonial rule. While this eventually failed, it began the discourse used to refer to the Vietnamese. It was also the beginning of the discourse the Vietnamese used to refer to themselves. Not everyone agreed on this issue, and this became part of the problem.

'Anticolonial,' 'Nationalist,' 'Communist'

These are the three labels that have been most often placed upon Vietnamese by foreigners. They are also the labels that Vietnamese have often placed upon themselves beginning when the French arrived with military forces in 1858. Underpinning each of these labels, however, is the much older, more durable, and singular pursuit of independence and freedom. This is why Ho Chi Minh's quote, "Không có gì quý hơn độc lập tự do" [Nothing is more precious than independence and freedom] was so easy to accept and understand. Whether a person was from the North or the South, independence and freedom was the reason for everything in Vietnamese history. This was certainly the case when the Trung sisters (Hai Ba Trung) battled the Chinese two thousand years ago as well as when Le Loi fought and defeated the Chinese 1,400 years later. Unfortunately, the notion of fighting for independence and freedom has often got lost in the politics and discourse of the nineteenth and twentieth centuries.

The first label, 'Anticolonial,' is relatively easy to understand. The French arrived and wanted to make Vietnam a colony and the Vietnamese rejected this just as they had when the Chinese wanted to do the same thing.

The second label, 'Nationalist,' is more complicated. In the early twentieth century, scholars such as Phan Boi Chau (1867–1940) and Phan Chu Trinh (1872–1926) began writing about and organizing campaigns that were more nationalistic in spirit. Driving the French out was assumed, but they were seeking something else; they wanted to build their own country. Sun Yat Sen was trying to do the same thing in China. For the Vietnamese, this included writing blood letters (letters written in the blood of the writer) about nationalism as well as the Dong Du (Eastern Study) movement which involved people such as Chau moving to Japan to study how to create a nation state. This point in history marks a turning point in Vietnam's pursuit of independence and freedom for nationalist rather than anticolonial reasons. It was probably hard for many people, especially outsiders, to understand the difference.

The label of 'Communist' was just as confusing, if not more so. For some observers, mainly those outside Vietnam, the country's pursuit of independence and freedom was considered for communist rather than for nationalist reasons. They could point to President Ho Chi Minh's writings, his travels to China and the Soviet Union, and his participation in French communist groups as evidence. The notion that he might be using communism as a tool to achieve nationalistic goals was lost on many. At the time, in the middle of the Cold War, there was only one way of looking at the communist issue. There was no room for any gray area or nuance. For the Americans, their Domino Theory of the Cold War era, whereby a communist Vietnam would be a domino at the behest of the Soviet Union and would eventually topple Thailand and then Malaysia and Indonesia, and so on, had to be stopped.

Although there may have been three labels used to define Vietnam, in each case the single objective of the Vietnamese was independence and freedom from foreign rule, be it Chinese, French, Japanese, or American rule. Unfortunately, too many people in history missed this point.

The Final Thirty of the Last 164 Years

Vietnam has long admired its heroes. As shown in the previous chapter, their names are placed all over the country, on streets, parks, schools, and numerous roundabouts in the form of martyr statues. These people represent the country's power of intention and resolve. The pursuit for independence and freedom was singular, and these had to happen before peace was secured. Only then could development of the country follow. Over the past 164 years (1858–2022), however, it has been only in the last thirty-two years that Vietnam has achieved independence, freedom, and peace, allowing it to freely pursue its development as a country.

Table 1. A 164-year pursuit for freedom and independence, 1858–2023

Era	Independence	Freedom	War or peace	Economy
1858–1900s	No	No	Anticolonial war against the French	Colonial economy to feed France
Early 1900s*–1940	No	No	Nationalist war against the French	Colonial economy to feed France
1940–1975	No	No	War against Japan, France, and the United States	Wartime economy
1975–1989	Yes	Yes	War against China and the Khmer Rouge	Debilitated by war and isolation
1989–2023	Yes	Yes	Peace	Free to develop

* The start of the nationalist campaigns by Phan Boi Chau and Phan Chu Trinh

As table 1 shows, it took a long time to achieve independence, freedom, and peace. Is it any wonder, therefore, that once it was achieved in 1989 it would take some time for Vietnamese leaders to figure out the 'What's next?' question? It will be left to historians and perhaps economists to determine how well Vietnam managed its first thirty years of development (1990–2020). In this and chapters 4–6 we offer some data and analysis on the issue to satisfy our curiosity about the next thirty years (2020–2050). What comes next is the real question for many Vietnamese. Fortunately, they have cultural traits that are going to help them answer this question.

Thanks to Grit and Pragmatism

Liberation in 1975 did not attract any seriously violent retributions characteristic of the end of so many civil and revolutionary wars in history. However, in its first ten years of unified rule, the new government of Vietnam implemented a series of poor policies that negatively impacted many people's lives. It rounded up the South's former army officers and many government officials and put them in re-education camps. It forced other people, especially the unfavored surplus population of Saigon, into 'New Economic Zones,' many of them little more than unproductive sections of rural and jungle land. The new tenants, most of whom were not farmers, were supposed to build new lives amid malaria, unexploded mines, and other war debris. In pursuit of a socialist utopia, the government nationalized all businesses and forced all farmers into unfamiliar and ultimately unproductive agriculture communes. It set up roadblocks to plan and control the flow of agricultural and other goods into the cities. This meant that while the cities starved, rural farmers had nowhere to sell their produce. Eventually, they stopped growing crops and Vietnam had to import food to survive. The new government changed the currency twice with little advance notice. Informers infiltrated many sectors of society. For example, Saigonese became worried about cooking meat at home because the smell would make neighbors jealous, and the police would show up demanding to know where the meat came from.

Those who tried to work around the system were stymied at every turn. An elementary schoolteacher shared a story with co-author Sam Korsmoe about the time she tried to smuggle rice from the Mekong Delta into Saigon simply to feed her family and sell some surplus to her neighbors. The new regime's roadblock police confiscated all her rice, leaving her penniless and deeply in debt. By comparison, she got off easy. Another post-Liberation story shared with the co-author is about two brothers who tried to smuggle into Saigon two pigs owned by another brother, a farmer in a nearby province. They were caught, arrested, and spent nearly one year in jail awaiting trial. Their crime was illegally bringing food into the city. Their case never came to court. After nearly a year of incarceration, the family bailed them out of prison.

By 1986 it was time for a change. Nguyen Van Linh, who was born in the northern province of Hung Yen and became a revolutionary in southern Vietnam in the 1930s (which included several years in French prisons), understood the situation clearly. Linh was a key figure on the Politburo of the Communist Party, and he spearheaded a series of efforts that culminated in the Doi Moi policies of the 6th Party Congress of 1986 when he became the general secretary of the Party (1986–91).

The words Doi Moi are most often translated into English as 'new change' or 'renovation'. The word *doi* means 'change' and *moi* means 'new'. In the English language press of the early 1990s, the term was often defined as the Vietnamese equivalent of *perestroika* and *glasnost* of the former Soviet Union, even though the Doi Moi policies were developed a few years before Mikhail Gorbachev introduced his reforms. Initially, the basic idea of the policies was to mix aspects of a free market economy with socialist planning objectives and to do this in a more decentralized manner than the top–down approach used immediately after Liberation.

Prior to the 6th Party Congress, Linh had published numerous articles in the state-run media on the problems that had been created by the government and the reforms needed for the country. He signed his articles with the acronym NVL, purportedly standing for *noi va lam* [speak and work] but also the initials of his own name. The NVL articles were the first steps towards something that many Vietnamese have come to expect from their government, namely, a frank assessment of what is wrong and a relatively honest attempt to fix it. By the mid-1980s, the country was in desperate straits and the Communist Party was determined to fix things.

Among the first steps was a liberalization of agriculture which had been set up as farmer communes in the Mekong Delta and the rest of southern Vietnam after Liberation.[1] The government now changed course and instructed farmers to grow and sell their crops on their own and without price controls or subsidies. When this decision was put into effect in 1988, Vietnam was not growing enough food and had to import it. However, by 1991 it was not only feeding itself but had also become the world's third largest exporter of rice. The government passed a revised land law in 1993 that gave farmers more ownership rights over their land. The new law guaranteed farmers five rights to do with their land as they wished: the right to transfer, exchange, inherit, rent, or mortgage their own land. The government also opened the doors to foreign trade, thus allowing foreign-made goods into the country.

While many commentators hail the Doi Moi policies of 1986 as the great turning point for Vietnam, the changes were initially slow to materialize. That was soon to change because of events in Eastern Europe. The primary catalyst for where Vietnam is today occurred thousands of miles away with the fall of the Berlin Wall in 1989, after months of protests and thousands of East Germans fleeing into Austria via an open border in Hungary. The final protest on the streets of East Berlin in early November was the last straw. The Berlin Wall, the key symbol separating East and West Germany, as well as two different views of how the world should work, fell and East Germans poured into West Berlin. There was no longer a barrier between East and West in the city of Berlin, the country of Germany, or ultimately in most of the world.

---

1. See Chapter 10, Case Study 5: Value-added Agriculture, pp. 107–22.

The predominant socialist policies of state control, command economies, and limited free market opportunities had been proven not to work and communism as a means of governing had been reduced to five countries, namely, China, Cuba, Laos, North Korea, and Vietnam.

Important Old Friends Disappear

Vietnam lost more than an ideological partner with the collapse of communism in Eastern Europe. The Soviet Union had been providing numerous subsidized goods as well as soft loans to Vietnam for its development. After April 1975 one of the first large-scale joint-venture companies was VietSovPetro. This oil and gas company was set up after the exit of international companies like Mobile, Exxon, and BP, who were forced to abandon the development of offshore oilfields at the end of the American War. VietSovPetro stepped in to pump up the crude and develop the gas fields that had been discovered and developed by the foreign oil and gas companies.

The Soviet Union and many Eastern European socialist countries also provided educational opportunities for Vietnamese students. If a survey was done among Hanoi intellectuals, many outsiders would probably be surprised at the number of Vietnamese who had obtained their undergraduate and postgraduate degrees in East European universities. These countries were also the source for many Vietnamese to work in factories and earn foreign currency for their families at home. All these opportunities dried up when the Berlin Wall fell and many countries, for example, Poland, Hungary, Bulgaria, Czechoslovakia, and the Soviet Union, had to plot new strategies for their own future. Helping a socialist outpost in Asia was not high on their priority list.

It was a nightmare come true for the leaders of Vietnam. The Soviet Union had helped to keep Vietnam afloat after Liberation and into the early 1980s. Even though the money had run out by the late 1980s, Vietnam still had an ideological friend. After the break-up of the Soviet Union, however, it still had a Russian friend, but Russia had neither aid money nor was it an ideological partner with which to face the world. The fall of the Berlin Wall, the reunification of Germany, and the eventual dismantling of the Soviet Union was not something most observers could have anticipated. Even among those who did or could, no one would have predicted the speed of the change.

Within a matter of months, the world as Vietnam knew it and the world as it knew itself was no longer. Vietnam was very much alone in the world. It was time to draw on its reservoir of the two things it had in abundance: grit and pragmatism.

Grit and Pragmatism

Grit is a cultural trait that Vietnam has long relied on. It essentially means putting in a sustained effort towards a long-term goal. Grit helps explain how the Vietnamese could persevere through so many years of war against nations much more powerful than its own. But simply working hard is not unique. Throughout history, citizens of many countries have worked hard for something they believed in, and the world today has a lot of hard-working people who have endured, and still endure, difficulties for something they believe in. Vietnam exhibited plenty of grit during the French War, especially at the end by carrying enough heavy artillery, piece by piece, into the mountains surrounding the French at Dien Bien Phu to force the French to surrender after more than fifty days of bombing. Another and perhaps better example of grit are the Vietnamese who built and managed the Ho Chi Minh Trail during the American War. This was a multiyear effort during which the bombing was constant. Yet, at the end of this gritty effort, their country was falling apart. Grit on its own was not enough. Grit on its own helped the Vietnamese win a thirty-year war against two very powerful countries, but it could not be used to successfully run a country. This is where another strong Vietnamese cultural trait—pragmatism—came into play.

President Fidel Castro of Cuba, one of Vietnam's ideological partners during the war years and after Liberation, was famous for his four- to five-hour speeches. He could endlessly harangue the capitalist world. Emitting a big puff of cigar smoke, he would pound his fist and shout *Socialismo hay muerte* [socialism or death] to the fanatical applause of his audience. He had a certain idea of how socialism should work for Cuba (e.g., full state control, command economy, and no market forces) and he pursued it relentlessly. Fortunately, this never happened in Vietnam because the Vietnamese are a very pragmatic people. Fidel Castro survived the reign of ten United States presidents without moving from his *socialismo hay muerte* stance. He refused to bend, which is an admirable trait in some cases, but not all. Vietnam tried its best with socialist policies for about ten years (1975–85) and then decided to try something new. This trait of abandoning what is not working and trying something new is something that happens time and time again in government policy settings and in the creation of laws in Vietnam.

Grit is a cultural trait that Vietnamese have in their DNA. But like talent on its own, grit on its own needs a booster. It needs another cultural trait. In the Vietnam case, it is pragmatism. Set out as an equation spanning the era since 1975, it might look like this:[2]

Grit x No Policy Change = No Opportunity to Succeed (1975–85)

Grit x Pragmatism = Opportunity to Succeed (from 1989 onwards)

While Vietnam's leaders in 1989 were undoubtedly nervous about the events of Eastern Europe, the notion of changing course or pivoting away from a certain policy direction that was not working was nothing new. As early as 1983 there were minor shifts in agricultural policy that started to turn the country away from full-blown commune-style rice farming in the Mekong Delta. These and other adjustments led to the formal adoption of Doi Moi at the 6th Party Congress in 1986, a full three years before the collapse of communism in Europe and well before Mikhail Gorbachev's *glasnost* and *perestroika* policies fundamentally changed the Soviet Union and ultimately all the Eastern European bloc nations. In other words, pragmatists were already on the job and trying to make changes during the turbulent decade after Liberation. Eastern European communist countries took several decades to initiate, execute, and then eventually abandon their ultra-socialist policies. In Vietnam this same realization and acceptance that these same types of policies were not going to work took less than a decade. The country was ready to try something new.

Vietnam in the 1990s was an opaque and often hard to understand place for doing business. Seemingly contradictory steps were taken all the time, or so it seemed to foreign and local investors. It was a socialist country with the Vietnamese Communist Party fully in charge. Yet, it had a market economy

---

2. This is a modified framework of a model developed by Dr Angela Lee Duckworth in her book *Grit: Why passion and resilience are the secrets to success* (Vermillion, 2016). In her work she argues that talent on its own cannot adequately explain success. It must be paired with effort (i.e., grit). In our modified framework of her model, we argue that grit on its own is not good enough. It must be paired with pragmatism.

or at least the start of one. It was allowing foreign investors into the country. It was beginning to trade with countries from around the world. It could boast several commodities, including crude oil, rice, shrimp, cashews, and coffee, that many markets in the world were ready to buy. For this reason, it was preparing to enter into a range of trading alliances and free trade agreements that were all based on free market economy principles.

More than thirty years later, Vietnam has answered the question that its leaders probably asked themselves after the Berlin Wall fell in 1989 about what they should do next. Its answer is to keep moving forward, adapting, and pivoting when needed, and to not allow labels or economic models to define who they are and what they intend to do with their country.

Vietnam is a nation of pragmatic people determined to overcome whatever obstacles are put in front of them. They are pragmatic by nature, and having survived countless challenges they now have little to fear. That is what happens when grit and pragmatism combine. As the country was forced to move forward on its own after 1989, the past was put behind them. The country had independence and freedom. It was no longer at war. It was time to open to the world and move forward. That is what it did.

Chapter 4

OPEN FOR BUSINESS

Vietnam was an exciting place to be in the 1990s. To kick off the decade, the government advertised its first official 'Year of Tourism.' It also passed a foreign investment law to encourage foreign companies to build businesses in the country, as well as a domestic investment law to encourage local entrepreneurs to do the same. Although it is likely that few Politburo members, government planners, or regular citizens really knew where the country was going, there were no complaints. Wherever it was going, it had to be better than where it had been.

In February 1994 the United States finally lifted its trade embargo on Vietnam. One year later, and after aggressive lobbying from two American veterans of the American War—United States Senators John McCain and John Kerry—official normalization of relations was agreed between Vietnam and the United States, and the two countries exchanged ambassadors. This boosted trade and investment for not only United States-Vietnam relations but also numerous other countries and organizations such as the World Bank and International Monetary Fund, who had been hamstrung by the politics of Washington DC. The embargo also impacted private companies, for example, Airbus and Boeing, who previously could not sell airplanes to Vietnam because they contained American-made components.

A Buzz in the Air

The lifting of the United States embargo and the eventual normalization of United States-Vietnam relations set off a chain of events for nearly everyone in Vietnam. It was deal-making season, which caused many Vietnamese to catch MOU fever (memorandums of understanding). They were being signed constantly. Vietnamese companies hosted fact-finding missions from numerous countries and international companies. On the foreign side, the goal was to simply look, but the Vietnamese side wanted more and asked visitors to sign an MOU. These never carried a lot of weight and certainly no legal obligations, but were signed anyway. However, some of those MOUs did begin to lead to something tangible, and suddenly there was a multitude of deals in the works.

Local entrepreneurs were opening all kinds of businesses, ranging from small, family-owned trading companies to home-based manufacturing companies. For much of the mid- to late 1990s, it seemed that a new coffee shop or restaurant was opening every week in Ho Chi Minh City. At the same time, the property market was booming, with investments in homes, apartments, undeveloped land, and high-end serviced apartments and condominiums.

Despite any doubts they might have had, the conservative members of the Party and Politburo must have been happy where things were heading. Vietnam was starting to grow. In fact, by the twentieth anniversary of the Liberation of Saigon in 1995, Vietnam was seriously booming. The national economy was moving along at 8–9 percent annual growth (much higher in the urban areas), exports were growing around 20–25 percent per year, and licensed FDI had hit close to US$10 billion per year by the end of 1995. Expectations of the future were wonderfully high, though often premature. Not everyone was entirely

Tomorrow Never Dies

In 1997, licenses were issued, hotel rooms had been booked, and equipment was on the way for a James Bond 007 movie to be filmed in Vietnam. The film crews and directors from England were on their way to Heathrow airport when word arrived that the film had been canceled. In a sign that not everyone was pleased with the new developments, one of the members of the Politburo scrapped the project at the last minute. He said James Bond was too anti-communist, or so the gossip was at the time. Though the filming of the movie was canceled, the story line for the movie was still 'set' in Vietnam, but it was filmed in Thailand. For this particular 007 movie, tomorrow may not have died for James Bond, but his permit to film in Vietnam did.

ready (see the story on James Bond), but many foreign companies were flocking in regardless. They set up joint ventures or 100 percent foreign-owned companies. They all wanted to cash in on the newest business frontier of Asia. China was old news. It was a chance to enter a country getting ready to skyrocket.

It was a great time to live and work in Vietnam. There were parties every week to celebrate a contract signing or the opening of a new joint venture, a representative office, or some other kind of foreign-invested company. In 1995 CNN sent a film crew to cover the twentieth anniversary of the 'Fall of Saigon.' Among journalists, expatriates, and local Vietnamese, there was almost a parlor game atmosphere to find and attend the opening ceremony parties that had the best food. The consensus at the time was that the Japanese provided the best food, the Americans the most beer, and the Koreans were usually the most fun.

The Asian Economic Crisis of 1997 did not lead to the collapse of the Vietnamese economy as it did in Thailand and many other countries in Asia, nor did it compel the government to reverse course. In neighboring countries, many people lost substantial amounts of wealth. Capital was being pulled out of those countries and local companies had debts they would never be able to repay. But in Vietnam things were different. At the time it had no stock market or a readily convertible currency. There was little foreign debt, so its economy was not too deeply connected to the rest of the world.

But it was not completely immune. Vietnam's bubble had started to burst before the regional financial crisis. It was not really a burst, more like a large balloon of expectations that slowly began to deflate. Investors, mostly foreign but also local, started to realize their unrealistic and unmet expectations. There were also a handful of scandals, one of the more significant ones known as Minh Phung EPCO. This scandal involved two companies—a private garment and construction company, Minh Phung, and a trading company, EPCO—that illegally obtained around US$280 million in loans from state banks by using phantom property as collateral. More than seventy people involved were convicted and some were sentenced to death. The scandal revealed just how far Vietnam still had to go to join the international business world.

Foreign companies were also beginning to realize that doing things 'the Vietnam way' really did mean 'the Vietnam way.' The government would not be bullied into reforms that the country was not ready for, and it made that clear in various venues. For example, the Swiss-based World Economic Forum hosted a seminar in Ho Chi Minh City in the mid-1990s. It was a big deal at the time and reflected the level of international attention that Vietnam was attracting around the world. The seminar featured various ministers and government leaders and the press covered it in detail. It was an important enough event to have simultaneous translation with headphones available for attendees at their seats, among them co-author Sam Korsmoe.

The speeches presented by the ministers were scripted and the words completely predictable about the role of the state, joint ventures (not 100 percent foreign-owned entities), and the need to keep certain industries in state hands. When the floor was opened for questions, a foreigner asked, "What will be the role for private sector companies in Vietnam?" The government leader who had the microphone on the dais seemed surprised by the question. There was a pause, and then he answered, "For various reasons, the state will maintain a leadership role in certain sectors of the economy such as telecommunications, banking, transportation, finance…." This went on for a bit as he listed the various sectors of the economy. He concluded with, "and any other major sector of the economy."

The real challenges were being experienced by foreign investors who had already entered joint ventures with local partners. The foreign partners quickly realized that their new local partners would not passively sit back and let them take control of the business to run as they saw fit. This was especially evident with the likes of major consumer goods companies who had established business models and strategies on how to do business successfully in the fast-moving consumer goods (FMCG) market. The local partners often had other ideas. The result was a litany of failed or severely adjusted joint ventures leading to questions about Vietnam's readiness to modernize its economy. A prime example of 'adjustment' was the American company Procter and Gamble (P&G), who formed a joint venture with a local state-owned company on a 70/30 share basis (70 percent for P&G and 30 percent for the local partner) in the mid- to late 1990s. A loan from a foreign bank got called and the joint venture could not pay, so the company had to recapitalize itself with more capital from the balance sheet of its owners. Since each side's balance sheet was quite different when the capital call was made, it forced a recalculation of the joint- venture terms. It became a 97/3 joint venture (97 percent for P&G and just 3 percent for the local partner) from its previous 70/30 agreement. Similar stories played out with Coca Cola, Pepsi, and Unilever at the end of the 1990s. Many of these ventures eventually were allowed to convert to 100 percent foreign-owned entities.

At the time investors had justifiable reasons to be concerned, but in fact it was more a matter of the country moving too far too fast. Nation-building does not go in straight lines and every now and again everyone's expectations can get ahead or fall behind what is realistically achievable. Vietnam, like other emerging countries, had a plethora of experienced foreign experts advising on what it could do better. However, this did not mean the anticipated changes, no matter how good they were, would immediately follow. This is exactly what co-author Brook Taylor found out when trying to enhance Vietnamese accounting standards. Patience is essential to nation-building because often it just takes time.

It Can Take a Generation

By Brook Taylor

In the late 1990s there was a move to standardize accounting standards around the world. Many countries were replacing their locally developed national accounting standards with the International Financial Reporting Standards (IFRS) or a modified version of it. At the time Vietnam had its own accounting system which all companies were expected to follow. It was appropriately called the Vietnamese Accounting System (VAS) and it was essentially a bookkeeping manual for state-owned companies. Its value to private companies was questionable and it was certainly not anything close to IFRS.

I was asked to introduce IFRS to the head of accounting policy at the Ministry of Finance and I was eager to get started. I figured it would be relatively easy for the authorities to see the benefits of IFRS. Vietnam would be the first country in Southeast Asia to adopt these important global standards. Armed with my copy of IFRS, my meeting with the director was cordial, but he said he had already heard of IFRS and was not interested in it. I left the meeting as another perplexed and frustrated foreigner.

It took time, several years in fact, but eventually I realized the problem. It was the lack of empathy on my part. The director was a career bureaucrat within the Ministry of Finance and had already achieved some success in his career. As the chief editor of VAS, he was 'comfortable' in his role. He had things under control. He did not want to endorse IFRS because it might put his job and legacy at risk. I thought promoting these new standards would immortalize him among the Vietnamese accounting fraternity, but to him the decision was one of risk management. He understood the importance of improving financial reporting in Vietnam and he understood IFRS much more than I had realized, but this did not matter.

The director would not endorse a new set of accounting standards because he did not know what the unintended consequences might be or how to manage them. It was also not just his decision to make. A change of this significance would need the approval of others in the Ministry of Finance, other ministries, and eventually the prime minister, most of whom would have little knowledge of accounting standards, whether VAS or IFRS, and so would need to be fully briefed before giving their endorsement. It would be a tough job to pull off. Obviously, the better move would be to simply wait until more people became familiar with the new standards and then the adoption process would be easier.

That is exactly what happened with IFRS. On March 16, 2020, the Ministry of Finance approved the IFRS road map which required all companies in Vietnam to apply the Vietnamese Financial Reporting Standard (VFRS), a modified version of the IFRS, by the year 2025. The long waiting time might be the cause of frustration to well-intended foreigners and outside experts, but some things cannot change overnight. Patience is required. It often takes time, even a generation, for some changes to occur.

After the 1997 Economic Crisis, Vietnam, along with everyone else in Asia, had to put its house in order and convince local and foreign investors that its growth fundamentals were still in place. This was new territory. Vietnam really had no experience marketing itself, but it managed well enough by once again drawing on its reservoir of the two things Vietnamese have in abundance: grit and pragmatism.

An enterprise law was enacted on the first day of the new millennium. It clarified the rules of investment for foreigners and resulted in a boom of new entrepreneurs opening private companies. An inordinate amount of time was spent getting a bilateral trade agreement (BTA) with the United States in place, but that finally happened at the end of 2001 and resulted in a 300 percent increase in Vietnamese exports to the United States in the first year of trade under the new BTA. Local governments were also more empowered to license bigger and more sophisticated foreign investment projects in their provinces. They then went on to build industrial parks and export-processing zones and began to market themselves as investment destinations to American, European, Japanese, Taiwanese, and South Korean manufacturers.

The stock market opened in July 2000 with a modest two listed companies—the Refrigeration Electrical Equipment Joint Stock Company (REE) and the Saigon Cable and Telecommunication Material Joint Stock Company (SACOM). Several more companies followed. The shares of these companies were held by management, staff, and some outside investors. The newly restructured and listed companies were the result of a process called 'equitization.' This was the means of moving the thousands of SOEs that previously dominated all business into the modern economy. In other countries, this process is called *privatization*, but in Vietnam that term was considered 'too capitalist' to use at the time and the word 'equitization' was adopted instead.

The process involved putting SOEs through a series of steps so that they were no longer controlled by the state. They would also no longer be entitled to any of the privileges SOEs received, such as subsidies, cheap loans, and market protection. They would be forced to fend for themselves in the new market-based economy that was emerging in the late 1990s and early 2000s.

The first step was to convert the SOEs into joint-stock companies with their capital divided into shares. The second step was to distribute these shares to the employees of the SOE. And then if needed, a third step might be to sell shares to strategic investors with the intention of either recapitalizing the companies and/or helping them with their transition to the free market.

The fourth step was to list the companies on the stock market so that employees could, if they still had shares, sell these at a fair price and get a cash payment. In fact, most employees sold their shares to management and speculators for cash on the day they received them. This meant that it was not the employees lining up at the stock market but the traders who had already purchased their shares on the informal market. Capitalism was alive and well in Vietnam as soon as there was a chance for it to appear. The company could, of course, raise additional capital by selling more shares on the stock market. These shares could be liquidated, purchased, gain value, lose value, or anything else that a normal stock market does. It was not the NYSE, nor the Nikkei, nor the LSE, but it was a start.

In its early months the stock market would be 'open for trading' for only several minutes before price swings forced its closure. There was a line of buyers and a line of sellers ready to go at the opening bell. Since share prices were not allowed to move more than three percent per day, all trading would end once this price swing was met for each company listed. For many listed companies, this generally took just a few minutes, and the market almost always went up. More companies were added in the first year and the market grew. In fact, the index grew more than 400 percent in 2001, its first full year of operation. At that time, it was the fastest growing stock market in the world.

Red Capitalists

The push to equitize SOEs and get a stock market up and running was part of the Vietnamese government's effort to do something constructive with all its SOEs. These were the big policy- driven state-owned companies that had too many employees who were paid unlivable wages to do or make whatever it was the SOE was supposed to. Whether there was market demand for what they did or made might have been irrelevant. Employees of these SOEs always had side jobs because it was impossible to live off an official state salary (sometimes less than US$20 per month).

Various policy reforms were attempted and one of them was to allow some SOEs to do, on their own, whatever they were already doing and then anything else they wanted to do. This meant management could essentially direct the company in whatever direction was needed to survive or make a profit without reporting to a ministry official or anyone else outside the company. In some cases, this meant pursuing non-core opportunities in real estate, tourism, or various services, even though they had nothing to do with their mandate as an SOE. For example, a SOE like the oil and gas behemoth PetroVietnam could go into real estate and open a chain of hotels for foreign tourists (not oil and gas employees) because it either already had the real estate or had enough cash to buy real estate in prime locations. It could also obtain licenses for a bank, insurance company, and several other regulated businesses in which it had no experience.

The Vietnamese have a term for this—*pha rao* or 'fence-breaking'—the idea being that the companies were breaking down the fences in which they had been confined and could venture into business on their own. This meant not just having all their bases covered, but also being allowed to do whatever they wanted, for example, buy land, open new companies in untested markets, build a hotel, etc., but still being covered by the state. The SOEs had a green light to pursue side deals and they could also petition the state for finance or state guarantees. Moreover, their side deals might include investing in and starting up a finance company, an existing bank, or purchasing shares in a start-up bank with some private investors as well as other SOEs. It was a bit of a black box with few, if any, regulators ensuring that the state's capital was used responsibly and that the debts were paid on time and with interest.

Despite the challenges, the campaign to 'equitize' the SOE sector continued. Good 'fence- breaking' companies could potentially pull together enough core deals and non-core deals and combine these with their access to capital and make good money. Perhaps this would push them down the road to become the Vietnamese equivalent of a South Korean conglomerate (*chaebol*), or so went the thinking prior to the implosion of VinaShin.

The VinaShin Saga

The most famous of the fence-breakers in the early 2000s was the Vietnam Shipbuilding Industry Group or VinaShin. It had dreams of becoming one of the world's largest shipbuilders. Perhaps the senior managers had researched South Korea's shipbuilding industry and thought it might be a good model for themselves. Perhaps they felt they were, or could become, a type of *chaebol* with the advantage of having the backing of the state.

In 2004 VinaShin won, with state support, a US$322 million contract to build fifteen bulk carriers (53,000 DWT ships) for a Welsh company. The state had to step in to seal the deal because neither private foreign banks nor, initially, state-owned Vietnamese banks would guarantee the deal. They argued that VinaShin was simply too new and inexperienced to pull off such a large contract for so many ships. The state banks stepped in only when ordered to do so by the government. Although the first completed ship off the construction dock reportedly sprung a leak, the leak was fixed, and the contract was successfully fulfilled. This led to VinaShin building several more bulk carriers. Foreign economists and pundits argued that the only reason the ships could be built was that they were being built at a loss due to the cheap capital that VinaShin could obtain from the state.

Successfully floating so many boats probably gave the aspiring *chaebol* the confidence to become more aggressive. The short story of the VinaShin scandal is that the company managed to pull together a consortium of foreign- and state-owned banks to obtain over US$600 million in loans for new projects, several of which were questionable from the start. One rumor at the time was that the company set up a taxi business and the CEO of the taxi company was formerly the chauffeur of the VinaShin chairman.

When VinaShin missed its first loan payment shortly after closing the deal, the finger- pointing and blame game began. Apparently, the VinaShin management ship had a lot of leaks and the mismanagement of the money caught up with them. Over the next few years (2008–12), several executives were sentenced to jail. The case was frequently reported in the local and international press. In the end, the loan had to be converted to bonds backed by the Ministry of Finance. Pundits cried foul and warned of the 'moral hazard' of bailing out an inefficient state-owned company that had clearly got in way over its head.

Optimism Prevails

How did the Vietnamese feel during the ups and downs of the early days of Vietnam's capitalist experiment? Since the early 1990s, and most of the time since then, Vietnamese have been among the sunniest, most satisfied, and most optimistic people in the world. There is evidence of that sentiment from an extensive worldwide survey of global attitudes. In 2002 the Washington DC-based PEW Research Center for the People and the Press surveyed more than 38,000 people in forty-four countries. It was called the Global Attitudes Project, and among its many purposes was to find out what people were thinking about themselves, their countries, their government, the United States, other countries, and the state of the world at large.

The overall conclusion? Twenty years ago, discontent and dissatisfaction were worldwide trends. There were very few people who seemed happy with their lot in life. This was particularly true of rich and powerful nations such as the United States and most of Western Europe. They had dismal views of the future, the state of their own nations, and the fate of their children. Rising above this discontent were a handful of nations, one of which was Vietnam, whose people consistently expressed optimistic attitudes about what was happening in their lives and the world around them. Below is a selection of Vietnamese responses to some of the questions from the survey.

Table 2. Vietnamese optimism compared to the rest of the world, 2002

Question/Issue posed in the survey	Vietnamese 'yes' response (%)	Vietnamese responses compared to citizens from the other 43 countries surveyed
Personally satisfied with the world at large	51	Highest rating in survey
Personally satisfied with their country	69	Highest rating in survey
Personally satisfied with their own lives	43	Second only to South Korea
Country has 'made progress' over the past 5 years	53	Highest in Asia; 4th highest worldwide
Optimistic about the next 5 years	69	Second highest in Asia
Satisfied with the state of your country	69	Highest in Asia; tied with Uzbekistan for highest
Economic situation is good vs. bad	92–good	Highest in survey (22 points ahead of 2nd place Canada)

Source: 'What the World Thinks in 2002,' Pew Global Attitudes Project, Pew Research Center, 2002.

Fewer than one in twenty Vietnamese believed the following five years (2002–7) were going to be worse than the previous five. By contrast, half of the Americans surveyed thought their children would be worse off when they grew up. The British were equally pessimistic, and the Italians, French, and Canadians were even more pessimistic about the future lives of their children. The 92 percent of the Vietnamese who believed their economic situation was 'good' is a true outlier; optimistic runner-up Canada was far behind. More than 50 percent of those surveyed from France, Germany, Italy, Japan, South Korea, and the United States, and most of the other forty-four countries surveyed said their economic situation was 'bad.'

At the beginning of the new millennium, Vietnam had an optimistic and simple outlook. The country had opened its doors to FDI, trade, and perhaps most importantly, to allowing its own citizens to do business and engage with the world. They had grit on their side as well as pragmatic leaders. Vietnam was ready to do business with the world. To do that well, it had to compete head-to-head with the rest of the world, and it had a plan to make that happen.

Chapter 5

FREE TRADE BETTER WORK

In 1776 Adam Smith published *The Wealth of Nations*, a treatise that captured the world's imagination. It portrayed a view of how the world should or, at least, could work. Smith argued that for the 'natural liberty of man' the free market was the best way to allocate resources and that government intervention should be limited. According to Smith, the free market was the final stage of man's four-stage development from hunting to nomadic agriculture to feudal agriculture and, finally, to commercial interdependence. In this final stage, Smith argued that free trade makes societies richer due to the existence of 'the invisible hand'—the concept that if individuals pursue their own self-interest, they are usually led to make decisions that are in the best interests of their society. His ideas were radical at the time, but they have since become the foundation of modern economics.

Summarizing the work of the man considered to be 'the Father of Economics' in a single paragraph is difficult, but it is an appropriate way of introducing this chapter and explaining its relevance to Vietnam. Maybe it was the pursuit of 'natural liberty' that took hold, or maybe it was because free trade had worked for so many countries in the world, but whatever the reason, since joining the World Trade Organization (WTO) in 2007, Vietnam has taken the idea of free trade to heart. For Vietnam, it is not just a commitment to the WTO. At the beginning of 2023, Vietnam was party to fifteen free trade agreements, with two more under negotiation. These include agreements linked with its membership in the Association of Southeast Asian Nations (ASEAN), as well as relatively new agreements negotiated independently with the European Union (EU) and the United Kingdom.[1]

Vietnam was also at the founding table in 2005 when twelve Pacific Rim nations committed to the Trans-Pacific Partnership (TPP) agreement, which then took another ten years of negotiating to conclude. The draft agreement was finalized in February 2016. In 2018 Vietnam's National Assembly unanimously ratified the agreement, making Vietnam the seventh nation to officially enter the TPP. By then the trade agreement had taken on a new name, the Comprehensive and Progressive Agreement for Trans-Pacific Partnership (CPTPP) and its membership had been reduced to eleven nations after the United States pulled out after the Trump administration came to power.

Vietnam's approach to free trade is not just about a flow of imports and exports through its ports. That aspect of trade has been going on for the last thirty years, with double-digit annual growth in recent years. Free trade in Vietnam encapsulates many things. It includes the inflow of capital in terms of foreign direct investment (FDI) and foreign indirect investment (FII). FDI is not just about joint ventures—the government's preferred structure of investment in the 1990s—but also about 100 percent foreign-owned enterprises. FII includes the flow of capital into and out of the country's stock and bond markets, which is unrestricted except for the foreign ownership limits applied to the shareholders' registers of certain companies.

The country's free trade philosophy also means an open border in terms of people who want to visit the country as well as an open border in terms of ideas that can be shared over the internet and social media platforms.[2] Many of the more recent free trade agreements that Vietnam has entered into, such as the CPTPP, also include commitments to addressing environmental, social, and governance (ESG) issues, such as protection of the environment and labor rights. The international engagement that comes with free trade also means partnering with other nations to address global issues, such as climate change.[3]

---

1. Center for WTO and World Trade and Vietnam Chamber of Commerce and Industry website, March 2023.

2. Blocking access to these platforms could be done with relatively simple firewall tools, but that is not happening to the same extent in Vietnam as it is in other countries.

3. Vietnam joined 127 other countries committed to net-zero greenhouse gas emissions by 2050 at the 26th Conference of the Parties of the United Nations Framework Convention on Climate Change (COP26) in Glasgow on November 1, 2021.

The breadth of Vietnam's commitments under its many trade agreements and the benefits already realized mean that the country has passed 'the point of no return' on the issue of free trade. Why, then, does a country with nearly one hundred million people have such a high commitment to free trade? It is not just odd, but rather counter-intuitive since one aspect of free trade that many countries worry about is increased competition for local firms. Socialist nations, one would think, would want to protect local SOEs, and controlling markets would be one way of doing this. Vietnam is seemingly ignoring this type of thinking and doing the opposite.

The reason is because free trade is an essential component of the version of the East Asian Development Model that Vietnam has chosen to build its economic wealth and development. While the application of the East Asian Development Model differs across countries, the general approach involves the government introducing policies that facilitate growth through the better use of the country's resources. In Vietnam's case, government policy changes have improved agricultural production and mobilized capital and the labor force to produce goods for export markets. Readers living in Western countries have probably observed similar versions of this export-driven version of the East Asian Development Model in action without being aware of its existence. Depending on your current age, you will recall that many of your childhood clothes and toys had labels stating where the products were made. They usually came from one or two countries. In the 1950s and 1960s, it was Japan. In the 1970s, it was Hong Kong and Taiwan. In the 1980s, it was South Korea. Since the 1990s, it has been China. However, from about 2010 Vietnam has taken an increasing share of this market from China. This movement of the manufacturing of labor-intensive products from country to country is one example of the East Asian Development Model being adopted by different countries over the last seventy years. Hence, the importance of trade and trade agreements.

The mobilization of idle labor and the movement of labor from sectors where it is less productive, such as in agriculture, into the manufacturing sector means labor is better utilized and creates more value. The process begins with the production of simple goods, such as garments, footwear, and toys. But as the skills, infrastructure, and technology in the country improve, the focus shifts up the value chain to producing more sophisticated and higher-value goods like computer chips and laptops.

Assuming that the right conditions are in place, and irrespective of the product produced, if the country is among the lowest cost producers it will be able to attract investors to build new factories to produce products to sell to other markets. Those sales earn foreign currency, which is then spent on acquiring additional machinery and equipment and the building of infrastructure. This leads to even more factories producing more and higher-value products. This cycle expands production over several decades until it is no longer a low-cost producer. At this point, the country needs to have transitioned its economy from predominately manufacturing to predominately services to sustain its growth. This has already happened in South Korea and Taiwan, where services now make up 57.3 percent and 64.9 percent of GDP, respectively.[4]

Vietnam's aggressive pursuit of free trade and an export-driven version of the East Asian Development Model has popularized the use of a metric to describe the country's current success in this endeavor—the Globalization Rate. This is the ratio of total trade to GDP. It is expressed as a percentage of the total value of imports plus the total value of exports divided by total GDP. For example, for 2019 the calculation would be as follows:[5]

Total size of Vietnam's GDP: US$255 billion
Exports (US$264 billion) + Imports (US$253 billion)
    = Total trade of US$517 billion
Total Trade (US$517 billion) / Total GDP (US$255 billion)
    = 203 percent Globalization Rate.

A globalization rate of more than 200 percent is very high when it comes to measuring the rating of a country on the globalization index. Among countries similar in population size to Vietnam, it is the highest. The second-placed country, Thailand, is 123 percent globalized (see table 3). Except for small, lightly populated nations and city-states like Hong Kong and Singapore, most countries do not have globalization indexes of more than 100 percent.

---

4. World Bank World Development Indicators Database, 2022.

5. *Authors' Note*: 2019 data is used for this illustration about globalization because 2020 and 2021 data have been impacted by COVID-19 and would not paint an accurate picture of what has been happening with trade since the year 2000. The authors consider COVID-19 a blip in terms of its impact on the Vietnamese economy and they expect trade to revert to pre-COVID-19 norms in 2023.

Also, the general norm is the more people that live in a country, the lower its globalization rate. This is certainly not the case for Vietnam today. In fact, based on the globalization index, Vietnam is one of the most globalized countries in the world and few nations of its size even come close.

Table 3. Globalization rates (%) of the top five nations based on segmented population data, 2018

Large city states to 10 m	10–20 m	21–50 m	More than 50 m
Hong Kong – 376	Belgium – 176	Malaysia – 132	Vietnam – 196
Singapore – 326	Netherlands – 155	Poland – 107	Thailand – 123
Ireland – 210	Czech Republic – 151	Ukraine – 99	Germany – 87
Slovak Republic – 193	Guinea – 132	Canada – 66	South Korea – 83
Hungary – 168	Cambodia – 125	Taiwan – 63	Congo Republic – 71

Source: World Bank and multiple industry sources.

The reason for this high globalization rate is because an early step in the export-driven model (manufacturing garments, footwear, and toys) involves the developing country (e.g., Vietnam) importing semi-processed raw materials and components for processing and then exporting the resulting finished products. It imports semi-processed raw materials and components because it does not yet have the factories needed to produce these items from basic raw materials, such as agricultural commodities and minerals.

These manufacturing arrangements are often part of the global supply chain of large foreign companies. The foreign company is both the provider of the materials and components and the recipient (buyer) of the finished products that are then distributed through its sales network. The primary input of the country processing the goods is labor. This kind of manufacturing is referred to as 'toll manufacturing' and it skews the globalization rate calculation. The numerator, total trade (imports plus exports) is large when the denominator (total GDP) is small because GDP only increases by the labor cost and ancillary materials and services sourced locally. Hence, Vietnam's high globalization rate is a product of toll manufacturing, which is an indicator that a country has started to apply an export-led version of the East Asian Development Model strategy.

Further evidence of this happening in Vietnam can be cited with examples of companies involved in these activities. Nike has been sourcing garments and footwear in Vietnam since 1992,[6] and now considers Vietnam its largest manufacturing hub.[7] Canon has been shipping components to Vietnam for assembly and re-export as light electronics since 1998,[8] and now manufactures most of its cameras, printers, and scanners for the Asia-Pacific region in Vietnam.

But the best and most interesting example of this in Vietnam is the South Korean *chaebol* Samsung Electronics. The *chaebol* has already invested US$18 billion in the country, and in 2022 it exported about US$65 billion worth of products from the country (20 percent of Vietnam's total exports).[9] Most of this is due to the Galaxy smartphone which is made in its factory in Thai Nguyen Province. Today, according to several industry sources, most of Samsung Electronics' smart phones are assembled in Vietnam by teams drawn from its over 200,000 workers in the country.[10]

The verb 'assembled' is appropriate here because many of the smartphone components are imported. The workers put these parts together and test them before the finished products are exported to global markets. For Vietnam this process makes for very large trade numbers. Although the amount of value derived in Vietnam and its impact on GDP is much smaller, the incomes generated by 200,000 people are very important. They likely support 400,000–600,000 people directly and millions more indirectly. The 200,000 employees are also gaining better skills for the future than if they were sewing garments and making shoes. The government understands this, and that is why companies like Samsung are given investment incentives to build factories in Vietnam.

As the manufacturing base expands, a key success factor in the process becomes the host country's ability to increase the share of locally produced components used in the products being assembled and exported so that a greater share of the value of exports remains in the country. This requires more advanced training of the workforce and the construction of factories producing semi-processed raw materials and components. To encourage this, host governments like Vietnam require that the items produced contain a

6. *About Us*, Nike website.

7. *Report*, Vietnam Business Forum.

8. *About Canon*, Canon's official global website.

9. *Report*, Vietnam Customs Department, March 2023.

10. 'Samsung Electronics to raise total investment in Vietnam to $20 billion,' Vietnam Investment Review, December 2022.

minimum proportion of locally sourced components for the manufacturer to receive tax incentives. Customs duty exemptions granted by foreign governments under trade agreements also encourage the localization of production, as local content is an important consideration when determining a product's 'Country of Origin.'

Localization is already happening in Vietnam. When Honda opened its first motorcycle plant in the mid-1990s, it was an assembly-line production facility that put various imported parts together to produce motorbikes for the local market. In the beginning, nearly all the parts were imported from Honda suppliers in the region to make primarily one model—the Honda Dream. Twenty-five years later, according to industry sources, the locally sourced ratio of parts in a Vietnam-made Honda motorcycle ranges from 35 percent to 55 percent for its Wave Alpha, Super Dream, and Future models. Not only did Honda parts suppliers follow their major customer to Vietnam, but local entrepreneurs also built factories to produce parts, thus negating the need to import them.

The more value that the country generates from expanding manufacturing and increasing local content increases household wealth through both salaries and wages and domestic consumption, thus supporting local businesses. This is particularly important for a country of nearly one hundred million people, because as time passes it is important that a higher proportion of GDP is derived from the provision of products and services locally. If this happens, we will see Vietnam's globalization rate decline to be more in line with its more developed peers.

The Numbers

To appreciate the progress that has been made over the past twenty years, we need to look at the numbers. These will reveal whether the changes have had a positive or negative impact on the economy and standard of living. In the following sections, we have included a selection of charts and tables that convey what has, or has not, been achieved from the economic reforms that have been adopted. These metrics also define where Vietnam stands today and show trends that may continue over the years to come.

To aid this analysis, we have presented below a diagram to explain the economic model being applied by Vietnam today. Economists use the

'Cobb-Douglas' economic model to attribute a country's economic growth to three key factors: (1) an increase in the country's workforce; (2) an increase in the amount of capital/machinery in the country; and (3) an increase in the country's productivity. There is evidence that all three of these factors are contributing to Vietnam's present growth.

The diagram below shows the relevant elements arranged with the inputs (demographics and capital) at the top and the outputs (standard of living and macroeconomics) at the bottom with the strategy (Vietnam Development Model) linking them in the middle. There are other inputs and outputs that could have been included, such as arable land, ODA funding, foreign indirect investment, infrastructure investment, interest rates, and government borrowing, but these would add unnecessary complexity and detract from the basic story. Moreover, for simplicity, we have not included all the relationships between the various components. If more of these linkages were presented, we would see that the process is circular. Increasing outputs leads to greater inputs; better health leads to a larger population and labor force; a better educated population leads to higher skilled workers and more productivity; more foreign reserves from exports enables the purchase of more equipment for production, and so on.

The story begins at the top left of the diagram with the country's population. Vietnam's large and growing labor force, combined with policies that stimulate the deployment of capital by foreign investors, the private sector, and the state sector, leads to production increases. This, in turn, leads to more exports and the generation of foreign exchange reserves. In Vietnam's case, the increase in the availability of capital, including from FDI, has been the main driver of the increase in the country's production, but productivity increases have also played a role, especially as the country adopts modern technology and management practices from abroad.

Higher production has increased household wealth via higher salaries and more household incomes, thus lowering the poverty rate and increasing consumption, including increased spending on health and education. Greater production and consumption also lead to an increase in government revenue which is spent on public services, such as health, education, and infrastructure (not shown on the diagram). The increase in production, consumption, and government spending has led to an increase in total GDP which, if it grows at a faster annual rate than the population, will result in higher GDP per capita.

Figure 1. Economic relationships being applied by Vietnam

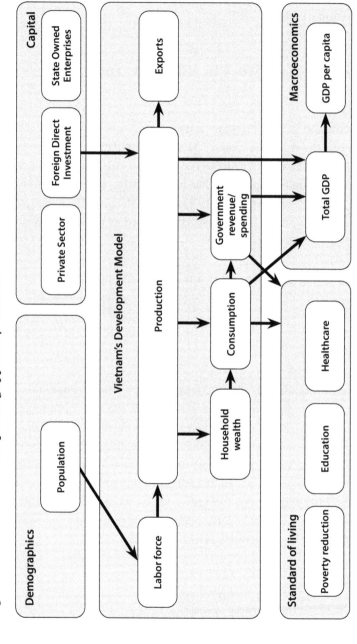

Source: Brook Taylor and Sam Korsmoe.

That is our descriptive narrative of the economic relationships ongoing in Vietnam. In the following pages, we test whether the numbers reflect these relationships and trends.

The Vietnam Story in Numbers, 1990–2020

Demographics

Any explanation of the Vietnam story in numbers must begin with its people. Within the next few years, Vietnam's population will exceed one hundred million people.[11] It will be the fifteenth country to achieve this milestone. The Vietnam population has been growing steadily over the last thirty years and, with an average age of 32.5 years, the population is relatively young. It has several decades of productivity ahead of it, and it has not yet reached its peak consumption years.[12]

Table 4. Vietnam's population, 1990–2020 (millions of people)

1990	1994	1998	2002	2006	2010	2014	2018	2020
68.0	73.6	78.1	81.5	84.6	88.0	91.7	95.5	97.5

Source: World Bank.

An important population-related consideration is where people live. Over the past century, people in nearly every country in the world have migrated from the rural to the urban areas of their countries. Vietnam is no exception. Vietnamese have been moving into the cities since at least 1990 to be closer to services and jobs. Vietnam has three urban centers—Hanoi, Danang, and Ho Chi Minh City—to attract rural residents, compared to countries like Thailand, the Philippines, and Indonesia which have just one—Bangkok, Manila, and Jakarta, respectively. Demographers forecast that the rural and urban population of Vietnam will be equal by 2030.

---

11. In this book, the authors have relied extensively on World Bank data, including population data which states Vietnam's population is approximately 97.5 million. There are other sources that state Vietnam has already surpassed the 100 million population threshold.

12. Individual productivity and consumption is highest between the age of 35 and 65.

Urbanization is important because it contributes to economic growth in many ways. Cities are more productive than rural areas because a large concentration of people and businesses in one place generates economies of scale, specialization, and innovation. It improves living standards because cities have more job opportunities and better access to education, healthcare, and other services compared to rural areas. There are also environmental benefits because cities are more energy-efficient than rural areas because they have a higher population density and use less energy per person. This trend is having a positive effect on Vietnam's economy and is set to continue for the next several decades.

Table 5. Share of the urban population in Vietnam, 2011–2020 (by %)

Year	Share
2011	31.08
2012	31.75
2013	32.43
2014	33.12
2015	33.81
2016	34.51
2017	35.12
2018	35.92
2019	36.63
2020	37.34

Source: Statista 2022, based on research by Minh-Ngoc Nguyen, March 8, 2021.

Capital

Economies need capital to grow. Capital is a key input in production because it is needed to purchase machinery, equipment, and other items to produce goods and services. However, sourcing capital for investment in production is difficult for many developing countries. They often do not have any savings as most of their money is spent on purchasing essentials, such as food, shelter, and energy. Moreover, developing countries often do not have the right policies in place to allocate capital effectively.

This was the situation in Vietnam in the 1980s and 1990s. The country was poor, and the capital it did have was controlled by state-owned enterprises. These enterprises were often inefficient and poorly managed, so they did not use capital effectively. As a result, Vietnam's economy grew slowly. However, over the last twenty years, the Vietnamese government has implemented important reforms to mobilize and attract capital. These have included land reforms, equitizing state-owned enterprises, encouraging the development of the private sector, improving the financial system and lending, and opening the economy to foreign investment and trade. The results can be seen in the increase in capital deployed and growth in economic activity.

Equitization of the State Sector

The privatization of state-owned businesses has been a global trend because it can lead to economic growth through increased efficiency, investment, competition, transparency, and accountability. However, Vietnam has taken a unique approach to its privatization program. Instead of fully privatizing state-owned enterprises (SOEs), Vietnam has implemented a process referred to as 'equitization,' which converts SOEs into joint-stock companies. The government retains discretion over the distribution of shares to employees or sale of shares to private investors, and often maintains a significant stake in companies deemed strategic or operating in sensitive sectors.

The equitization process in Vietnam began in the 1990s. There were basically two and possibly a third step: (1) converting SOEs into joint-stock companies with the capital divided into share; (2) distributing these shares to the employees and management of the SOEs; (3) the possible third step is to sell the shares to strategic investors and/or list the joint-stock company on the stock market.[13] Initially, this process was very slow, but it has sped up over time. While many large state-controlled companies remain, there are very few sectors where one SOE has a monopoly, for example, in electricity distribution. There are also many cases where SOEs compete aggressively with one another, such as telecommunications, and/or against the private sector, as in banking. As a result, many of the benefits of privatization have been realized even if the state continues to own certain companies.

Expanding the Private Sector

The development of the private sector is important in economies because it is usually a more efficient user of capital, and it also supports job creation, innovation, exports, and competition. The private sector in Vietnam has grown

---

13. These steps are explained in more detail in Chapter 4, Open For Business.

in tandem with the equitization of the state sector because the policies are often related. Many equitized SOEs are now privately owned (i.e., they have been fully privatized) or listed on the stock market, and the establishment of new companies founded by entrepreneurs has flourished. These developments, along with reform of the banking sector, have increased the amount of capital allocated to the private sector and thus contributed to economic growth.

Table 6. Private sector companies in Vietnam, 2011–2017

Year	Total number of companies	Number of active companies	Actual increase in active companies
2011	576,876	324,691	45,331
2012	646,750	346,777	22,086
2013	723,705	373,213	26,436
2014	798,547	402,236	29,113
2015	893,301	442,485	40,159
2016	1,003,401	477,808	35,323
2017	1,132,260	561,064	83,256

Source: *Vietnam Private Sector: Productivity and Prosperity*, Mekong Business Institute, Ha Noi, 2018.

Attracting Foreign Direct Investment

Foreign direct investment (FDI) is where a company from one country invests capital in a company in another country. Vietnam has implemented policies to attract foreign direct investment through various means, including the establishment of special economic zones that offer incentives such as tax breaks and relaxed regulations, the liberalization of the investment regime, the signing of trade agreements, and measures to improve the business environment by reducing corruption, improving infrastructure, and strengthening the legal system. These policies, coupled with geopolitical tensions, have resulted in Vietnam attracting significant FDI capital for investment in factories and infrastructure over the last twenty years. Along with this capital, advanced technologies and manufacturing techniques have arrived in the country, as well as the training and development of workers.

Table 7. Foreign direct investment in Vietnam, 2000–2020 (in US$ billion)

2000	2001	2002	2003	2004	2005	2006	2007	2008	2009	2010
1.3	1.3	1.4	1.4	1.6	2.0	2.4	6.7	10.0	7.6	8.0

2011	2012	2013	2014	2015	2016	2017	2018	2019	2020
7.4	8.4	8.9	9.2	11.8	12.6	14.1	15.5	20.4	26.4

Source: World Bank; Ministry of Planning and Investment.

Labor force

Vietnam's current labor force of about sixty million workers is estimated to be the eleventh largest in the world.[14] Its labor force is only slightly smaller than that of Japan but larger than that of other important emerging countries such as Mexico, the Philippines, and Thailand. Perhaps more interesting is that Vietnam's population is larger than that of South Korea and double that of Taiwan, the two nations against whom we are comparing Vietnam's growth path. Based on this data, it is foreseeable that Vietnam might one day have an economy that is larger than both these countries.

A key reason the workforce is so large is the female participation rate. Unlike many countries which have cultures or religions that restrict the role of women in the workforce, Vietnam has few such barriers. The percentage of men of working age (20–64 years) who are working and the percentage of women of working age who are working is quite similar—96 percent and 88 percent, respectively.[15] The value and similarity of these numbers means that nearly everyone is included in the country's development because nearly everyone is part of the country's workforce. It is a team approach rather than a male-centric one, which is a very different story compared to many other countries.[16]

---

14. Calculated from International Labour Organization data, 2022.

15. Cimigo presentations, Vietnam 2021 Consumer Trends.

16. This issue is covered in more detail and with various data sources in Chapter 10, Case Study 3: The Role of Women, pp. 158–66.

Table 8. Female labor force participation rates, 2021 (%)

	Ratio of female to male labor force participation rate
Vietnam	87.7
Cambodia	86.1
United States	83.1
China	82.9
European Union	81.6
Thailand	78.6
Singapore	77.3
Japan	75.0
South Korea	73.7
Malaysia	66.0
Indonesia	65.8
Philippines	64.2
India	27.4

Source: International Labour Organization, 2021 estimate.

Production Output

Production output growth is a key objective of any East Asian Development Model strategy. Without growth, none of the subsequent benefits can be realized. From 2005 to 2020, Vietnam increased its manufacturing output by 15.5 percent per year from US$10.8 billion to US$83.0 billion due to the policies adopted. This compares very favorably against global manufacturing output growth of 2.7 percent over the same period.[17]

Figure 2. Vietnam's manufacturing output, 2005–2020 (in US$ billion)

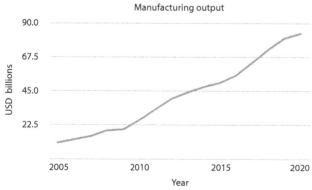

Source: World Bank, World Development Indicators.

---

17. Calculated from World Bank Development Indicators.

Household Wealth

Economic growth, driven by an increase in production output, boosts household wealth by providing higher incomes for households from increasing employment and wages. Over the last twenty years, the average household income has increased from US$280 to US$2,196 per year.

Table 9. Annual household income, 1996–2018 (in US$)

2000	2002	2004	2006	2008	2010	2012	2014	2016	2018	2020
280	369	478	732	894	1,152	1,496	1,695	2,057	2,236	2,196

Source: CEIC

The increase in household incomes has resulted in the expansion of the middle class and more households becoming economically secure, an especially important achievement.

Table 10. Population of Vietnamese by economic class, 2010–2016 (%)

Economic class	2010	2012	2014	2016
Middle class	7.7	7.9	9.6	13.3
Economically secure	41.5	47.6	54.2	57.0
Economically vulnerable	32.0	28.9	24.4	21.1
Moderately poor	13.8	11.6	8.8	6.6
Extremely poor	5.0	4.0	3.0	2.0

Note:
    Middle class: More than US$15 per person per day
    Economically secure: US$5.50–$15 per person per day
    Economically vulnerable: US$3.20–$5.50 per person per day
    Moderately poor: US$1.90–$3.20 per person per day
    Extremely poor: Less than US$1.90 per person per day

Source: Mekong Development Research Institute.

Consumption

Growing household wealth and a reduction in economic vulnerability leads to increased consumption. In Vietnam's case, consumption per capita has risen from US$682 in 2000 to US$1,924 in 2020.

Figure 3. Annual consumption per capita, 200–2020 (in US$)

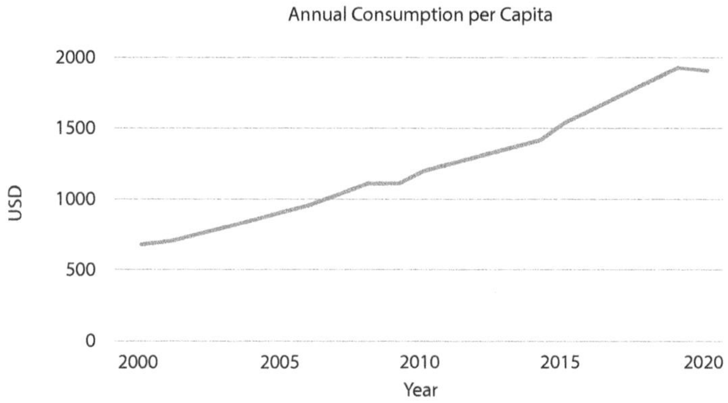

Annual Consumption per Capita

Source: World Bank, World Development Indicators.

Government Revenue and Spending

If the right policies are adopted, economic growth will lead to an increase in government tax revenues and a corresponding increase in government spending, thus expanding the economy and improving the lives of people. Over twenty years, the Vietnamese government's consumption expenditure has increased sixteen-fold, from US$2.0 billion in 2000 to US$32.9 billion in 2020.

Figure 4. Government consumption, 2000–2020 (in US$ billion)

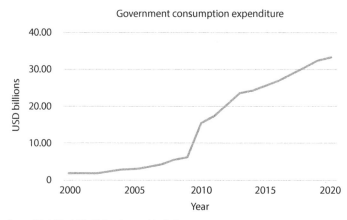

Government consumption expenditure

Source: World Bank, World Development Indicators.

Exports

Vietnam's numbers story is not contained within the country's borders. Vietnam has chosen a growth model dependent on free trade, and the numbers confirm this is happening. Over the past ten years, Vietnam's trade growth has been rapid, a direct result of Vietnam joining the World Trade Organization in 2007 as well as its numerous bi- and multilateral trade agreements. For this and other reasons, the appearance of 'Made in Vietnam' labels on goods in global markets is a recent phenomenon, but it is one that is likely to increase in the years to come.

Figure 5. Total trade in Vietnam, 2000–2020 (in US$ billion)

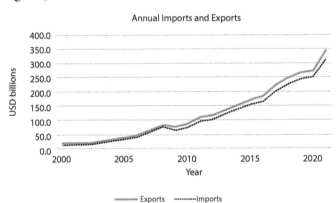

Source: World Bank, World Development Indicators.

Improved Education

Economic growth can improve education levels in many ways. Increased household wealth and government spending provide more funding for education and higher standards of education. Improved infrastructure and better access to information does the same. These factors and others are having a positive impact on the quantity and quality of education in Vietnam, and the numbers support this.

Table 11. Mean years of schooling in Vietnam, 1990–2017

1990	1995	2000	2005	2010	2015	2016	2017
3.9	4.6	5.4	6.4	7.5	8.0	8.1	8.2

Source: Reducing Rural Poverty in Vietnam, Mekong Development Research Institute Report, 27 February–1 March 2019.

Academic achievement has always been important in Vietnam due to the well-established Confucian value placed on education. For this reason, Vietnam's literacy rates are consistently high, with an estimated 95 percent of the country fully literate according to the United Nations Development Program. Based on a more contemporary metric, the Program for International Student Assessment (PISA) ranking developed by the Organization for Economic Co-operation and Development (OECD), Vietnam also rates high. In fact, Vietnam is an outlier on this metric. There is normally a strong correlation between high PISA scores and high GDP per capita countries. However, Vietnam's PISA ranking is now among the top ten nations in the world, which makes it higher than many developed and wealthy countries such as Australia, France, and the United States.[18]

Table 12. PISA worldwide ranking, 2018

Above 500[19]	450–500	Below 450
Singapore – 556	Australia – 499	Serbia – 442
Macao – 542	Switzerland – 498	Cyprus – 438
Hong Kong – 530	Norway – 496	Chile – 437
Estonia – 525	Czechia – 495	United Arab Emirates – 433
Japan – 520	United States – 495	Malaysia – 431
South Korea – 519	France – 493	Romania – 428
Canada – 516	Portugal – 492	Bulgaria – 426
Taiwan – 516	Austria – 491	Moldova – 424
Finland – 516	Latvia – 487	Uruguay – 423
Vietnam – 514	Russia – 487	Brunei – 423
Poland – 513	Iceland – 481	Montenegro – 422

Source: OECD, 2018, 2019.

18. Vietnam's national media published numerous stories about Vietnam not being included in the 2018 OECD report. It had ranked 19th out of 65 countries in 2012 and 32nd out of 70 countries in 2015. Sources claim that Vietnamese education officials missed a publishing deadline due to use of paper tests which took too long to mark and submit.

19. China was also listed in the PISA ranking with a score of 578, but it collected data from four provinces only (Beijing, Shanghai, Jiangsu, and Zhejiang), not the entire country. The OECD published China's score with a footnote that it was from just these four provinces, and we have referenced this same fact here.

Better Healthcare

Economic growth can also improve health in several ways. Increased income can be used to purchase better food, housing, and medical services which all contribute to a healthier population. More government spending on hospitals and equipment, as well as health education and infrastructure such as clean water and waste management, will also lead to better health-related outcomes. These and other factors are having a positive impact on the quality of healthcare in Vietnam, and the numbers support this.

Table 13. Infant mortality rate of Vietnamese, 1990–2020 (per 1,000 live births)

1990	1995	2000	2005	2010	2015	2020
36.9	29.5	23.4	19.8	18.3	17.2	15.9

Source: UN Interagency Group for Child Mortality; UNICEF; World Health Organization; World Bank.

Table 14. Life expectancy of Vietnamese at birth, 1990–2020 (by year)

1990	1995	2000	2005	2010	2015	2020
70.5	72.0	73.3	74.3	74.8	75.1	75.5

Source: World Bank.

Lowering the Poverty Rate

Thomas Jefferson, the third president of the United States, wrote, "The measure of society is how it treats the weakest members." If we accept this statement as true, Vietnam can be rightly proud of what it has achieved over the last thirty years. During this time, the extreme poverty rate fell from over 50 percent in 1993 to less than 0.7 percent today.[20] This remarkable achievement is a testament to the country's economic progress which has helped reduce poverty by increasing the incomes of all Vietnamese people. The poor can now purchase necessities, such as food, water, shelter, and clothing from new and higher sources of income. Economic development has also increased government spending on social programs, such as education, healthcare, and welfare, which are especially important to improving the lives of the poor and reducing poverty.

---

20. *Source*: World Bank.

Table 15. Vietnam's poverty rate, 2002–2020 (% of population)

Year	2002	2004	2006	2008	2010	2012	2014	2016	2018	2020
Extreme poverty rate	29.9	20.1	14.9	11.1	2.9	1.7	1.9	1.3	1.2	0.7
Moderately poor	65.6	54.1	44.6	39.7	14.0	10.2	8.8	6.4	5.3	3.8

Source: World Bank.

Macroeconomic

Total GDP is the total market value of all final goods and services produced within a country's borders in a specific time frame. It is a comprehensive measure of a country's economic activity and is often used as a measure of a country's economic health. Again, there is clear evidence that the policies and activities being undertaken in Vietnam are delivering economic growth in the form of increasing GDP.

Table 16. Gross domestic product in Vietnam, 2000–2020 (in US$ billion)

2000	2001	2002	2003	2004	2005	2006	2007	2008	2009	2010
39.6	41.3	44.6	50.2	62.9	73.2	84.3	98.4	124.8	129.0	143.2

2011	2012	2013	2014	2015	2016	2017	2018	2019	2020
171.3	195.2	212.7	232.9	236.8	252.1	277.1	303.1	327.9	342.9

Source: International Monetary Fund and the World Economic Outlook Database, April 2022.

GDP per capita also shows a similar trend. It has increased to US$3,521 in 2020 from just US$499 in 2000. This has advanced Vietnam from a low-income nation to a lower-middle income nation according to World Bank metrics.

Table 17. Gross domestic product per capita in Vietnam, 2000–2020 (in US$)

2000	2001	2002	2003	2004	2005	2006	2007	2008	2009	2010
499	513	547	610	757	873	996	1,152	1,447	1,481	1,628

2011	2012	2013	2014	2015	2016	2017	2018	2019	2020
1,950	2,198	2,370	2,567	2,582	2,720	2,958	3,202	3,398	3,521

Source: International Monetary Fund and the World Economic Outlook Database, April 2022.

The charts and graphs presented in the previous pages have painted a mostly positive picture of how Vietnam's economy and society have developed over the previous twenty plus years. Vietnam has been relentlessly pursuing growth, and to a large extent it has succeeded. The results have been impressive, but a key question is what is happening in Vietnam now and where is it heading. There are many analysts who attempt to answer this question by comparing Vietnam to countries they know and understand better. Some companies take on the task of trying to determine a list of top performing countries for the year 2050. For example, in 2017 the consulting firm PwC produced a report containing the long-term growth projections to 2050 for 32 of the largest economies in the world, accounting for around 85% of world GDP. Among other trends, the report states that Vietnam will be the fastest growing economy in the thirty-five years between 2016 and 2050 and will increase its overall GDP (based on PPP) to become a member of the G20 as the twentieth largest economy in the world. This is a twelve-place movement up the ladder, from thirty-second in 2016.[21] No other country has that level of projected growth.

The charts presented in this chapter tell a story about Vietnam. The trends are positive, and a good foundation has been established for the run to becoming a high-income nation. Whether Vietnam can continue to move these numbers in the right direction is the essence of the questions we are seeking to answer in this book. But like every country in the world, there is a political element to almost every facet of life in Vietnam. We explore this in the next chapter.

---

21. *The World in 2050*, PwC, February 2017.

Chapter 6

POLICYMAKERS

Learning how Vietnam's political system works has been one of the most challenging aspects of this book project. A clear understanding of how policies are made and how laws are executed is vital to describing a potential future for Vietnam. Researching news reports in the Vietnamese or international press about a new law or a revision of a new law is not sufficient. Such news stories are usually descriptions of how laws are or are not working, not about how they were made.

Regardless of its political system, every country in the world has a method for how its laws are created. In most, if not all cases, this is a combination of discussion, analysis, debate, testing, bargaining, and other types of negotiations among political leaders who probably have different interests and expectations in the outcome of a policy. This type of endeavor is often about politics, and it occurs in all countries when policies are formulated and executed. Vietnam is no exception.

In the case of Vietnam, there is an obvious challenge when researching this topic. While new laws and revisions are frequently promulgated, it is near impossible to find people who are confident in their description of how politics work in Vietnam. We met plenty of people who were ready to talk about politics, but most simply did not know very much. In many cases, the discussions were an opportunity for people to share views on the things that were not working to their satisfaction. Topics ranged from comments on petty bureaucratic corruption and poor infrastructure to the inability to get the various licenses or approvals to move a project forward. Ultimately, these interviews were not about politics but more about the challenges of doing business in Vietnam.

To get a better sense of the roots of this criticism, we asked interviewees questions that probed deeper and forced them to think more carefully about the issue. The first question was whether the quality of life for most Vietnamese today is better than in the years 2000 and 2010. Predictably, the answers were almost always "Yes." We followed that by asking whether there are any reasons or evidence that the quality of life in 2030 is going to be worse than today. While this question took longer to respond to, there was a consensus that there were no strong reasons preventing the current trend from continuing. In fact, there was an expectation that the quality of life would continue to get better over the next decade despite any concerns having previously been voiced.

We also asked interviewees if they thought the citizens of South Korea and Taiwan in the 1980s and 1990s would have been frustrated with and critical of their own government's inability to address the same issues Vietnamese are facing today. The question was rhetorical because nobody we interviewed was there at those times or had otherwise considered such a question, but there was an acknowledgement and comfort in the realization that similar concerns were likely to have been expressed in South Korea and Taiwan.

The reality is the concerns and frustrations we hear about politics today in Vietnam are no different from what we heard in Vietnam twenty years ago, nor significantly different to what is being voiced in other countries today and in the past. The topic of politics and the discontent it arouses is a general point of discussion for every citizen in every country. Vietnam is no exception. From the 1970s to 2000, South Korea and Taiwan dealt with multiple political issues when they were Tiger Economy countries and were pursuing and eventually achieving high-income country status. These political processes, and the complaints about them, exist in Vietnam today. Vietnam has a political system, and based on the economic progress that has been made, it is working even if it is not entirely clear how it works. We will explain this dynamic.

We do not have unique access to the political dynamic in Vietnam or the politicking that occurs behind closed doors at the highest levels, but based on our experience and observations, we can provide a framework to better understand how policy is made and how the Vietnamese system works.

The Government

Politics in Vietnam begins with the Communist Party of Vietnam. Any relevant official of the government will be a Communist Party member. The four most important and powerful positions are the following:

1. **General Secretary** of the Communist Party who is also the leader of the Politburo;
2. **President,** who is the head of state as well as the head of the Vietnam People's Army and police force;
3. **Prime Minister,** who leads the government and manages the execution of the law and the sixteen ministries of the government; and
4. **Chairman** of the **National Assembly,** who runs the legislature when it is in session.

There are several key entities and groups which form the power structures of the Vietnamese system. Any new policy or revision of an old policy must work its way through these entities to become a law that the Prime Minister is duty-bound to execute. These entities include the following:

1. **Communist Party,** which is comprised of around 5.2 million members according to various media sources. They elect the delegates for the National Party Congress.
2. **National Party Congress,** which meets every five years and is comprised of around 1,600 delegates. Its primary job is to establish the policy direction of the Party and the country every five years.
3. **Central Committee,** which is comprised of 200 members elected by the National Party Congress. It meets twice a year to continue the work of the Party Congress.
4. **Politburo,** which is chaired by the General Secretary and has (as of 2021) eighteen members who are elected by the Central Committee and meet to ensure implementation of the work of the National Party Congress and the Central Committee.
5. **National Assembly,** which is comprised of 500 members who represent specific provinces and cities and are elected to four-year terms by the people in those jurisdictions. It meets twice a year to develop, write, and pass laws.
6. **Standing Committee,** which meets between the National Assembly sessions to continue the work of the National Assembly.

7. **Fatherland Front**, which is an umbrella organization comprised of all the various groups that represent the political base of the people. This includes the Communist Party itself plus labor groups, the youth communist league, the women's union, and others. It theoretically acts like a monitor of all the activities of the above-mentioned groups to ensure that they are working on behalf of the people.

8. **Judiciary**, which is responsible for ensuring the constitutionality of the laws as well as the appeal and review of laws. The highest level of the judiciary is the Supreme People's Court.

The above describes the national government. At the provincial and local level, there are fifty-eight provinces and five centrally planned cities, each with its own government. They are managed by People's Councils that create the People's Committees which are the local administrative authority for their jurisdiction (e.g., a province such as Binh Duong will have its own People's Committee). There are chairs (mayors) and vice-chairs (vice-mayors), as well as numerous department heads within each province or city. There are districts, wards, and hamlets under each province/city, with various leaders in charge of each jurisdiction who must report to the authority directly above them.

Every five years the Communist Party hosts a National Party Congress to set out its objectives for the following five years. Political scientists commonly say the Party Congress produces the 'road map' for the direction of the country and then the National Assembly and the government is responsible for how this road is navigated.

At the core of the 1986 Doi Moi policies was a decentralization of the national government's power. The 6th Party Congress agreed with then-General Secretary Nguyen Van Linh that more decisions needed to be made by provincial People's Committees because they were closer to the reality on the ground in each of their jurisdictions. By no means did the Doi Moi policies make the national government irrelevant, but it did bring more power to local People's Committees, and some of them became quite savvy about how to attract investors to their communities and otherwise spur economic development using the assets they had within their provinces and cities. These were the leaders who invested in industrial parks, export-processing zones, and hi-tech centers, and who launched new companies with their newly gained power. They inspired a new sense of the old idea of independence and freedom.

Independence and Freedom

In the mid-1990s a foreign investor visiting Dong Nai or Binh Duong Province could be forgiven if he or she thought that the local People's Committee had somehow been granted unlimited power to do whatever it took to get a factory off the ground. The national government and Hanoi were barely mentioned as the local investment team rolled out the red carpet with numerous incentives for foreign investors to do business directly with the provincial leaders. Initially, these provinces had to request permission for this, but once received they could pursue their own goals. The result was that the more astute provincial leaders were able to set up their own industrial parks, hi-tech zones, and export-processing zones. The truly aggressive could try to build airports and seaports, as well as launch and implement their own investment programs or tourism strategies.

In some cases, relatively strong companies were set up and managed by local governments. For example, in the 1990s Saigon Tourist, a company formed in 1975 by the local government, was an important player in the tourism and hotel sector. Shortly after unification, it took over Saigon's iconic hotels, such as the Rex, Caravelle, Majestic, and Palace. Because it owned a lot of properties, it was an important company. Although these companies were state-owned, their profits remained with the local government rather than being delivered to the central government. The number of profitable local government-owned companies a province or city has was important to its bottom line and its ability to invest and grow.

How the money is distributed and what amounts are distributed is a key question for the provinces and cities. A financial analyst for the southern province of Binh Duong estimates that only ten provinces and cities can live on their own revenue streams. These are the provinces/cities that send money to the national government. The other fifty-three provincial/city governments receive more money from the national government than they remit.

The revenue streams for all the provinces and cities come from three sources, according to the analyst. First, there are import taxes, export taxes, and big company income taxes. The term 'big company' is generally defined as one large enough to have several branches. One hundred percent of the taxes collected by the local government from these sources must be sent to the national government. Second, there are revenues collected for land rents, registration fees, and other kinds of government services. One hundred percent of this revenue pool is kept by the local government. Third, the final pool is derived from income taxes from local companies, personal income taxes from residents, and value-added taxes (VAT) from product sales. The revenue from this pool is divided between the local government and the national government. The ratio of the division depends on the wealth of the province, and most likely on the political skills and maneuvering ability of the provincial leaders. For example, Binh Duong Province is allowed to keep 36 percent of its revenue from the third pool and sends the remaining 64 percent to the national government. This is a lot, but it is better than the situation in Ho Chi Minh City, which reverts all but 18 percent of its revenue base to Hanoi. Unsurprisingly, Ho Chi Minh City has been petitioning the national government to keep more of its own revenue base so it can continue to invest in the city on its own.

Aside from the politicking skills of leaders required to negotiate good deals for their own locale, the official status of the province or city is important. The issue of who reports to who and what they are required to say and do or allowed to do is important. It often comes down to what kind of local government they are. For example, in 2020 the important tourism island of Phu Quoc reportedly petitioned to become the sixth 'city' in Vietnam (i.e., a city that is centrally controlled rather than provincially managed). If approved, Phu Quoc Island would be a city like Hanoi, Ho Chi Minh City, Hai Phong, Danang, and Can Tho. It would no longer fall under the jurisdiction and management of Kien Giang Province. Instead, it would have a direct reporting line to the national government in Hanoi and negotiate its own revenue-sharing formula for the third pool of revenue noted above.

The Great Debate

It is common to read an article about Vietnam in the international media which includes references to communism when there is no obvious need to do so. It is one of those labels that Vietnam is forced to accept, even if today nobody really understands what it means. Globally, since at least 1954, political arguments have often centered on a 'Communism versus Democracy' debate. This approach drew a clear line between the two ideologies. National governments from around the world, leaders, academics, politicians, corporations, and citizens of all countries were supposed to choose one side or the other. There was no room for nuance or gray areas. Communism was good/bad and democracy was bad/good, and there was a plethora of easily available language, models, examples, and evidence to support each side of the argument. The vast majority of the world's people accept these arguments without further consideration.

But things change and today the vocabulary of the 'Communism versus Democracy' debate is an outdated relic of the Cold War between the United States and the Soviet Union. That war finished more than thirty years ago, and the Soviet Union no longer exists. Yet, many people continue to compare the two systems as if they were the only two governmental systems that have ever existed. Not only is this incorrect, but it has become increasingly unclear what these words and similar vocabulary really mean. It is also unclear which systems they are supposed to define.

The terms communism, socialism, democracy, capitalism, etc. are a mixture of philosophical, social, political, and economic ideologies that have different meanings for different people at different times. During the Cold War, the meanings were clear and there was little or no overlap in the definitions and the systems they referred to. But things have moved on since then. Today, the term 'democracy' has been oversimplified as 'one person one vote.' Is it appropriate to call a country a democracy when its voters are increasingly disenfranchised by the electoral system supporting it? Ironically, the countries that are often touted as the ones with the highest degree of democratic participation, such as Norway, Sweden, New Zealand, and Denmark, also have extensive socialist-oriented policies like welfare programs and collective labor-bargaining practices.

The debate gets especially muddled when describing countries with one-party systems. Conventional wisdom used to dictate that a single-party state meant a communist state with a command, non-market economy controlled by the government. That is no longer the case. For example, Vietnam is a one-party state, but its pursuit of a free trade philosophy that invites in foreign direct investment, empowers the private sector, and demands that its SOEs compete or fail, is hardly a command, non-market economy designed to support the state. It is the opposite. In Asia there are other countries that are clearly one-party states with capitalist economies that are considered communist countries (e.g., China), while there are other countries who also have one-party states and capitalist economies that are, or have been, somehow labeled differently. This list would include Singapore, which has been ruled by the same political party since 1965, Taiwan from the 1950s to at least 2000, and South Korea from the 1950s to 1970s and well into the 1980s and 1990s.[1]

Then there are the oligarchies where the nation's power resides in the hands of several families that seemingly take turns running the country. Asia watchers claim that a handful of Filipino families have owned land and exerted influence since Spanish colonial times. Thailand is even more complicated with control of the government rotating between the military and political parties controlled by wealthy families. Since 1932, Thailand has had thirteen coups d'états with several more failed attempts.[2] In some countries vote-buying is also quite common. Is it correct to refer to these countries as democracies?

In February 2021, the London-based Economist Intelligence Unit (EIU) published a report on democracy. Rather than provide a single definition of 'democracy,' it contained a democracy index which categorized 167 nations in the world into four groups: Full Democracies, Flawed Democracies, Hybrid Regimes, and Authoritarian Regimes. Vietnam was labeled an authoritarian regime by virtue of the fact it is ruled by one party (an important distinction with many other authoritarian regimes which are ruled by one individual or family). The United States, the world's champion of democracy, was designated a flawed democracy. South Korea and Taiwan were considered full democracies, with Taiwan making the biggest move upwards on the 'Democracy Index' scale over the previous twelve months.

We are not political scientists. However, we believe nuance is or at least should be more the norm than the exception when trying to decipher the Communist Party's decision-making process. We have already made the point that Vietnam has had to fight against being labeled as anticolonial, nationalist, and communist while pursuing independence and freedom for much of its

---

1. There are more than ten political parties in Singapore, but one party, the People's Action Party (PAP) has won a majority of seats in parliament in every major election since 1965. Singapore has only had three prime ministers since its founding as a nation in 1965, and all three—Lee Kwan Yew, Goh Chok Tong, and Lee Hsien Loong—are PAP members. Lee Hsien Loong is also the son of the late Lee Kuan Yew.

2. "Thailand's 'Wicked' Development Trap" by Peerasit Kamnuansilpa and Le Anh Khan Minh, *Bangkok Post*, 19 September 2019.

THE GREAT DEBATE 83

modern history. Though the words might be different, the labeling issue still prevails and needs to change if we are going to eliminate the biases that come with such labels.

We encourage readers to ignore the labels and to think about politics in another light: 'Good Government versus Bad Government.' In Chapter 10 we describe this issue as one of the five lenses for the case studies and label it 'Governance.' This means a measurement of how well or how poorly the government responds to the country's overall needs. Irrespective of the political system in place, a 'Good Government' works towards serving the needs of its people. It does this because there is accountability. If it fails to deliver on these needs, the party, the government, the system, and often the individual in power will be held accountable for its failure. Historically, Western countries and liberal democracies have been taught that a government can only be accountable to its people if it is a democracy and that democracies are always accountable to their people. But as noted above and documented by media groups like the EIU, there are many flawed and failed democracies in the world. Thus, this latter point is factually incorrect. We would also argue that a country does not need to be a democracy for its government to be held accountable to its people and that this situation exists in Vietnam today. In fact, while it might not have always been obvious, accountability has been an integral part of the Party's psyche since the national constitution was drafted by the country's forebears. Article Four (subsections 1 and 2) of Chapter 1 of Vietnam's national constitution is all about accountability. It states that the Party is accountable to the people.

There is still plenty of nuance, but there is more accountability in Vietnam than the country is often given credit by outsiders. The Party has been aware for a long time that corruption undermines its legitimacy, which is why few weeks go by without an article in the state press about an ongoing or upcoming anticorruption campaign or an investigation. In fact, the Party's efforts to reduce corruption seem to have ratcheted up after an event off the coast of Vietnam in 2016, which provides evidence of the Party's accountability, as well as how it will respond to environmental risks and damage. The event is worth retelling. It involves a Taiwanese conglomerate, a huge steel manufacturing plant, a lax attitude towards the environment, an inept response from a Taiwanese manager, and—fish.

We Choose Fish

In the first week of April 2016, Vietnamese fishermen off the coast of the central Vietnam provinces of Ha Tinh, Quang Binh, Quang Tri, and Thua Thien-Hue noticed something strange. They were not catching their normal number of fish. Neither were they seeing them. The fish had simply disappeared. First hundreds and then thousands of dead fish began to wash up on the beaches of Ha Tinh Province. Something had killed them, but no one knew what. By the second week of April, an estimated 70 tons of dead fish of various species had washed ashore in all four provinces.

Fingers began pointing at the Formosa Ha Tinh Steel Corporation, a project of the Formosa Plastics Group from Taiwan, a huge company that had a dubious environmental track record in other countries. The company was building a US$10 billion steel manufacturing plant, together with a power plant and deep seaport. At the time it was one of the largest foreign investment projects in Vietnam. Local Vietnamese claimed the steel plant had discharged poisonous toxins into the sea and this was what was killing the fish.

In response, the Taiwanese company pointed their fingers back. It denied any responsibility and claimed the dead fish were the result of red tides (algal blooms that can be toxic) and toxins generated and thrown into the sea by the local people. It was nature's fault and the people's fault, not theirs. In an April 27 press conference, a deputy minister from Vietnam's Ministry of Natural Resources and Environment backed the Taiwanese claims. The Vietnamese Fisheries Society, an NGO set up in 2000 to support Vietnamese fishermen, immediately rejected the red tide argument. At least two Vietnamese journalists who tried to report on the disaster were jailed. Then, Chou Chun Fan, the head of Formosa's business operations in Vietnam, infamously inflamed the controversy by stating in an interview with local journalists that "You must decide whether you want to catch fish and shrimp or build a modern steel industry. You cannot choose both." The Vietnamese public chose fish.

By early May, the volume of dead fish washed ashore was around 100 tons according to local new sources. Protests erupted around the country, not just in the central provinces where the disaster had occurred, and the livelihoods of thousands of Vietnamese had been impacted. From the south to the north, tens of thousands of Vietnamese marched on the streets of the country's major cities to protest the Taiwanese project. They held up signs reading "We Choose Fish."

The government launched a formal investigation. In late June 2016, the Formosa Corporation admitted it was responsible for the dead fish. The cause was a variety of toxic industrial waste materials that had been discharged through sewage pipes extending from the steel plant out into the ocean. The company made a formal apology in front of several provincial leaders and pledged US$500 million for the clean-up and compensation.

Several conclusions can be drawn from this disaster. At the time, Prime Minister Nguyen Xuan Phuc (2016–21) called it "the most serious environmental disaster that Vietnam has ever faced."[3] The attempted cover-up of the disaster did not last a week. The people were emboldened enough to protest on the streets of Vietnam, forcing the authorities to act. The government eventually refused to continue backing the claims of a company that was building a US$10 billion plant in the country.

This incident also sheds light on the frustratingly paradoxical statement that is constantly quoted by Party and government leaders whenever they talk about the economy: Vietnam "will grow, develop, and become rich as a socialist-oriented market economy," without explaining what the latter part of the statement means. By choosing fish over steel, the government respected the people's desire for a clean environment and respected their traditional rights over unrestrained economic development. The most important lesson learned was that accountability to the people counts for something even when you first try to deny and/or avoid responsibility. Look no further than how the nations of the world defended themselves and their citizens against the COVID-19 pandemic. Some nations managed the pandemic horrendously while others proved to be quite adept. Some leaders appeared to care more about maintaining their power base and less about ensuring their citizens would not catch COVID-19.

A key reason for Taiwan's rapid rise on the EIU's democracy index was its management of the COVID-19 pandemic. By the end of 2020 Taiwan had recorded only 802 cases and 7 deaths. This is remarkable for a country of 23.8 million people. But more remarkable was Vietnam's record—a case count of 1,474 and 35 deaths during the same period, especially for a country whose population is four times greater than Taiwan's, is much poorer, and shares

---

3. Bloomberg News, May 4, 2016.

a land border with China. When the Delta variant of COVID-19 arrived in May 2021, it was a much more difficult challenge and an even more important measure of accountability. While over 11 million Vietnamese contracted COVID-19 and more than 43,000 died as of early December 2022,[4] the government also managed to provide vaccinations to 92 percent of Vietnamese with one shot and 86.3 percent were fully vaccinated.[5]

COVID-19 is just one of the issues that Vietnamese political leaders from Lang Son in the north to Ca Mau in the south have to juggle. There are many issues that must be balanced in an appropriate way. Failure to do so could mean a derailment of the entire Doi Moi experiment or at least permanent status as a middle-income country. How well these challenges are dealt with becomes an exercise in smart politics.

Pragmatic Grit in Politics Too

Beginning in the 1950s and into the 1970s, the Canadian-born political scientist David Easton introduced a new means of looking at how politics works. He argued that the creation of any policy follows a loop starting with input (new proposal or idea) to conversion (creation of a policy by the political system, i.e., the government) to output (distribution of the policy through laws and regulations) to feedback (response from the public about the new laws and regulations, i.e., accountability) and then back through the loop again for revisions depending on the demands from the environment (we would argue that this is, once again, accountability). The process is neither top down nor bottom up, but a constant flow that responds to its environment.

Whether it was by design or not, Vietnamese political leaders appear to have been using Easton's model of politics. For centuries Vietnamese society has valued independence and freedom. Since at least 1858, when French forces first arrived to implement and cement French colonial rule, Vietnamese policies were developed and implemented to fight against this rule. It took a long time to win that battle. Then, for the first ten years after unification in 1975, the 'societal value' espoused by the country's leaders was to build a

---

4. Worldometer, COVID-19 Data. Of the 11.5 million cases, this same data source notes that 10.6 million have fully recovered and COVID deaths have completely flattened out.

5. Our World in Data, November 2022.

prosperous socialist state. That did not work out, so new ideas were attempted, the most important being the Doi Moi policies which, among other impacts, has put the country on its current free trade path. The constant tinkering with policies to make things more efficient, one small step at a time, is part of the Vietnamese political process. This method is often criticized for being too slow and not comprehensive enough, but it is occurring.

A final note about politics in Vietnam. There is limited value in pointing fingers and asking questions about the mistakes of the past, the sanctity of the voting process, or some essential need to have a 'democracy' for a country to advance, because the progress made by Vietnam over the last twenty years has shown these to be irrelevant. What is important is that there is accountability in Vietnam. It has a political process that has been working effectively to improve the quality of life for most Vietnamese. This is a good start to begin the 2020s.

Chapter 7

IS VIETNAM A TIGER AND CAN IT JUMP?

With the most important trends of history, culture, business, and politics covered in the previous chapters, we now return to the hypothesis of this book which we detailed in Chapter 1: 'Vietnam is the next Tiger Economy of Asia, and it will grow and develop in a similar way to how South Korea and Taiwan grew as Tiger Economies of Asia.' There are two questions embedded within this hypothesis. The first is whether Vietnam is or will be a Tiger Economy. The second is whether Vietnam as a Tiger Economy can grow and develop in the same way that South Korea and Taiwan grew and developed when they were the Tiger Economies of Asia in the 1980s and 1990s.

Question 1: Can Vietnam call itself a Tiger Economy?

Google the words 'Tiger Economy' and most sources offer a relatively simple definition: 'A Tiger Economy is the economy of a country which undergoes rapid economic growth, usually accompanied by an increase in the standard of living.' Over a relatively short time, the quality of life of the citizens of Tiger Economy countries improves and they get richer. Parents send their children abroad for higher education and they return to launch innovative companies, set up businesses that make machinery, equipment, and componentry, create firms to deliver professional services, and join their government to figure out new laws and negotiate complicated trade agreements. They each falter here and there amidst global crises and local challenges, but the overall upward trend is clear. There is GDP growth in or near the 6–10 percent range over consecutive years. There are trade surpluses that keep growing because of access to large export markets. Foreign currency reserves grow. Debt is manageable. The currency is stable. Products are manufactured that other countries want. They start by manufacturing footwear, garments, and toys, but they do not stay in that lane for long. They move up the value chain where larger margins can be earned. Sometimes they even pull off a global event like hosting the Olympic Games or the Football World Cup.

The poster children of this phenomenon are South Korea and Taiwan and the country looking at them with envy is Vietnam. It also wants to do what many Tiger Economy look-alikes in the past could not do but South Korea and Taiwan could. It wants to join the elite group of high-income nations. With increasing frequency, senior government and Party leaders, including the prime minister, have stated that a national goal for the country is to become a high-income nation by 2045.

There are plenty of detractors, but an argument can be made that Vietnam is already a 'Tiger Economy,' at least as far as the term is defined above. Since 2010 and even earlier, GDP growth has averaged 6–7 percent per year on the back of even faster export growth. But relying only on economic data is simplistic as there are other qualitative factors that provide better evidence of a Tiger Economy.

There are statement markers. These are events or projects that offer some evidence that the country is on its way to, or already is, a Tiger Economy. These include a relatively new privately owned auto manufacturer (VinFast) being able to produce an electric car for the international market within five years of its manufacturing plant breaking ground.[1] They also include how a start-up airline company, VietJet, could acquire a fleet of nearly 80 airplanes operating more than 400 daily flights to over 120 domestic and international routes within eleven years of its inaugural flight in December 2011. On the foreign investment side, it includes the 90-year-old Danish toy company Lego investing in a billion-dollar carbon-neutral factory to manufacture its toys for the Southeast Asian market. And in what was a surprising move for a communist country considering the *bourgeois-ness* of the sport, Hanoi would have been the twenty-second city/country in the world to host a Formula One Grand Prix motor race.[2]

---

1. See Chapter 10, Case Study 2: Leapfrog Technology, pp. 151–57.

2. The Inaugural Vietnam Grand Prix was scheduled for April 2020, but it was rescheduled due to COVID-19 and eventually cancelled outright. The fact that Vietnam had been awarded the Formula 1 race was significant because it pointed to sufficient direct sponsorship as well as the size of a future market for auto sports.

But this is all anecdotal. What really makes an economy a Tiger Economy? It must get more than a few things right beyond the numbers, building a few large corporations, and hosting international events. Vietnam is still in the lower half of the middle-income group of countries, but has it earned the title of Tiger Economy? To better test the central hypothesis of this book, we proposed six criteria or 'tiger metrics' in Chapter 1 to measure whether Vietnam can credibly call itself a Tiger: (1) Numbers; (2) Exports; (3) Industrialization; (4) Expertise; (5) Markets; and (6) Leaders.

These metrics were achieved, in varying levels of success, by Hong Kong, Singapore, Taiwan, and South Korea during their Tiger Economy runs from the 1970s to 2000. The metrics were part of the reason they became Tiger Economies. What does Vietnam have, or not yet have, or may never obtain? How does the Vietnam case in the early 2020s compare to the Taiwan and South Korea cases of the 1970s to 1990s?

1. Numbers

The numbers that Vietnam has accumulated over the past 10–20 years fit the proposed definition of a 'Tiger Economy.'[3] In early interviews with key informants, respondents were confident that the current growth rates of GDP, trade, foreign currency reserves, FDI, and other metrics would continue to grow over the next decade. For illustration purposes, below is a selection of three metrics (GDP, imports, and exports) that compare South Korea and Taiwan to Vietnam. The trends are strikingly similar, though decades apart.

The growth trend for the twenty years from 2000 to 2021 for Vietnam's GDP, exports, and imports have a 'hockey stick' look (i.e., the indicators start slightly flat, then shoot up).

Table 18. Vietnam GDP and trade data, 2001–2021 (in US$ billion)

	2001	2002	2003	2004	2005	2006	2007	2008	2009	2010
Imports	16.2	19.7	25.3	32.0	36.8	44.9	62.8	80.7	69.9	84.83
Exports	15.0	16.7	20.1	26.5	32.4	39.8	48.6	62.7	57.1	72.2
GDP	32.7	35.1	39.6	45.4	57.6	66.4	77.4	99.1	106.0	115.9

	2011	2012	2013	2014	2015	2016	2017	2018	2019	2020	2021
Imports	105.8	114.3	131.3	148.1	165.0	173.3	211.0	236.7	253.1	270.0	332.2
Exports	96.3	114.6	132.2	150.1	162.0	175.9	214.0	243.5	264.2	300.0	336.3
GDP	135.5	155.8	171.2	186.2	193.2	205.3	223.8	245.2	255.0	271.0	290.0

Source: World Bank.

---

3. See Chapter 5, 'The Numbers' data section, pp. 59–74.

South Korea and Taiwan had similar 'hockey stick' growth from 1980 to 2000. They became high-income countries at the end of this period. They escaped the Middle-Income Trap. Most observers say that Vietnam is 'twenty years behind' South Korea and Taiwan in terms of total GDP growth. If these trends continue, it will indicate that Vietnam would reach high-income status around 2040.

Table 19. South Korea GDP and trade data, 1980–2000 (in US$ billion)

	1980	1981	1982	1983	1984	1985	1986	1987	1988	1989
Imports	24.3	27.1	25.7	26.3	27.8	26.1	32.8	41.7	52.3	63.1
Exports	18.6	21.8	21.4	24.5	28.2	27.2	37.3	51.5	64.8	67.6
GDP	65.4	72.9	78.4	87.8	97.5	101.3	116.8	147.9	199.6	246.9

	1990	1991	1992	1993	1994	1995	1996	1997	1998	1999	2000
Imports	69.8	81.5	81.8	83.8	102.3	135.1	150.3	144.6	93.3	119.8	160.5
Exports	65.0	71.9	76.6	82.2	96.0	125.1	129.7	136.2	132.3	143.7	172.3
GDP	283.3	330.6	355.5	392.7	463.6	566.6	610.1	569.7	383.3	497.5	576.1

Source: World Bank.

Table 20. Taiwan GDP and trade data (US$ billions)[4]

	1980	1981	1982	1983	1984	1985	1986	1987	1988	1989
Imports	N/A	N/A	N/A	N/A	N/A	N/A	N/A	N/A	N/A	N/A
Exports	N/A	N/A	N/A	N/A	N/A	N/A	N/A	N/A	N/A	N/A
GDP	42.3	49.0	49.5	54.1	64.1	63.6	78.2	105.0	126.5	152.7

	1990	1991	1992	1993	1994	1995	1996	1997	1998	1999	2000
Imports	54.8	63.4	72.6	77.4	84.8	104.1	103.0	114.1	114.1	111.3	140.5
Exports	67.2	76.5	82.0	85.7	94.1	113.0	117.3	122.8	122.8	123.4	151.2
GDP	166.6	187.1	222.9	236.6	256.2	279.1	292.5	303.3	280.0	303.8	330.7

Source: World Bank.

---

4. The authors were unable to identify a reliable data source for the total value of the imports and exports of goods from/to Taiwan in the 1980s. This was the first decade of the People's Republic of China (PRC) becoming 'the real China' for most of the world while Taiwan, the Republic of China, was considered to be different. In the authors' opinions, this possibly impacted data collection for many organizations including multi-lateral organizations who published trade and economic data on the PRC without any reference to Taiwan. However by 1990, there were reliable, including multi-laterals, data sources available on Taiwan's economic and trade activities.

2. Exports

As early as the mid-1990s, Vietnamese factories produced an estimated 50 percent of Nike's apparel and 20 percent of its footwear through Taiwanese, South Korean, and Vietnamese-owned factories that employed tens of thousands of workers. This indicates that the country checked off the 'footwear and garments' manufacturing criteria early on and was ready to move up the value chain by the beginning of the new millennium. Early evidence that Vietnam was also moving up the value chain ladder in electronics came from Intel, which opened a representative office in Ho Chi Minh City in 1997. In 2010 Intel opened a US$1 billion chip testing facility which supplied 80 percent of Intel's global production by 2014. When the plant initially opened, only three local companies could supply the parts needed, while the rest were imported, but by 2014 this had grown to sixteen local suppliers. The company boasted that it took Intel plants in China fifteen years and the one in Malaysia forty years to reach full capacity. Vietnam did the same in just four years.

For readers who have a Samsung mobile phone, it was probably assembled in Vietnam. According to industry sources, Samsung factories in Vietnam produce over 50 percent of the company's total annual global production of smartphones. In 2020 the Apple Corporation began manufacturing its popular Airpods wireless earphones in Vietnam, and in January 2023 it announced it would also start manufacturing MacBooks, Apple Watches, and HomePods in Vietnam.[5] Another example is the toy company Lego. Towards the end of 2021, the toymaker announced plans to build a US$1 billion plant in Binh Duong Province in southern Vietnam. In addition to employing four thousand people, it would be Lego's first carbon neutral plant and only use energy generated from renewable sources. It would export its toys to markets throughout Southeast Asia. While a relatively simple product, Lego has achieved remarkable success through technical innovation and is a clear tech leader in its segment. Lego Vietnam will not simply import components, assemble them, and then export finished products like Samsung's smartphones. Instead, Lego will make its products entirely within Vietnam and become a regional manufacturer and exporter for the company while also helping blaze a new trail in carbon neutral production techniques. Examples like Intel, Samsung, Apple, and Lego, show that Vietnam is moving up the export value chain very quickly.

---

5. *Apple To Diversify Its Supply Chain By Producing MacBooks In Vietnam*, Forbes, January 1, 2023.

3. Industrialization

One of the key reasons that South Korea and Taiwan developed so rapidly was their successful transition from an agrarian-based economy to an industrialized one. From the 1950s to the 1980s, and with the support of American ODA capital and other types of assistance, the governments of these countries focused on export manufacturing as the primary means for growing their economies. This was accompanied by poverty reduction programs and, in Taiwan in particular, land reform that incentivized farmers and boosted agricultural output. These policy moves coincided with the early stages of what is now known as the East Asian Development Model, whereby both countries began exporting higher value products to outside markets. The constant pursuit of free trade and the East Asian Development Model led to industrialization that eventually included a robust service sector. For example, from 1960 to 1975 in South Korea, agriculture's share of GDP declined to 25 percent from 45 percent while manufacturing's share increased to 27 percent from 9 percent. By 2020, the South Korean services sector comprised around 57 percent of GDP, with industry providing 33 percent and agriculture less than 2 percent.[6] These trends signify an increasingly industrialized country.

The trends in Vietnam are not on the same scale yet, but in at least two areas that are important to an industrialized future—policy and infrastructure—the seeds have been sown. In the years leading up to Vietnam's entry into the WTO on January 1, 2007, the government began to restructure its state-owned enterprise sector. The private sector was legitimized with the Enterprise Law in 1999. This led to the launch of thousands of new companies owned by private Vietnamese citizens. The country had already begun to move away from a centrally planned economy to one driven by market forces. This included the phasing out of import-substitution policies that protected SOEs to more open and competitive policies that forced them to compete. Many SOEs were also either closed or merged into large general corporations, perhaps with the intention of trying to replicate the *chaebol* model of development from South Korea. They were given a freer rein to pursue their own business objectives. This effort had mixed success.[7] But as noted in various chapters of this book, and especially with relation to the case studies, considerable emphasis is now

---

6. Statista, 2020.

7. See the narrative on 'fence-breaking' and the VinaShin saga in Chapter 4, pp. 48–50.

being placed on the private and foreign direct sectors as the key drivers of economic growth.

While the lack of infrastructure is often highly visible and sometimes an impediment to progress, steps have been taken that provide optimism. Numerous industrial parks, export-processing zones, and hi-tech centers that host companies from around the world have been built and are producing international standard products for export. Vietnam, unlike South Korea and Taiwan, also has extensive natural resources which can be used in its transition from an agriculture-based economy to an industrial-based one. These include both agriculture and mineral resources, including some of the largest untapped deposits of rare earth minerals and nickel, both of which are in high demand across a range of high-tech industries.

Vietnam's policy innovations have outpaced infrastructure developments on its journey to becoming an industrialized economy. However, that is not unusual. Every industrialized country, including Germany, Japan, the United Kingdom, and the United States traveled a similar path to development. Vietnam has begun this journey.

4. Expertise

There is a scarcity of quality universities in Vietnam and the K-to-12 education infrastructure is generally overburdened, underfunded, and not highly regarded by many Vietnamese parents. Although there are several good programs and gifted schools for the best and the brightest, more needs to be done. Change is happening too slowly to suit most parents and employers, not to mention impatient students who want to pursue their academic dreams.[8] These shortcomings can, however, be offset by positive developments. The average age of its nearly one hundred million people is around thirty-two years. There is a great deal of foreign and local investment in schools, training centers, and private international schools. The number of students who have studied abroad, or are currently studying abroad, and/or are preparing to study abroad, is growing every year. For example, there are around 25,000 university students in the United States (the sixth highest among foreign students), over 60,000 in Japan (2017 data), and over 27,000 in South Korea (second only to China in the total number of foreign students). In these three countries, as well as many others, the total numbers are increasing while numerous agents,

---

8. See Chapter 10, Case Study 1: Education, pp. 143–50.

foreign universities, and training centers vie for more Vietnamese students who want to study at universities around the world.

Education is a rapidly growing market segment. It is also something that South Korea and Taiwan handled well during their Tiger Economy runs. By 2014 South Korea had the seventh highest number of Ph.D.s by citizenship in the world (13,000). The United States has the most with 67,449, followed by Germany with 28,147, according to the OECD. For the year 2020 alone, Taiwan's Ministry of Education reported that nearly 200,000 Taiwanese were pursuing graduate degrees (masters and Ph.D.s) at local universities. As we discuss in later chapters, for cultural reasons, Vietnam could experience the same type of growth.

5. Markets

The question of whether to open its markets to the world has been answered in Vietnam. The country is already party to fifteen free trade agreements with two more under negotiation. Within a few years of the introduction of the Doi Moi policies in the late 1980s, Vietnam was eager to trade and engage with the world. Initially, Vietnamese businesses cut numerous deals. Foreign Direct Investment (FDI), seen as a curse by some countries because of a fear of being taken over by outside interests, has blossomed in Vietnam and continues to grow.

The best measure for this 'Tiger metric' is probably the rate of globalization of the economy, which was covered in Chapter 5. It measures how significantly the economy is exposed to, and relies on, the world economy. Vietnam is very exposed, and this has been advantageous. Vietnam's globalization rate is close to that of Hong Kong and Singapore (the other two Tiger Economy countries of Asia) even though they are effectively city-states with small local markets and thus need to export to grow their economies. Vietnam is an aberration in a good way. It wants to trade, and the world is ready to oblige. Moreover, the benefits of free trade have been spread relatively fairly. The extreme poverty rate, measured as living on US$1.90 per day, was in the 50 percent range for the entire country in the 1990s, but today is 2 percent.

6. Leadership

Early interviews conducted with local Vietnamese for this book revealed a negative attitude towards the government's ability to continue to grow the economy beyond the next five years. Most cited corruption and/or the inability of Vietnam's leadership to provide what it takes to steer the nation to prosperity. Many did, however, acknowledge some improvements in transparency and corruption prevention, but felt that the consensual decision-making process was too slow and would ultimately lead to Vietnam's downfall. There were too few appropriately skilled technocrats in positions of power and involved in key decision-making.

Identifying strong leadership skills in a person is difficult. Most often you just know it when you see it. However, for the public to have confidence in the people who will run the country in the future, they need to know who these people are and have confidence in their leadership skills. This level of transparency and disclosure does not yet exist in Vietnam. There are sure to be strong leaders within the Politburo and government, but how can anyone outside a small circle of people know for certain? One of the biggest complaints about their government expressed by politically aware Vietnamese is the constant reliance on a consensus-based decision-making process. It is not only too slow, but it also means that the true leaders and decision-makers are not always apparent. This could hamper Vietnam in the long term.

Lee Kuan Yew, Singapore's first prime minister, was frequently mentioned as a model leader. In many interviews when our Tiger Economy hypothesis was offered up for comment, local Vietnamese jumped to the Singapore model—not the South Korea and Taiwan models—as the one Vietnam should follow. However, they also acknowledged that their country could not emulate what Lee Kuan Yew did for Singapore. It was not only a case of not having a similar figure, but also that the Vietnamese system did not have a civil society apparatus in place. They noted that high-level government employees in Singapore earned high salaries compared to the paltry sums earned by their counterparts in Vietnam. It is no wonder, many claimed, that corruption is endemic.

This tiger metric is fraught with unanswered questions. Will a strong leader with a vision for the country emerge or can the country emerge without such a leader? Will government offices be filled with Vietnamese who have the training and skills needed to build the country? Will the existing leadership listen to these technocrats and follow their advice? Will ideological debates derail the entire process? These questions are difficult to answer at this time, but they must be considered.

To return to the first question of the hypothesis, 'Is Vietnam already or will it become a Tiger Economy?' we recap the tiger metrics and the questions each one posed:

Numbers. This is a resounding 'Yes.' The raw economic data economists use to measure the strength of an economy and country are impressive in the Vietnam case. GDP growth, trade growth, foreign currency reserves, inflation, and other metrics have been positive for more than a decade. There is no evidence to support any argument that Vietnam has not exhibited 'Tiger Economy' data trends. Nor is there any evidence that this trend will not continue.

Exports. This is 'Inconclusive' but beginning to lean towards 'Yes.' The positive news is that Vietnam has already started to manufacture export-quality products. It has been making footwear, garments, plastics, furniture, processed and packaged food, and various electronics for more than twenty years. In some areas, it has been able to produce (either by manufacturing or assembling) higher-value products, such as Samsung smartphones. Though assembling smartphones is not the same as manufacturing them using locally sourced high-end components, there are other manufacturers, such as Intel, Canon, Honda, and Lego, that source components locally and invest in R&D within Vietnam. This is a positive trend.

Industrialization. This is a soft 'No' because there is a long way to go, but the process has begun. The concept of 'Industrialization' can also be hard to define. Most analysts would categorize Hong Kong and Singapore as 'Service Sector Driven' economies rather than industrial economies although they are both developed and wealthy countries. South Korea's *chaebol*, such as Samsung, Hyundai, and LG, provide a clear model of what companies can look like in an industrialized country. Taiwan provides examples of the kind of technological innovations and software/hardware companies that can be developed within an 'industrialized economy country.' If the definition of 'industrialization' is the existence of appropriate policies *and* infrastructure to see those policies to fruition, Vietnam still has a long way to go. South Korea and Taiwan had to go through these processes. There are no shortcuts to becoming an industrialized country.

Expertise. This is a very soft 'Yes' because there is also a very long way to go. Vietnam has always had the energy, willingness, cultural imperative, and basic brainpower to train its smartest citizens in the way South Korea and Taiwan trained theirs in the 1970s–1990s. However, there are simply not enough high-quality local high schools or universities to accomplish this. Not every family can afford to send their children abroad. They must wait for the domestic education infrastructure to improve. This investment is happening, but it is too early to judge its impact. There has not been enough reform of the country's education sector to be convinced of a certain 'yes' on this issue.[9]

Markets. This is a definite 'Yes.' As detailed in Chapter 5, Vietnam's aggressive promotion and action on free trade has resulted in access to markets around the globe. The country's globalization index is exceptionally high due to this trade. Vietnam is taking a leading role in the Comprehensive and Progressive Agreement for Trans-Pacific Partnership (CPTPP). The country is in a good position to supply products to CPTPP nations while also receiving them on favorable terms. It potentially can do the same in European markets/countries since the adoption and passage of a trade agreement with the European Union as well as with a post-Brexit Great Britain.

Leadership. This is 'Inconclusive' because most observers simply do not know the real situation behind closed doors. But there is some good news on this issue. The 13th National Party Congress, held in January 2021, revealed an influx of well-trained technocrats who are being appointed to key positions within the government. There is also evidence that the leadership is committed to delivering prosperity to the whole country, not just to an elite few. This is aligned with its socialist ethos. This metric is still a 'wait and see' issue, but there are reasons for optimism.

The analysis above reveals three 'Yes' answers, two 'Inconclusive' answers, and one 'No, not quite yet' answer. This is not a firm 'Yes,' but it does suggest that, on the balance of probabilities, Vietnam already deserves recognition as a Tiger Economy.

Question 2: Can a Vietnamese Tiger Jump?

From the above we have concluded that Vietnam is a Tiger Economy. The next question is whether Vietnam can replicate what South Korea and Taiwan accomplished more than thirty years ago. The goal of such a journey is thus clear, but will it join the ranks of high-income countries or will it become a

---

9. See Chapter 10, Case Study 1: Education, pp. 143–50.

victim of 'The Middle-Income Trap'? This is the second part of the hypothesis and arguably the more important part for determining the future of Vietnam.

To answer this second, more challenging, question, we have developed a three-step approach that will require the next three chapters to fully answer.

> **Step 1, Chapter 8.** Assess the comparative advantages South Korea and Taiwan had when they became Tiger Economies in the 1980s and 1990s and determine whether Vietnam has some of those same advantages for the 2020s and 2030s.

> **Step 2, Chapter 9.** Document the comparative advantages that Vietnam has for its Tiger Economy run that South Korea and Taiwan did not have for their runs in the 1980s and 1990s.

> **Step 3, Chapter 10.** Present a range of case studies on specific themes and economic sectors that the authors believe will have a significant impact on Vietnam's future and may lead to the country replicating the South Korea and Taiwan cases.

'Jumping out of' or Escaping from the Middle-Income Trap

Most analysts and investors are bullish on Vietnam in the short term and believe, barring any major catastrophes or significant changes in direction, the country will keep growing for around ten years. They are less certain about how much growth and development can be achieved beyond then. Any discussion of Vietnam being 'trapped' as a middle-income nation may appear premature in the early 2020s, but it is an important issue that will inevitably emerge—as it did in every other country that has been able to grow and develop. Many of these countries simply stopped growing and became mired in the Middle-Income Trap, such as Argentina, Brazil, Greece, Malaysia, and South Africa, among other nations. Taiwan and South Korea are two countries that offer good examples of how to escape the trap and never look back.

It is worth looking into the background of Taiwan and Korea to see how they took full advantage of the tools at their disposal to become Tiger Economies and then to eventually break out of the Middle-Income Trap.[10]

---

10. This is covered in detail in Chapter 8, What the Asian Tigers Had, pp. 107–22.

After thirty years of direct American support, Taiwan had to stand on its own two feet beginning January 1, 1979, when the United States established diplomatic relations with the People's Republic of China (PRC). Exactly a year later, the Sino-American Mutual Defense Treaty, a pact between Taiwan and the United States that protected Taiwan from being taken over by Mainland China, expired. Taiwan, officially called the Republic of China, was on its own. The PRC, which had always been referred to as 'Red China' or 'The Mainland' by much of the world, was now 'the real China' of Asia. Taiwan was different, and so began its political juggling act that continues today to explain what Taiwan is, and is not, in the global world of politics and business.

Rather than wring their hands over the country's new and undesirable fate, the Taiwanese went back to work. This included boarding flights to Hong Kong before transiting to planes, trains, and automobiles for destinations within Southeast China. They brought with them capital, equipment, technology and, importantly, the desire to erect factories and start producing manufactured goods for customers in the United States and other large markets. They helped to kick-start the 'Made in China' phenomenon and in doing so laid the foundations for a high-tech future in the world of IT hardware. Within a generation, Taiwanese factories in the mainland were manufacturing the majority of the world's notebook and laptop computers, while high-tech manufacturers in Taiwan produced the computer chips that went into those laptops, as well as vehicles and other machinery from around the world.

South Korea's incredible rise from the ashes of the Korean War (1950–53), fought between North Korea, supported by China and the Soviet Union, and South Korea, supported by the United States, was dubbed 'the Miracle on the Han.' For the next several decades, South Korea simply outhustled, outworked, and outinnovated the rest of the world. It grew its economy by a factor of 31,000 times, from US$40.9 million in 1953 to US$1.3 trillion in 2015.[11] One of its *chaebol*, Hyundai, built the world's largest car factory at Ulsan, while another, Samsung, vies with Apple Corporation as the world's leading seller of smartphones. The country's work ethic and speed of development caught the attention of the International Olympic Committee in 1981, who chose South Korea to host the 1988 Summer Olympic Games in Seoul, and later, in 2018, the Winter Olympic Games in Pyeongchang. It also co-hosted, with Japan, the Football World Cup in 2002.

---

11. *Korea Herald*, August 10, 2015.

When the Korean War ceasefire took place in 1953, over half the citizens of the country were illiterate and its per capita income was around US$67 per year. Yet, South Korea went on to host two Olympic Games and one Football World Cup.

South Korea and Taiwan became high-income countries using two different but similar approaches. The Taiwanese built small- and medium-sized enterprises (SMEs) that became world leaders in semiconductors, robotics, and other sectors. The South Koreans built huge conglomerates called *chaebol* that could compete with the developed world. But for South Korea, it is not just about money, market share, or global events like the Olympics. In 2020 a South Korean film director won the Academy Award for Best Picture with a movie called *Parasite*. Towards the end of 2021, the nine-part Netflix special *Squid Game* became a global sensation. The South Korean K-pop boy band BTS is known worldwide for its musical style, lyricism, discography, and fashion. BTS concerts sell out within minutes of ticket sales opening to the public. Both countries have achieved global pinnacles in various fields, and they accomplished these in less than fifty years. They did something right. Both countries thus offer Vietnam something to emulate as it grows into its Tiger Economy role in the 2020s, as well as something to replicate over the next thirty years as it aspires to become a high-income country.

The Middle-Income Trap Journey

Our analysis of a Tiger Economy requires an understanding of economic growth numbers and references to low-, middle-, and high-income countries. The World Bank and others provide monetary amounts for the countries in different income ranges. In 2020, and on a nominal GDP per capita basis, the range is US$1,000–4,000 for 'lower middle-income' countries and approximately US$4,000–12,000 for 'upper middle-income' countries. Any country that has a GDP per capita of less than US$1,000 is defined as a 'low-income' country, and if a country can consistently maintain GDP per capita of over US$12,000 it is considered a 'high-income' country.

The good news is that all countries start, or have started, as low-income countries and are becoming better places in which to live. Based on any measurable socioeconomic metric (e.g., literacy, child mortality, extreme poverty, girls' education, mass starvation, and nutrition), the trends are clearly moving in one direction. Despite what we see in the news, the world is a safer, healthier, and more peaceful place than it has ever been in its history.

These trends are the outcomes of human nature. In the last two hundred years of global industrialization, many nations have achieved high-income status together with a relatively fair distribution of wealth. Over the last one hundred years, however, the growth rates of individual countries have accelerated at different times, with the acceleration of each country corresponding with the industrialization at that time. GDP growth spiked when the conditions were right, and then the countries just kept on growing. There are many historical cases that can be studied. For example, the United States saw an acceleration of growth right after the end of World War Two, Japan's growth began in the 1960s, Taiwan in the 1970s, South Korea in the 1980s, and China in the 1990s.

These countries did not, of course, grow at the same rate, and not all of them 'made it' to high-income status like South Korea and Taiwan. But for those newly arrived immigrants from the ranks of low-income countries, their new status as a middle-income country provides some comfort that they are heading in the right direction. Life is getting better.

Table 21. Number of countries by income category (GDP per capita US$)

Low-income	Lower middle income	Upper middle income	High income
Less than 1,000	1,000–4,000	4,000–12,000	More than 12,000
31	51	53	81
14.4%	23.6%	24.5%	37.5%

Source: World Bank, 2018.

Although global trends are positive, there are many countries that consistently fall within the US$4,000–12,000 range. Sometimes they clear the high-income US$12,000 GDP per capita bar, then fall below the bar after a short time. These are the countries that analysts refer to as being 'stuck' in the Middle-Income Trap. Conventional wisdom would indicate that some of these countries already are or should be high-income countries because of the wealth they have, including the BRICS countries—Brazil, Russia, India, China, and South Africa—which some observers might think are already high-income nations. This is because they are wealthy in some respects. Despite having oil and gas resources (Russia), agricultural wealth (Brazil), mineral wealth (South

Africa), or manufacturing juggernauts with an enormous labor force as well as high-tech industries (China and India), the BRICS are currently considered middle-income countries. Whether they can permanently become high-income nations is uncertain.

Although a daunting challenge for Vietnam, the Middle-Income Trap is not inescapable. According to the World Bank, in 2018 there were eighty-one high-income nations around the globe. A brief look at the list shows that these countries do not necessarily need to have expansive natural resources or large populations. The original 'Tiger Economies' of Asia did not have significant oil and gas resources, agricultural wealth, mineral wealth, or large workforces. However, they have all risen to the level of being permanently labeled high-income nations.

Table 22. Asian tiger economies, 1980–2018 (GDP per capita US$)

	1980	1985	1990	1995	2000	2005	2010	2015	2018
South Korea	1,704	2,457	6,516	12,332	11,947	18,639	22,086	27,105	31,362
Taiwan	2,389	3,314	8,205	13,119	14,908	16,456	19,197	22,780	25,525
Hong Kong	5,700	6,543	13,485	23,497	25,756	26,650	32,550	42,432	48,676
Singapore	4,928	7,002	11,862	24,917	23,852	29,961	47,236	55,646	64,582

Source: World Bank.

Sources vary as to the exact date, but both Taiwan and South Korea grew steadily from the 1970s and 1980s and left the Middle-Income Trap around the years 1995 and 2000, respectively. Most importantly, they kept on growing. Unlike other countries, they did not fall back after crossing the bar.

Vietnam, with a GDP per capita of around US$4,121 in 2022, is a couple of decades behind those countries because its development started later. However, if the data trends in these tables are compared and our hypothesis holds true, Vietnam will reach a GDP per capita level of US$12,000 within the next twenty years.

Table 23. Vietnam, 1990–2022 (GDP per capita US$)

1990	1995	2001	2005	2010	2015	2018	2019	2020	2022
95	276	513	873	1,628	2,582	3,202	3,398	3,521	4,121

Source: IMF and World Economic Outlook Database, April 2022.

How, when, or if this happens is the point of the second question of the hypothesis. Today's high-income country club comprises a broad range of countries that are very different from each other. There is no precise formula for what it takes to be a high-income nation, although several tangibles and comparative advantages need to be lined up.

Can Vietnam grow into a high-income nation like South Korea and Taiwan and, if so, when? Most forecasts and analyses are bullish about the next ten years, and current trends in FDI, manufacturing, and trade support this. However, the broader and more long-term issue is what happens after ten years of growth because Vietnam will need more than ten years to accomplish what South Korea and Taiwan did. The reality is that it is not going to be easy to get a Vietnamese tiger to escape the Middle-Income Trap. But if Vietnam is going to replicate the South Korea and Taiwan experience, it must face that challenge head on. It must be a Tiger that can jump.

Chapter 8

WHAT THE ASIAN TIGERS HAD

In August 1987, with US$125 in his pocket, co-author Sam Korsmoe arrived at Chiang Kai Shek International Airport in Taipei City, Taiwan. He had just completed a two-year stint as a United States Peace Corps Volunteer in the Philippines and was not ready to return home. Instead, he moved to Taipei City to teach English. Taipei City at the time had the look and feel of "a very Chinese city." There were very few English signs or recognizable brands visible. The streets were clogged with motorcycles, taxis, and large commuter buses that spewed smoke out of their exhausts when the drivers sped away from the bus stops and onto the city's crowded streets. Everyone, it seemed, was in a rush to get somewhere because they had to get something done.

In 1987 the size of Taiwan's economy was around US$105 billion. South Korea was a bit larger with a total GDP of about US$146 billion. For comparative purposes and without calculating the different values of the US$ between these time periods, Vietnam's GDP was about US$106 billion in 2009. Both South Korea and Taiwan were very much middle-income countries, yet both were also flirting with and envisioning a new future for themselves.

On July 15, 1987, the government of Taiwan lifted Martial Law, imposed in 1949. The Kuomintang (KMT) still had a firm grip on power, but there was a movement brewing underground that eventually became the Democratic Progressive Party (DPP). Such political movements were visible to all, even total novices like the co-author, who knew nothing of the country's politics or history.

Tensions with 'The Mainland' never completely ceased, but during the four years Sam spent in Taiwan the infamous 'Three No's'—No Contact, No Compromise, No Negotiation—became the 'Three Maybe's.' Taiwanese were allowed to travel to China for home visits provided they went via Hong Kong. There were no direct flights, but Taiwanese entrepreneurs had already started doing business with their factory counterparts, often distant family members, in Fujian Province, directly across the Taiwan Straits. The Fujianese and Taiwanese dialects of Chinese are quite similar. Amid the tension, there were small progressive steps being taken.

At the same time in South Korea, the students of Yonsei University were staging massive demonstrations on the streets of Seoul to protest President Chun Doo Hwan's regime. These included huge public battles with the police. Students were leaping off buildings. There were hunger strikes and even self-immolations. These events were broadcast all over the news in Taiwan. Sam also heard numerous first-hand accounts from teachers who had taught in Seoul and then moved to Taipei City. While all this was happening, Seoul was also preparing for, and then successfully hosting, the 1988 Olympic Games.

South Korea and Taiwan might go down in history as among the most puzzling aberrations of economic development. The fate of Hong Kong and Singapore, the other two Asian Tigers, is more easily explained because they are city-states in ideal locations for economic growth, fueled by trade and commerce. South Korea and Taiwan are different. They were not large in population nor rich in natural resources, but they succeeded. There is no simple answer to how this was achieved. There are numerous ways to look at it and numerous factors at play.

The Development Model

As described earlier, the East Asian Development Model is straightforward. Countries use their labor resources to generate low-cost exports that in turn generate foreign reserves and increase internal consumption. Over time, they move up the export value chain to produce high-value products and eventually become rich. They essentially export themselves to wealth.

As noted in Chapter 7, South Korea and Taiwan adopted different approaches to their East Asian Development Model strategies and had different starting points, but they shared a number of similarities, including a strong national government that had little interest in democratic elections, a large market and strategic partner in the United States, a supplementary military shield provided by the United States military, successful forays into high-tech industries, and an incredibly hardworking labor force. If fully researched, the differences between the two countries are most likely numerous, but one key difference is South Korea's development of large, family-owned private corporations called *chaebols* compared to Taiwan's reliance on a range of SMEs. Whether the firms were large behemoths or SMEs, they pursued the development of export-quality products with a vengeance. Their investment in technology, infrastructure, and especially people, paid off. They broke through the Middle-Income Trap barrier of US$12,000 per capita GDP by the year 2000. More than twenty years later, the best companies from Taiwan, and especially from South Korea, are global players in the world economy as well as big investors in Vietnam.

Can Vietnam achieve something similar and, if so, by when and how? Currently, the country is about twenty years behind the former Tigers on most metrics. That said, the world was a very different place twenty years ago when South Korea and Taiwan were leaving the ranks of middle-income countries. Some of the comparative advantages they enjoyed are fixed to a historical point in time while others are not. Nevertheless, there were distinct reasons for South Korea and Taiwan's economic rise. In the analysis that follows, we offer nine observations to help understand their success. We then apply these observations to Vietnam's situation and ask if these same comparative advantages apply.

1. The Priority of Education

The so called 'chopstick nations' of Asia—those that predominantly use chopsticks for eating—are also the nations that have adopted an education system that is over 2,500 years old. It is fundamentally a Confucian-oriented concept. This is the Mandarin exam system of China. It is based on the passing of a series of tests. It is still in use today in China in the form of the *gao kao*, or university entrance exam, which is given to high school seniors once a year. Vietnam has the same test as does South Korea, Taiwan, Hong Kong, Singapore, and Japan.

This is why education is so important in these nations. From an early age, the standardized tests play an essential role in what a person will be able to achieve in life—job, family, career, where one lives, etc. There is a type of *gao kao* for each step of the education system: one to determine which middle school a child gets into upon leaving primary school; another to determine which high school a child gets into upon leaving middle school; and, finally, the big *gao kao* test to determine which university a student can go to. Although there might not always be actual tests, parents of school children in all the chopstick nations fret, stress, stand in line, beg, plead, bribe (if that works), and pray at temples that their four- or five-year-old child gets into the best preschools available.

The *gao kao* system is hated by most East Asians as well as criticized by education observers from around the world as nothing more than rote learning. It does not measure creativity, problem-solving, or any kind of real intelligence, say the critics. It is, however, a type of meritocracy in that everyone takes the same test, and the results determine who goes to a top middle school/high school/university and who does not. It is a measure of raw intelligence. While it is also a measure of how well a person can take a test, it is an even better measure of a student's study ethic and how hard they are willing to work. To a significant degree, it is a measure of grit.

In all chopstick countries, preparing for the national exams is a family affair. There are legions of training centers, online programs, and private tutors who provide courses and guidance on how to prepare for the tests. These programs are only as good as the student's willingness to show up, sit down, and get to work. This same work/study ethic applies to the students who decide to study abroad and must take the IELTS, TOEFL, SAT, ACT, GRE, LSAT, GMAT, MCATs, or any of the range of standardized tests required in countries around the world. In the chopstick nations, the children line up to do this. The parents, who wake up early to get their children up early, line up too. The work and study ethic of the South Korean and Taiwanese citizens that made these countries so successful began well before these same citizens attended kindergarten.

Does Vietnam also prioritize education? Do Vietnamese parents consider education as an investment rather than an expense? This is a definite 'Yes', and it is one of many cultural traits shared by all three countries. South Korean and Taiwanese factory managers who have the choice of running a factory in Indonesia or Vietnam always choose Vietnam, say various businesspeople. It is an automatic decision. A higher salary in other countries does not attract them. Vietnam gives South Korean and Taiwanese expatriates a comfort level that other countries do not. The three countries are extremely similar, and education is one of the most important shared values.

Vietnam might even have an edge in this space. As observed by co-author Sam Korsmoe, Taiwan in the late 1980s did not have many young people who were fluent in English. It also did not have the internet or many teaching tools or online learning programs. Vietnam in the 2020s will have many bilingual youths, and the online education trend will create even more. The treatment of education as a priority is already paying dividends and this will be significant for the country's future.[1]

2. Investment in High Tech

In the early to mid-1990s, South Korean and Taiwanese footwear and garment companies flooded into Vietnam. They wanted to cash in on the relatively cheap land, take on the offers from industrial park managers who were begging for their business, and employ the millions of workers who were lining up to go to work for an average salary of US$50 a month. By then South Korean and Taiwanese businessmen had mastered the art of putting down a concrete slab, erecting steel walls and a roof, and setting up sewing lines, all in a matter of months, so they could begin filling orders for American and European buyers of footwear and garments. It was all about the numbers. How much is the land? How high are the tariffs? What is the cost of labor? The same thing occurred in South Korea and Taiwan, but now it has been exported because South Koreans and Taiwanese do not want to make footwear and garments anymore. They have moved on. Instead, high-end manufacturing took its place in South Korea and Taiwan

The South Koreans and Taiwanese are hardly the first group of businesspeople to learn that making footwear and garments (or toys, plastics, ceramics, cheap gadgets, etc.) is mundane work that does not offer much of a financial future for either the workers or the factory owners. When it is all about the numbers, there will always be a location offering better numbers. It was a low margin game reliant on cheap labor, and that kind of game is hard to win over the long term. They needed to make a change and they did.

Both nations leveraged their Cold War partnerships to make smart investments in high-tech facilities. These were industrial parks with clean rooms and automated lines. These were research centers with significant R&D budgets. In the case of Taiwan, there was a call put out to the expansive diaspora of Overseas Chinese to return home and help make Taiwan an industrial leader of high tech. This all dovetailed with an education push and a desire to send their best and brightest children to the top universities in

---

1. See Chapter 10, Case Study 1: Education, pp. 143–50.

the United States and Europe. They studied engineering, physics, computer science, finance, medicine, law, and a range of subjects that were needed to build a high-tech country.

This all came together through a combination of impatience with being a 'shoe and garment country,' good timing with leapfrog technology opportunities, and the return of the children who had, at their parents' insistence, studied abroad and were ready to come home and get down to work. Had these things not happened, it would have been hard to see Samsung overtake Apple in the smartphone market and Hyundai build the world's largest automated car plant in Ulsan. Nor would Taiwan Semiconductor Manufacturing Company become the world's largest producer of computer chips and other Taiwanese companies lead the world in robotic manufacturing and semiconductors. It is also unlikely that Seoul would have hosted the 1988 Olympic Games or that Taipei City would have been home to the world's tallest building (Taipei 101) from 2004 to 2010.

Vietnam does not have a high-tech industry today, but a fairer assessment is 'Not Yet.' The term 'high tech' is ambiguous because it depends on what is being measured as high tech or low tech. For example, Hyundai's automated car plant in Ulsan, which can produce 1.6 million cars a year, is obviously high tech. It took decades to develop and is the only one of its kind in the world. Or if high-tech is defined by what is produced, as opposed to how it is produced, Samsung's plant in Vietnam producing Samsung's smartphones could be high tech. But Vietnam's share of this business is its ability to assemble small components that are shipped in from abroad, put these together into operating smartphones, test the phones, then package them for shipment to consumer markets around the world. A smartphone is a high-tech product, but simply putting the pieces together is not a high-tech endeavor. It is a labor endeavor. But it is a start, and it is not unreasonable to expect that eventually more high-tech componentry will be manufactured in Vietnam closer to the assembly lines.

The good news is that there are hundreds of assembly lines in the country, and they are building a broad range of products. Some are still low-end goods like footwear and garments while others are motorbikes, cars, electronic goods, and even lines to test computer chips. Some are high-tech robotic ventures, such as VinFast's car plant in Hai Phong, which is highly automated and is manufacturing electric vehicles.[2] Vietnam's tech industry is not like Taiwan's or South Korea's, but the assembly lines are up and running and component manufacturers are beginning to move into the country. It is only a matter of time before foreign and local companies begin to build more sophisticated research facilities in Vietnam.

3. Postwar Grit: The Greatest Generation

Tom Brokaw, the American newsman who anchored the NBC Nightly News for decades, is probably best remembered not for being a television news anchor or an award-winning journalist, but for writing a book called *The Greatest Generation*.[3] It was about the generation of Americans who grew up as children in the Great Depression and then fought in World War II. After the war they returned home and got to work building or rebuilding the United States. No whining. No bitterness. No blaming. Just going to work to rebuild a country that was not even destroyed by World War II. Much of Europe was destroyed, but Europeans did the same thing. Brokaw may have coined the phrase, but it was the Japanese that outshone everyone. Amid the rubble of Tokyo and other major cities, the Japanese got back to work to rebuild their country. The past was in the past. It was all about the future, and almost everyone in Japan was ready to do the heavy lifting necessary to move on. In a very short time, Japan became an industrial juggernaut again, selling its products around the world. Within twenty years of the atomic bombing of Hiroshima and Nagasaki, Japan hosted the 1964 Tokyo Olympic Games.

The same thing has occurred in many other countries around the world. When a generation of people manage to survive a horribly violent war, the last thing most of them want to do is to remember the events of the war. Nor do they want to tell their children all about it. Instead, they get to work. They put in incredibly long hours working on assembly lines, pouring concrete, pounding nails, working the phones, or typing away in front of a computer. This is an attribute that is beyond grit. It is a postwar work ethic that is not shared by many nations to the extent that it existed among the citizens of countries like Japan, South Korea, and Taiwan.

---

2. See Chapter 10, Case Study 2: Leapfrog Technology, for more details on VinFast, pp. 152–53.

3. Published by Random House Trade Paperbacks, New York, 1998.

The postwar generation of East Asians were ready to do whatever it took to make up for the previous generation's loss. Moreover, they were more than ready to make sure the next generation, their children, would never have to go through what they experienced. In doing so, they created economic miracles by showing up and outworking everyone else in the marketplace.

Vietnam has the same traits. It is all about the value of grit, which we discussed in Chapter 3. But taking our grit analysis further, we can add two more values relevant to Vietnam: 'postwar grit' and 'pragmatic grit.' One of these values (postwar grit) fits South Korea perfectly as well as Taiwan, though to a lesser extent. The other value (pragmatic grit) might fit both South Korea and Taiwan, but it is elementary for Vietnam. In 1953 and 1990, respectively, South Korea and Vietnam had to rebuild their countries from the ashes of war. It was the charge and responsibility of the postwar generation, and they were up to the challenge. There was no other choice: escape severe poverty or stay in it. To escape meant the development of postwar grit and the creation of what can be called 'the Greatest Generation.'

The primary driver for most parents to work so hard to succeed is their children, or the extended family if they do not have children. This is nothing new. To work hard for future generations is one of the most human emotions. Making life better for those to come is how most people are built. But the notion of only working hard as a means for economic success is not true. Poor families in developing countries tend to work very hard regardless of their country's history, religion, ethnicity, political model, or any other characteristic. Yet, in some countries, these families, and their countries overall, remain poor despite all their best efforts.

Taiwan, South Korea, and Vietnam share a similar work ethic. The citizens of each country all work hard to improve the lives of their families and for future generations. In this sense they are no different than poor families from Indonesia, Malaysia, Thailand, or the BRICS nations. However, Vietnam can add a postwar element to its work ethic as well as a sense of pragmatism and intention. Although the war ended on the last day of April 1975, Vietnam's postwar grit did not begin on May 1. The disastrous policies of the postwar unification government did the opposite of country-building, but this was reversed with Doi Moi in 1986.

The reason for the turn-around was that pragmatic intentions entered the formula. These intentions (the Doi Moi policies) mixed with postwar grit, or better still, post-poverty grit, meant that by the mid-1990s Vietnam began to look like a country that might make it. By 2010 it looked like a Tiger Economy. By 2020 it had become a country that has sparked interest from around the world. It is not unusual to see a luxury car like a Rolls Royce or Mercedes Benz outside a streetside *pho* shop because everyone comes from humble roots. When COVID-19 hit, Vietnamese friends of the authors would make statements like, "I'm not afraid of being poor. I was poor before, and I know that I can be rich again if I work hard."

4. Most Coveted Nation Status

Most observers of international affairs are familiar with the term Most Favored Nation (MFN) status. It is granted by the United States, the world's biggest economy, to select countries that it trades with. It can be vitally important for manufacturers who want to export to the largest market in the world. Without this status they cannot compete with manufacturers from other countries that have preferential trading rights and are selling products to the United States because the difference in tariff rates is too great. From the very beginning, South Korea and Taiwan had MFN status with the United States. The key reason was the Cold War.

These two nations also had an even more important status—Most Coveted Nation (MCN). This is a different deal (as well as a verbal creation of the authors). By our definition, MCN status is not only about economics and trade, it is also about politics. Geography and the Cold War between the United States and the Soviet Union meant that both South Korea and Taiwan played outsized roles. They were important to the United States for a host of reasons that had nothing to do with tariff rates. The United States needed to keep both nations in its orbit while fighting the war in Vietnam, keeping an eye on 'Red' China, and not succumbing to the Soviet Union and its numerous Cold War plays. South Korea and Taiwan were important chess pieces in the game. Granting them something more significant than MFN status was part of the deal. This would include ODA, technology transfers, scholarship programs, and joint-venture deals. It would also include military bases and a significant military presence and partnership, especially in South Korea. In effect, the United States provided a military shield for both countries. It had the look and feel of a 'Big Brother' to 'Little Brother' relationship, and that was fine with most South Korean and Taiwanese citizens in the early years. They had only recently been removed from severe poverty, and the swallowing of some national pride was the price to be paid. By the time the Cold War ended in 1989, both countries were in a strong enough position to go their own way, which included continued and expanded trade with the United States.

Vietnam never had this status. Until 1995, the United States embargo on Vietnam remained in place and permanent trade status (this time around called PNTR—Permanent Normal Trade Relations) was not issued until 2007. But this situation is changing fast. The historical animosities between Vietnam and the United States are in the past, and Vietnam's aggressive pursuit of free trade and FDI is one of the assets it must move forward and keep growing. Its comparative advantage in this respect is like that of South Korea and Taiwan, but in a different era and without an overt political purpose. This, too, is perhaps due to change. There is a growing 'Cold War' environment between China and the United States. While Vietnam is not a party to this fight, there could be an opportunity for Vietnam to receive a similar type of favoritism and even leverage that South Korea and Taiwan enjoyed during the Cold War of the 1970s and 1980s.

5. Commitment to Global Trade and Integration

Throughout this book, and especially in Chapter 5, Free Trade Better Work, the authors have been describing Vietnam's aggressive opening of its economy to the outside world. This is most visible in the numerous free trade agreements that the country has joined. Another important metric is how much attention a country attracts from outsiders or, more specifically, how much investment it attracts. Vietnam's National Assembly passed a foreign investment law in 1996, which allowed for the formation of joint ventures (JVs), 100 percent foreign-owned enterprises (FOEs), business cooperation contracts (BCCs), and various types of build-operate-transfer (BOT) projects, among other investment vehicles. This was Vietnam not just saying it wanted to trade with the world, it was also inviting foreign investors to set up operations inside the country. South Korea and Taiwan companies also worked with foreign companies in terms of technology, patents, and manufacturing. They built strong partnerships.

It is no surprise, therefore, that the first ones through Vietnam's open door were companies from South Korea and Taiwan. They saw something, and it is hard not to believe that they saw a bit of themselves. They have invested tens of billions of dollars. China, Germany, Japan, the United States, and most global organizations like the World Bank, the Asian Development Bank, and the International Monetary Fund are all in Vietnam. These same countries and multilateral organizations are investing significant amounts of ODA in the country. The money is not only pledged but is disbursed and invested into projects. In 2016, Vietnam ranked sixth in terms of ODA disbursements, according to Development Aid, an international organization that collects and collates aid information for the international development sector.

FDI investment is also booming. On its own, just one corporation, Samsung from South Korea, has invested US$17 billion in the country. It employs around 160,000 Vietnamese. If outsiders are looking for proof of concept, ask the *chaebol*. That kind of investment is quite a statement about the credibility of Vietnam's future.

6. Geography

The size, shape, and location of countries can have profound impacts on how they develop. Sometimes, however, these metrics are overlooked or not given due credit. Hong Kong and Singapore are city-states ideally suited for trade and investment and in superb locations for growth. For decades Hong Kong was the gateway to China, while Singapore was in an ideal location for global shipping. That is part of the reason they were Tiger Economies.

South Korea and Taiwan are also well located, and small enough in size that government and business did not have too much trouble reaching its furthest communities during its growth stages. Getting the last mile of infrastructure built was easier in South Korea and Taiwan than in most countries. China, India, and Russia are far too large in geographical terms to cover the last mile of infrastructure and services easily and affordably. In such large countries, there will inevitably be large disparities of wealth, as is clearly observed in the socioeconomic differences between eastern and western China. On its own, eastern China would be one of the wealthier 'nation states' in the world, but it is not on its own. It has western China to consider. A similar comparison could be made with the United States, where most of the wealth accrues to people living near the coasts.

Geography impacts the development of a country in multiple ways. This includes the geographical size of the country, its weather, and the amount of arable land available to produce food and soft commodities. For trade, it includes the number of air, sea, and river ports, plus the distances from the furthest reaches of the country to these ports as well as the country's proximity to global shipping routes. For tourism, it includes the availability of beaches and other destinations for development. For infrastructure development and the movement of people within the country, it includes the proximity of key metro areas and whether the country is a single landmass or a group of islands.

Vietnam's long and skinny footprint offers several geographical advantages that also exist in South Korea and Taiwan. It is a coastal nation and there are many airports and seaports along its north to south geography. The ports have good proximity to global shipping routes. The overall distance from the furthest reaches of the country to these ports as well as to metro areas is not extreme. The fact that Vietnam is one landmass, as opposed to an island nation like the Philippines and Indonesia, has also made it easier for the country to connect remote communities and ensure everyone has access to the electricity, communications, internet, water, and logistic services they need. This is one of the key reasons that the extreme poverty rate declined so rapidly post-1990. The country's economic growth was more evenly shared than in other developing countries because it was easier to do this. Vietnam's geography means that the rural poor are less disadvantaged than the rural poor of many developing countries, and arguably they have a clearer road to the middle class.

7. Culture

Culture is more complicated than geography when describing a country. It helps explain many issues, but also creates several questions. Making cultural arguments to explain any issue is fraught with challenges. Whether it is a fear of overgeneralizing or outright racism, cultural anthropologists have a demanding job. It is difficult to explain, culturally, why some countries are poor and others are rich. What is known and accepted is that cultures are different, and a wide diversity of cultures within a country creates added complexity to how it is governed and how its resources are shared. South Korea and Taiwan are homogenous nations. They have Mandarin-style education systems that rely on rote learning. Adhering to a national government is less problematic because there are fewer ethnic issues and, in the case of these two Tigers, less inequality among the population.

Vietnam's location on the border of Northeast Asia and Southeast Asia makes it a compelling study. Is it a Southeast Asian country because of where it sits geographically, or a Northeast Asian country because that is where it sits culturally? In terms of education, religion, and work ethic, Vietnam is more like South Korea and Taiwan than Indonesia and Thailand. It features Confucian values that are not as prominent as in Southeast Asian cultures and countries. The adherence to authority, a work and study ethic that propelled its workforce up the value chain of export manufacturing, and sheer grit are some of the key reasons why South Korea and Taiwan have been so successful. These traits, combined with a relatively homogenous population in terms of ethnicity, made it easier for the central governments in both countries to set the rules in place for growth. In both countries there were few to no restrictions based on religion or gender. In comparison with other nations, women have played outsized roles in the Asian Tigers, especially in Vietnam.[4]

Throughout history, Vietnam has also been more open to other cultures than many other countries in the region. Part of this can be explained by its colonial past and its integration of Chinese, French, and American culture into Vietnamese culture. This creates a more open environment for accepting new ideas, learning, and global integration, among other influences, compared to its Southeast and Northeast Asian neighbors.

In our opinion, Vietnam is more like South Korea and Taiwan than any other nation. It is also like China, but without the enormous geographical challenges or the ethnic complexities of a large, heavily populated country. Whether these cultural traits will help Vietnam pass through the Middle-Income Trap to become a high-income nation is hard to tell. However, it is fair to say that these cultural traits will not impede its attempt to do so. They are almost certainly going to help rather than hurt. The cultural traits held by the South Koreans and Taiwanese pushed them through the Middle-Income Trap. If Vietnam is quite similar culturally, why would not the same thing happen for the Vietnamese?

8. Wealth Disparity

As the world enters the decade of the 2020s, a hot topic in the mainstream press and most certainly on social media is about wealth inequality, in particular the top '1 percenters' and how much money and power they have. In 1912, Corrado Gini, an Italian statistician and sociologist, developed a statistical model that measures wealth and income distribution. It ranges from 0 (everyone has the same amount of wealth) to 1 (one person owns everything). It is called the Gini Coefficient and globally it is trending more towards 1 than 0. It is not a measure of the country's overall wealth. Some of the poorest countries in the world have the highest Gini Coefficients. Wealthy nations can go either way. For example, South Africa is measured at 0.63. More

---

4. See Chapter 10, Case Study: The Role of Women, pp. 158–66.

than half of South Africans live on less than US$83 per month. The United States' Gini Coefficient is 0.49, the highest it has been in fifty years according to the United States Census Bureau. Many wealthy European countries have Gini Coefficients in the 0.25 to 0.35 range which represents egalitarian societies. A high Gini Coefficient is likely to lead to entrenched interests ensuring their way of life. This makes the playing field unlevel, access to capital and technology more difficult for the less wealthy and connected, and tax structures that maintain the status quo.

Vietnam's Gini Coefficient is 0.36. For the Asian Tigers, Taiwan has an index of 0.34, South Korea 0.35, Singapore 0.46, and Hong Kong, the most unequal, 0.53.[5] One of the results of Vietnam's relatively equitable Gini Coefficient is the reduction of the extreme poverty rate from around 50 percent in the early 1990s to 2 percent today. Since the beginning of the Doi Moi era, the government has focused on increasing the household incomes of rural families to be closer to those in urban areas. There are still plenty of cracks for Vietnam's poorest households to fall into, but many of these cracks are being filled. It is too early to know what Vietnam's Gini-Coefficient might be in ten years' time, but the country's history so far, and semi-embedding socialist values, bode well for Vietnam's journey forward as it keeps growing.

9. Political Stability and Intent

Politicians around the world, regardless of their form of government, are the same in at least one respect: they make promises to their citizens and then they either deliver on their promises or they don't. For example, Vietnamese leaders' 'intent' to lower the extreme poverty rate was a simple promise in the early 1990s. When half the country lives on less than US$2 a day, something needs to be done. When half of South Koreans lived in poverty and more than half were illiterate after the Korean War in 1953, the leaders of a postwar South Korea had the same intentions. They had to make structural changes and they did. Promises have been kept in both countries.

Not all countries do this well. Many have entrenched interests that are able to cement their positions in government and society and ensure their own status quo. It is hardly surprising that those countries with strongly entrenched interests are also those with high Gini Coefficients. These countries have rich and powerful people/families who want to remain rich and powerful. The

---

5. *Source*: World Bank and other compiled sources.

middle-income group is full of countries that seem to have little intention of changing their status quo. South Korea and Taiwan have maintained relatively low Gini Coefficients because their governments deliver on their promises, and this has led to a relatively stable political environment. There are rich families in both nations, but these same families are not firmly entrenched within the government like in many countries around the world.

We have yet to see if Vietnam can achieve what South Korea and Taiwan have done and avoid creating an entrenched political and business elite, but for the time being things look promising. The Vietnamese government makes plenty of promises to the people and, as we argued in Chapter 6, there is accountability for these promises. The country's aggressive pursuit of free trade goes together with the concept of fair competition, so the notion of controlling resources or markets to protect the elite has not caught on. This could change, but as the 2020s proceed, the entrenched interests will have to work hard to gain an undeserved edge in terms of business development and wealth creation.

The Future Awaits

Vietnam, like South Korea and Taiwan, was a low-income country and it has become a lower middle-income country. Within the span of a few years, it will be an upper middle-income country. Then it has a challenging road ahead to leave the middle-income rankings. Vietnam's leaders are optimistic; one of the post-National Party Congress announcements made at the beginning of 2021 directly referred to Vietnam leaving the ranks of middle-income countries by 2045.

South Korea and Taiwan had what they needed to keep going and Vietnam shares many of the characteristics that those two countries had to escape the Middle-Income Trap. Whether Vietnam can do the same thing is the key question. The nine comparative advantages noted above were relevant for South Korea and Taiwan in the 1980s and 1990s. Most of them also seem relevant for Vietnam in the coming decades. But Vietnam also holds other 'cards' it can play to escape the Middle-Income Trap.

Chapter 9

THE CARDS IT HOLDS

This is a book about the future of Vietnam, but in a broader sense the hypothesis poses a more fundamental question about the future of all countries. How do they become rich? Becoming a rich country requires many tangible and intangible issues to be almost perfectly aligned. In the previous chapter, we identified nine of those issues relevant to South Korea and Taiwan, and we will offer more in this chapter that are specific to Vietnam. While some of these factors can be omitted, most must align for success. If not, the country runs the risk of not becoming rich and remaining stuck as a middle-income country.

Getting almost everything right and nothing wrong is a very high bar to clear. It is no wonder that economists created the term 'Middle-Income Trap' to describe nations that cannot seemingly get everything together for a sustained period, as well as the term 'Asian Economic Miracle' to describe the four Asian Tiger Economies that did succeed. Getting all the elements for growth in place without any one of them disrupting the entire effort and strategy is rare. Perhaps that is why, according to World Bank data, there are more nations quantified as middle income (103) than high income (81). Vietnam is still a lower middle-income country although it is consistently moving up the ranks. It would be impossible to find a Vietnamese person who is satisfied with the status quo. They want to keep moving up and will not stop until their country is a high-income nation.

In the first five chapters of this book, we described how the past has impacted present-day Vietnam and, most importantly, how it set the stage for the future. We argued that 'the point of no return' for Vietnam's reform efforts was its entry into the WTO at the beginning of 2007. This was a full commitment to free trade. It meant not just multiple trade agreements, but also a mostly unrestricted flow of capital, people, technology, and especially ideas and entrepreneurship into and out of the country. It also meant allowing in foreign companies that were much larger, better financed, and had superior technology compared to Vietnamese SOEs. Rather than try to protect local markets and limit competition for the SOE sector so it can catch up to the rest of the world, the government has indicated that it will allow free trade market principles to run their course providing there is an overall net gain for the country.

This free trade bet has been placed. This means Vietnam must rely on the assets it has within its own borders, along with what it can import and then manufacture for outside markets, to keep its economy growing. We have already concluded that Vietnam deserves the status of a Tiger Economy and that it shares many characteristics that South Korea and Taiwan had when they were Tiger Economies. This chapter takes the discussion one step further to discuss the additional 'cards'—comparative advantages and tools—that Vietnam has in its hand to continue its East Asian Development Model strategy. These are the cards that South Korea and Taiwan *did not have* or were less important to their eventual development.

It is not just about free trade and the East Asian Development Model strategy. There are several other factors relevant to the Vietnam story. Some of these factors have been discussed in previous chapters and will also be described in more detail in the Chapter 10 case studies. At the risk of repeating ourselves in some areas, we offer below seven additional advantages or cards that Vietnam can leverage for its journey to high-income status.

1. Global Manufacturing: China Plus One

One of the biggest questions for global business as COVID-19 begins to wind down is who is going to come out on top in the world of manufacturing? The pandemic revealed, among other issues, the precariousness of relying too much on a single country like China as the primary manufacturing destination for global supply chains. This has spurred a more aggressive search for an alternative, or a 'China Plus One' strategy and destination for manufacturers. Vietnam has the capacity to take on this role and this makes it one of the country's cards for the 2020s and 2030s.

At its core, the East Asian Development Model requires a stable and predictable environment for factories to manufacture export-quality products.

Since the 1990s, the primary location for global supply chains has been China, but this is changing. The migration of manufacturers exiting China began several years ago (i.e., well before COVID-19). It also started before the first volleys of the China-United States trade war began during the Trump Administration (2016–20). For a variety of reasons that include labor rates, land rents, and high and/or unpredictable tariffs, regional analysts say an estimated 20 percent of the manufacturing in China will leave that country in the next 5–10 years.

But where will it go? There is a border country just to the south that mostly escaped the ravages of COVID-19 and is pursuing a 'Live with COVID' strategy as opposed to a 'Zero COVID Policy.' It has a labor force of nearly sixty million people and decently competitive labor rates along with a relatively open economy for trade and investment. Over the past twenty-five years, Vietnam-based manufacturers have been producing 'Made in Vietnam' household products (e.g., footwear, garments, and furniture) as well as more sophisticated toll manufacturing products like assembling Samsung smartphones.[1] This trend, combined with Vietnam's relatively good economic health, will contribute to making Vietnam popular for manufacturers seeking alternatives for their China operations.

This is happening while Vietnam is intent on replicating the East Asian Development Model by courting more global manufacturers to come to Vietnam, as well as encouraging local investors to also build factories that manufacture higher-value products that earn higher margins. The good news about this movement is that it has all been done before. Japan (the 1950s and 1960s), Hong Kong and Taiwan (the 1970s), South Korea (the 1980s), and China (since the 1990s) have all pursued this journey. Historically, countries like Germany and the United States took the same steps. This was how many developed countries that started out poor became rich. They have also provided numerous blueprints on how to keep moving up the value chain ladder. No country wants to get stuck on a single rung by making footwear and garments for generations even though quite a few countries do. Vietnam's manufacturing sector is ready to take on this challenge. This is one of its cards.

Consider this potential chain of events. Over the next 5–10 years, an estimated 20 percent of all manufacturing in China (foreign-invested and Chinese-owned factories) will leave. Vietnam is clearly the most attractive

---

1. See Chapter 5, Free Trade Better Work, pp. 53–74, for more analysis on this issue.

destination. This will put pressure on all the existing resources for manufacturing in Vietnam, such as industrial real estate, labor, logistics, energy, and waste management. The prices for all these requirements will increase and only those companies with the highest margins will remain standing. Initially, the lower-margin companies will have to leave the industrial parks that they are in now and which surround the metro areas of Ho Chi Minh City and Hanoi. They will move to more remote provinces within the country that have opened their own industrial parks and have begun to train their own new labor pools. This is a positive trend for the country because it takes jobs to otherwise underemployed provinces and regions of Vietnam. Ultimately, the manufacturers, both foreign-owned and local, will have to make these moves or they will end up closing down. If they are not determined to move up the value chain ladder or move to more remote provinces, there might not be any affordable land and labor available for them in Vietnam.

Vietnam has the advantage of more than twenty-five years' experience in manufacturing a huge array of goods. Most of these products have been low-tech and cheap, but they still require manufacturing processes, workers, and a level of infrastructure sufficient to get the finished products to the market. In addition, Vietnam has signed fifteen trade agreements (with two more under negotiation) to gain preferred access to international markets. Not only does it have a set of operating rules in place, but it also has the experience of many other countries who have already made the East Asian Development Model journey that it can observe, replicate, reinvent, and make up as they go. Vietnam is ready for this next step.

2. Mass Mobilization

In Chapter 2 we covered the many ways that Vietnamese leaders and groups mobilized their citizens for the country's fight for independence and freedom. In Chapter 6, we covered the Communist Party and its need for accountability while it mobilizes the citizens for common causes, such as the fight against COVID-19. For much of its history, Vietnam has relied on its citizens to come together to combat a common foe, whether a physical enemy, such as China, France, or the United States, or a less-tangible force, such as illiteracy or extreme poverty. Overall, it has done this well.

The comparative cases of South Korea and Taiwan from the 1980s and 1990s do not help to clarify a model of governing and addressing significant challenges. Although they were one-party states at that time like Vietnam is today, the era of the 1970s, 1980s, and 1990s and the opportunities for development were quite different than today. A more useful study can perhaps be found in the Philippines, Thailand, and in some South American nations where political and business elites pass legislation to keep themselves in power. In doing so, they keep poor families poor, and hence the nation cannot escape the Middle-Income Trap. One of the reasons for this is the difficulty of kick-starting any kind of mass mobilization movement that benefits the many rather than the few.

Vietnam is not likely to follow those political models, but a couple of core questions remain: Does the political and business elite of Vietnam understand that wealth must be shared for growth to be sustainable? Will Vietnam be a meritocracy or an oligarchy? From our analysis, it appears that the Communist Party is more focused on its own accountability to keep it in power than it is to adhering to the business and political elite of Vietnam. It would be incorrect to say that there are not some connections between these groups (they exist in every country), but there is evidence that the current power structures in Vietnam are geared more towards mass campaigns and mass mobilizations for the betterment of all rather than small, micro policies that benefit a narrow elite. We have no doubt that there are people who will challenge this assessment, but we consider it to be a fair and viable argument when Vietnam is compared with other countries and in the context of what needs to be in place for Vietnam to escape the Middle-Income Trap.

Arguably the biggest test of this ability that Vietnam has faced in more than a generation was COVID-19. As detailed in Chapter 1, Vietnam's aggressive mass mobilization ability defeated COVID I and COVID II. This included a full-scale lockdown of all its citizens in their homes, the military stepping up to man city barriers and deliver food, and an ongoing massive vaccination campaign where citizens were lined up to receive vaccinations. Within eight months 86.3 percent of the adult population was fully vaccinated.[2] The fact that just over 43,000 people died[3] from COVID-19 in Vietnam is a testament to the government's actions and the peoples' willingness to comply, thus providing evidence that the Vietnamese people are willing to do what is required to get their country through the crisis. This is an important card for the country's growth and development.

---

2. Our World in Data, November 2022.
3. Worldometer COVID-19 Data.

3. Demographics and Urbanization

Vietnam is demographically blessed. Within the next few years, it will be the fifteenth nation in the world with a hundred million citizens. The average age of these citizens is around thirty-two years. Vietnam has a workforce of close to sixty million people. Another compelling metric is the peak spending demographic of 35–45-year-old people. This market segment is just beginning to grow. Nearly a quarter of the country is still under fourteen years of age. Two-thirds of the people are between fifteen and sixty-four. The current and future middle class of Vietnam will come from these two groups.

According to the market research firm Cimigo and based on government statistics combined with the research firm's household surveys, there are 27,335,221 households in Vietnam and 44 percent of them have monthly household incomes of more than VND 10 million (US$430), with 20 percent of them earning at least VND 15 million (almost US$650 a month). The latter group is considered middle class for Vietnam. In 2019, consumers within these households purchased 8,900 motorbikes a day (a 4 percent decrease over the previous year) and 885 cars per day (a 46 percent increase over the previous year).[4] These metrics will increase as more Vietnamese enter the peak spending cohort of 35–45-year-old residents.

While the income numbers are still small, these are enviable metrics because they are continually growing. In terms of population, South Korea and Taiwan in 1990 had 20.3 million and 42.8 million people, respectively. In other words, Vietnam's labor force is about the same size as the total population of both countries' 1990 population combined. As Vietnam enters the decade of the 2020s, it will be roughly four times larger in population than Taiwan and two times larger than South Korea. This represents a significant labor force that those two countries did not have when they were launching factories and making their Tiger Economy runs prior to the year 2000. It also represents a much larger consumer market. It is estimated that by 2030 Vietnam will have the tenth largest consumer market in the world.[5] While many Asian countries are dealing with an aging and declining population, Vietnam is still growing. It will eventually have to deal with an aging population, but the country will have at least two decades of productive workers to help solve the issue when it arrives.

---

4. Cimigo Presentation, Vietnam 2021 Consumer Trends.
5. HSBC Asia Consumer Market Report 2030, September 2022.

Like nearly every developing country, Vietnam is becoming more urbanized. Young Vietnamese are flocking to the cities just as they do everywhere in the world. In 2000, an estimated 25 percent of the country was urbanized. Demographers say more than one-third lived in urban areas by 2014 and the population could be split evenly between urban and rural areas by 2030. This trend is not unique, but one of the key differences between the urban-rural divide in Vietnam compared to many other countries is the geographical footprint of the country. Vietnam's 'long and skinny' footprint means the journey to the cities is often significantly shorter than in countries with 'wide and deep' footprints like Brazil, China, and India. It becomes even more challenging for island nations like Indonesia and the Philippines. This means returning home to the countryside for Vietnamese is easier and cheaper than the same journey for citizens in many other countries. There are also three major urban areas in Vietnam—Hanoi, Danang, and Ho Chi Minh City—for the young to migrate to compared to just one or two metro destinations, such as Bangkok for the Thais, Manila for the Filipinos, and Jakarta for the Indonesians.

Whether this issue is viewed through an economic, geographic, or age-and-income trends lens, the outlook is positive. Vietnam's demographics and its urban-rural divide is an asset, or card, that most developing countries in the world would probably love to have.

4. The Role of Women

We have referenced the role of women in the Vietnamese economy several times in earlier chapters and we have dedicated an entire case study to the topic.[6] Many countries and cultures have strict mores that identify the roles that women should play. For example, in many countries women *should* stay at home to care for the children. They *should* go to work after completing their schooling, but then work less after marrying. If they do work, they *should* be working in traditional roles such as office work, teaching, day care, nursing, or small businesses. They *should not* be working in the same roles as men, nor become successful entrepreneurs or manage large companies.

Anecdotal interviews with South Koreans and Taiwanese about the work habits of their parents and grandparents in the 1980s and 1990s tell a similar story. Dad went to work while Mum stayed at home and took care of the

---

6. See Chapter 10, Case Study 3: The Role of Women, pp. 158–66.

household. Dad held more than one job and worked 60-hour weeks while Mum might have had a normal 8-to-5 job, but her cultural priority was to maintain a more traditional household. The *shoulds* noted in the previous paragraph were mostly upheld in South Korea and Taiwan.

The *shoulds* and *should nots* for Vietnamese women are different. While they still have many traditional responsibilities defined by culture, Vietnamese women do not appear to have any strict *should nots*. This possibly started with the women who carried artillery into the mountains surrounding the valley floor of Dien Bien Phu. Perhaps it started a couple a millennium earlier when the Trung sisters organized an army to fight the Chinese. For the purposes of the hypothesis that has driven this book, women have played an enormously important role in Vietnam. We could multiply nearly every economic and business metric by a factor of two rather than just one. In many countries, the factory labor force, business management, education, and entrepreneurship are predominantly male-centric environments. In Vietnam, that is not the case. Women fulfill many, if not all, of the roles one might otherwise consider male working roles and there are many successful female entrepreneurs. They manage large companies and are well-known for their accomplishments.

Whether Vietnam fully replicates the South Korea and Taiwan experience or not, it will not be because of the lack of inclusion of women. There are few, if any, cultural constraints against women working outside the home. Compared to many countries in the world, there has always been more of a 'team approach' to the work and the development of the country and the economy. Women are in the mix and will continue to be part of the Vietnam growth story.

5. Natural Resources and Agricultural Wealth

Access to natural resources such as oil and gas or other carbon-based energy deposits, mineral wealth, and land for food production is crucial for economic growth. The conventional wisdom is that without most of these assets in place it would be impossible to grow, develop, and eventually break free of the Middle-Income Trap. However, this line of reasoning is more nuanced than conventional wisdom allows. For example, the BRICS nations have many of these resources, and some of them in abundance (e.g., Russia's oil and gas deposits, Brazil's agriculture wealth, and South Africa's mineral deposits), but they are stuck in the trap. South Korea and Taiwan, as well as the other two Asian Tigers, Hong Kong, and Singapore, did not and do not have many of these resources, but they have been high-income countries for the past two decades.

What does Vietnam have in this regard? The country has many significant natural resources to help fuel constant economic growth. This started with the country's offshore oil and gas fields that have been earning foreign currency since 1975. From 2010 to 2020 Vietnam's crude oil exports averaged about 125,000 barrels per day. Its natural gas production averaged 8,680 million cubic meters per annum, which is enough to cover most local needs, i.e., no liquified gas is imported for domestic production.[7] The energy industry has been a strong foreign currency earner for years, but the country's offshore deposits are declining. Vietnam is now importing some energy resources to fill different supply gaps as demand rises.[8] At the same time, it is rapidly moving forward with renewable energy generation such as wind and solar to help energize its future. Vietnam has already installed more solar energy generation capacity than any other nation in Southeast Asia. Its wind and solar locations are considered ideal for further growth, as detailed below.

The beginning of Vietnam's economic run was the liberalization of agriculture in the late 1980s. Policy changes meant that Vietnamese farmers could legally own their land, sell their produce to local and international markets at market prices, and eventually incorporate these efforts into legal companies. The same was true for South Korea and Taiwan. However, Vietnam is far richer in agricultural wealth than the other two countries. The Mekong Delta and Red River Delta can produce two and sometimes three crops of rice per year. This has led to Vietnam being the third largest exporter of rice in the world and the fifth largest producer of rice overall.[9] The total tonnage of cashews, coffee, and rubber from Vietnam makes it the number one, two, and three largest producers of these commodities in the world.[10]

There is a lot of agricultural wealth in the country compared to many other countries in the world. It has been a net food exporter for decades. Vietnam's geographical location and shape allow for this strength to be more beneficial than in other countries because the most remote farm is not far from a

---

7. CEIC Data and Organization for Petroleum Exporting Countries.

8. 'Vietnam becomes an energy importer: Not a good sign,' Vietnam Net, February 2, 2022.

9. See Chapter 10 Case Study 5: Value-added agriculture for information on the potential impact of climate change on rice farming in the Mekong Delta.

10. See Chapter 10, Case Study 5: Value-added Agriculture, pp. 176–83.

market or an international port. This is not the case for other countries with agricultural wealth, such as Brazil, China, and India which have 'wide and deep' geographies as opposed to 'long and skinny' ones that hug the coastline.

The country is also rich underground. Since at least 2010, the global demand for mobile technologies and batteries for vehicles and other products has grown. These products all need various rare earth elements and minerals. China has among the highest reserves in the world, and it also produces the most for itself and for export. The United States has some reserves, but not enough to meet its own demand. Vietnam stands out because it has significant reserves but there is still very little mining and production. This is an untapped resource for the country, especially in the northern regions where there are significant nickel and rare earth metal deposits.

Although the country's power supply is still reliant on carbon-based energy (coal and natural gas) and hydro power for most of its electricity generation, there has been strong growth in renewable energy. This development is being led by Vietnamese developers, not foreign companies, and has been helped by government incentives. From 2017 to 2020 local developers added 16.5 GW of solar installations. Installed wind power is currently around 700 MW, but government planners are forecasting 12 GW of wind power generation by 2025 and 20 GW by 2030. More importantly than the added capacity is the reason for these new developments—a local backlash against more coal-fired projects. Concerns about air quality and the environment overall have spurred a series of policies that have led to these new developments with Vietnamese companies leading the way.[11]

6. The Vietnamese Diaspora

In the 1980s, the government of Taiwan reached out to the immense Overseas Chinese community that had left China and spread to numerous countries around the world over the previous two hundred years. By some estimates, there are more than forty million Overseas Chinese. Most of them are still within Asia, but many ended up in Australia and the United States in the 1880s as well as in European countries after World War II. In the guise of a formal campaign, Taiwan called them back to help the country become a global player in technology. It offered research positions in industrial parks

---

11. See 'The Next Renewable Energy Powerhouse of Asia,' *Energy Tracker Asia Report*, September 2021.

and think tanks. Many responded to the call and became part of the Taiwan economic miracle.

In terms of a formal campaign, Vietnam has not yet done the same thing, nor are there the same numbers of Overseas Vietnamese (Viet Kieu).[12] The Overseas Chinese had capital as well as strong educational qualifications to contribute to Taiwan. The Viet Kieu community is not the same. While they may not have the financial capacity of the Overseas Chinese community, they do have similar expertise and solid educations. As with the Overseas Chinese, many of them have been encouraged to 'return home' to help build up the country of their parents and grandparents.

However, there is a community of expatriate Vietnamese who do not quite fit the mold of the traditional Viet Kieu community. These are the Vietnamese who studied, lived, and worked in a variety of Eastern European countries from the 1960s to the late 1980s. Many of the current Ph.D. recipients in Vietnam earned their doctoral degrees in East Germany, Poland, the Soviet Union, and other countries that were part of the Soviet Bloc. These countries hosted not just students but also workers who earned foreign currency that they sent home to their families. Some of them became successful businesspeople on their own in their adopted countries and then returned to Vietnam to continue their entrepreneurial goals. The most striking examples of this are Pham Nhat Vuong, the founder and chairman of Vingroup, who built businesses in Ukraine, and Nguyen Thi Phuong Thao, the founder of VietJet, who studied in the Soviet Union and traded goods throughout Eastern Europe before returning to Vietnam.

Apart from the likes of Vuong and Thao, there are approximately five million ethnic Vietnamese living in foreign countries. Some of them have been in their new countries for generations. Others are relatively recent arrivals. The United States has the largest Viet Kieu community because of the American War. Whether they were students or immigrants from the former South Vietnam or war refugees and 'Boat People' who arrived after 1975, many Vietnamese settled in the United States between 1975 and 1985. In the United States, they are generally considered 'model immigrants' because of their work

---

12. In terms of population, the Vietnam diaspora (Viet Kieu) is comprised of around five million people and concentrated in the mostly wealthy nations of the United States (2.2 million), Japan (372,000), France (350,000), Australia (300,000), Canada (250,000), Taiwan (200,000), and Germany (170,000).

ethic and commitment to education and their communities. While there are some groups who are still disgruntled with the current regime in Vietnam, the majority are more curious than angry. The Vietnamese community in California has never mustered up the kind of political force that the Cuban community in Florida did against the Castro regime and against United States normalization of relations with Cuba. It has been the opposite. There is an interest from the younger generation to engage with their heritage, perhaps do business in or even move back to Vietnam on a semipermanent basis.

The government of Vietnam has not been entirely idle on this issue. While it took some time to put in place, a positive response to the Viet Kieu community is taking shape. For example, there is a group under the Ministry of Foreign Affairs called the State Commission for Overseas Vietnamese Affairs (SCOV). Shortly after the 13th National Party Congress, local newspapers published stories about a new portal for information about living and working in Vietnam. There were general statements made about the Viet Kieu community being "an inseparable part of the Vietnamese nation and an important resource to contribute to national development."[13] While these are general statements of intent, and probably made mostly for political and public relations purposes, there were very few such statements made or similar sentiments expressed prior to 2000. This is a relatively new outreach to those ethnic Vietnamese who left and want to return. It may be an indication that Vietnamese leaders intend to tap its expatriate community in the way Taiwan did in the 1980s. This will be a net gain for Vietnam and an important card as it keeps moving forward and integrates with the rest of the world.

7. Digitalization and the Internet

As noted earlier and, in particular with the case study on leapfrog technology,[14] the youth of Vietnam as well as older workers will have in the palm of their hands (smartphones) technologies that South Koreans and Taiwanese would not have dreamt of in the 1980s and 1990s. New technologies are always opportunities for countries, as well as companies and entrepreneurs, to leap into new products, markets, brainstorming sessions, and learning. Open-source platforms allow for the free use of software codes that would

---

13. 'State Commission for Overseas Vietnamese Affairs Launches Portal,' Vietnam News Agency, October 24, 2021.

14. See Chapter 10, Case Study 2: Leapfrog Technology, pp. 151–57.

have taken months or years to develop. These also arrive or are available immediately rather than via a set of blueprints that are faxed or expressed-delivered. Laptops and smartphones have become innovation centers that store downloaded codes and applications from around the world. These codes can then be applied to the specific needs of a company or entrepreneur. Instead of waiting for programmers to develop new diagnostic tools and solutions, these needs can now be addressed almost immediately. One of the reasons for this immediacy in Vietnam is the government's decision to keep the internet open and mostly free of firewalls.

South Korean and Taiwanese entrepreneurs had the 1980s and 1990s equivalent of new technologies. These tools were also the leapfrog technologies of that era, and it is obvious that they were used to good effect. It is also obvious that South Korea and Taiwan used them better than other countries because they became Tiger Economies and then high-income nations largely on the backs of technology (e.g., robotics and computer chips in Taiwan and automobiles and telecommunications in South Korea).

Vietnam has begun to prove itself in this tech space. Companies designing block chain systems have been able to raise outside venture capital for innovative products applicable to digital currencies, inventory management, and global supply chain networks. The environment is ripe for this kind of development. The coders, open digital borders, and tech entrepreneurs are in place and have begun to innovate.

We do not yet know what the open source, leapfrog technologies of the 2020s offer or where machine learning and artificial intelligence (AI) will take the world of business. However, it is highly unlikely that the technologies will not continue to become more sophisticated, faster, cheaper, and more focused on specific needs of the business world. Countries need to be open to these new technologies. If Vietnam expects to continue growing, the government cannot arbitrarily set up internet firewalls or try to protect SOE or private sector interests from the transformational power of digitalization. If it can avoid these moves, which are common in many developing countries, the 2020s and beyond should offer a very progressive and interesting future. There are almost certainly more unicorn companies on Vietnam's horizon.

8. A Leverage Point

There is a final issue that could be considered a 'card' or, at a minimum, an opportunity for Vietnam to seek out and establish a strong leverage point for the country in an increasingly globalized world. South Korea and Taiwan had a similar tool when they were on their Tiger Economy runs in the 1970s and 1980s and both countries leveraged this tool well. For Vietnam, the tool is 'The China-United States Card.' It is complex, global, and will require a high level of political skill to respond to a mostly rhetorical question that also has an automatic and predictable response in Vietnam. The question is: Whose side is Vietnam going to be on in the pending Cold War between China and the United States? The current answer from any level of leadership within Vietnam is 'Neither side. We are on Vietnam's side only.'

When Lee Kuan Yew of Singapore was asked this question during the Cold War between the United States and the USSR in the 1960s, 1970s, and 1980s, and probably in various forms up to his death in 2015, he always said, 'We're on Singapore's side.' For Lee, it was an easy and automatic political answer to a rhetorical question. If the same question was asked of South Korea and Taiwan at that time, the answer would also be automatic though not so bluntly stated. It would be something like, 'Well, of course, we're on the United States' side.'

How Vietnam answers 'The China-United States Card' issue will have a longer lasting impact. China will continue to pursue its 'One Belt, One Road' strategy and Vietnam will have to decide how it should respond to this Chinese outreach campaign. It has already arrived in Vietnam in various forms. For example, Chinese ODA financed part of the Hanoi Metro system of which one commuter line has begun operation. The Chinese people have also been arriving en masse to Vietnam. In 2019, before COVID-19, there were more than eighteen million international tourist arrivals and around one-third of them came from China. Chinese companies are entrenched in the business economy, and it is hard to know clearly how much real estate is owned by Chinese interests. In various 'man-on-the-street' interviews we conducted, a frequent answer to this question was that they already own too much and there are worries that Ho Chi Minh City and Hanoi could become like Phnom Penh, Cambodia, where Chinese capital has been invested in many or even most of the prime real estate locations in the city. That said, the migration of China-based manufacturers to Vietnam will probably continue and Vietnamese exports to the United States are likely to continue growing. For all these developments to move forward smoothly for Vietnam, political finesse of 'The China-United States Card' will be necessary if a trade war between the China and the United States continues to heat up.

The combination of real estate ownership, FDI, and global trade is just one part of the puzzle. The bigger and more complicated issue is in the East Sea/South China Sea. There are multiple claims to the various islands and archipelagos in the Spratly (Truong Sa) and Paracel (Hoang Sa) Islands. International shipping routes pass through the area, which is also potentially rich in oil and gas resources. It is hard to know much about the latter since oil and gas exploration by either side would raise tensions just like China's propensity to build airstrips on coral reefs has been doing for the past decade.

Vietnam has 'The China-United States Card' in its hand. It may not yet have the same leverage as 'The American Card' had for South Korea and Taiwan in the 1970s and 1980s, but there is some leverage to be employed. How well Vietnam can play this card will be a fascinating issue in the 2020s. The present-day strategy of remaining neutral on the current, pending, and possible future Cold War issues is likely to continue. Vietnam will not be forced into deciding or even leaning one way or another despite political and/or economic pressure to do so. The status quo is working for Vietnam and alliances that would threaten this trend are not likely to be considered.

Vietnam's Metrics

Even before the Trump Administration started a trade war with China, Vietnam was attracting attention as a 'safe place' for manufacturing. For many international manufacturers, the pursuit of global trade opportunities meant building global partnerships in numerous countries. Keeping up with so many partnerships and country rules was not becoming easier, especially with the rise of nationalism and political uncertainty in many parts of the world. Thus, the search was on for a country that was open to investment, had a large and well-trained workforce, offered something resembling a rule of law regime that was not too opaque, and had enough infrastructure to move a product from a factory floor in a hopefully well-designed industrial park to a port that was preferably not too far away. Vietnam hits these and other metrics for many manufacturers.

With so many global uncertainties today, it is difficult to predict what the future world will look like and which countries will succeed. Political and social stability will be a plus, as will a health care system that did not implode during the crisis. An ability to marshal forces towards a common goal will also be useful. Having an infrastructure network that works and an education infrastructure that is at least trying to meet the needs of the twenty-first century will be basic requirements. Pragmatic grit with intention will probably be the most valuable asset in an era which no one can predict but everyone in the world is looking at with nervous anticipation. What will business be like? What about free trade? Will international travel be the same? So many questions and still no solid answers. Vietnam has a lot of cards in its hand. These are its comparative advantages for the 2020s and beyond. They are also the potential answers to the many questions about the future that no one seems able to answer. We address some of these questions in the case studies in the next chapter.

Chapter 10

SIX CASE STUDIES

In the preceding nine chapters we have analyzed the various drivers of growth in Vietnam over the past thirty years. In this chapter we take another step towards testing the hypothesis and understanding what is happening by applying these drivers to topics and sectors of the economy and the people within them through six case studies that we believe are highly relevant to Vietnam's future.

The case studies have been selected from a diverse range of economic sectors and societal themes. The topics include sectors of the economy (e.g., education and infrastructure), human resources (e.g., the role of women), and trends (e.g., the role of technology, Vietnam as a popular tourist destination, and the adding of value to agricultural commodities). In this chapter we explore these in more detail to learn more about how Vietnam will develop from 2020 to 2050. They also offer interesting and informative stories about Vietnam's past, present, and future.

Many sectors and topics (e.g., industry, finance, manufacturing, and trade) might be used to highlight what is driving Vietnam's economic future, but for a sector or topic to qualify as one of our case studies at least three of the following four questions had to be answered in the affirmative:

1. Is there an interesting trend in this sector (i.e., a good story that should be shared)?
2. Is Vietnam doing something in this sector that other countries are not doing or not doing as well?
3. Will the case study help us to test the book's hypothesis?
4. Is the activity happening in this sector part of, and leading to, an improvement in the quality of life for people in Vietnam?

After screening a range of sectors and topics we chose the following six to explore further:

1. Education

Main theme. The influx of investment in private education, combined with a cultural mandate for making the education of children a family priority, will mean a continuing trend of Vietnamese studying overseas and becoming fluent in English, but also the enhancement of the nation's own institutions and intellectual capital base.

2. Leapfrog Technology

Main theme. The country's access to many of the world's latest technologies and innovations, combined with the absence of any legacy investments, means Vietnam can leapfrog countries saddled with latent technologies and infrastructure. Vietnam can build a tech-enabled society and modern tech industries more freely and probably faster than many other countries because it can begin with the newest technologies available.

3. The Role of Women

Main theme. The role of women in the economy is one of Vietnam's most important assets. There are few cultural constraints for women in the workforce and there is a more equal environment for the treatment of women in terms of legal rights rather than a bias towards men. This means there is a much stronger 'team approach' towards economic development compared to many other countries.

4. Tourism, Cuisine, Art, and Olympic Dreams

Main theme. Prior to COVID-19, Vietnam was a favored destination for tourism, the food was popular, its art was selling, and its football team had become a regional powerhouse. Whether it is sporting events, the arts, culture, or cuisine, the Vietnam brand is gaining a presence on the global stage, attested to by the millions of tourists arriving each month. Tourism and events will eventually return from their COVID-caused isolation, and how well Vietnam can show off its food, culture, beaches, and other assets will be important for its long-term economic growth and its position in the world.

5. Value-added Agriculture

Main theme. Unlike South Korea and Taiwan, Vietnam has significant agricultural wealth. About 40 percent of Vietnamese households are dependent on agriculture as their primary source of employment, and how well Vietnam leverages its agricultural resources will have a significant impact on the lives of many people. Will Vietnam continue to be a major producer and exporter of raw agricultural commodities, or will it move up the value chain to become a nation that exports high-quality agricultural-based consumer products?

6. Public Works

Main theme. To sustain economic growth, Vietnam requires substantial investment in its infrastructure, such as roads, bridges, ports, railroads, airports, and power grids. It has already attracted considerable ODA and has been successful in using this capital to build many essential infrastructure projects, but can the country continue to attract and deploy sufficient capital into infrastructure projects that are essential to the building of a modern nation?

To help us understand how these six sectors and topics will help Vietnam grow and develop like South Korea and Taiwan did in the 1980s and 1990s, we have developed a set of testing lenses to understand how they—and therefore the theories they illustrate—either move Vietnam closer to or further away from affirming our hypothesis (Vietnam is the next Tiger Economy of Asia, and it will grow and develop in a similar way to how South Korea and Taiwan grew as Tiger Economies of Asia) is correct. The lenses, explained in detail in Chapter 1, to view each of the case studies are reiterated as follows:

1. **Culture.** Are there enough Vietnamese cultural traits that will lead to success in this sector or topic?
2. **Technology.** Are the new technologies available in this sector or topic obtainable and significant to its success?
3. **Environment.** Can this sector or topic absorb the inevitable impacts of climate change and environmental disruption that are due in the 2020s and 2030s?
4. **Policy.** Are the government's policies and directives conducive to success within this sector or topic?
5. **Governance.** Is the government able to manage issues like rent-seeking, corruption, and a lack of experience which can make success in this sector or topic difficult or nearly impossible to achieve?

The Final Analysis

A schematic template appears at the end of each case study. It shows how we have used each testing lens to understand how the sector or topic under study might impact the hypothesis. We wanted to assess how each case study supports, negates, or remains neutral to the hypothesis when viewed through the five lenses of culture, technology, the environment, policy, and governance. The most positive outcome overall for Vietnam is, of course, for the hypothesis to be true because this means Vietnam will continue to grow and ultimately become a high-income country like South Korea and Taiwan. For this to happen, most of the influences must point to a positive outcome (support) and as few as possible to a negative outcome (negate).

Figure 6. Case study template

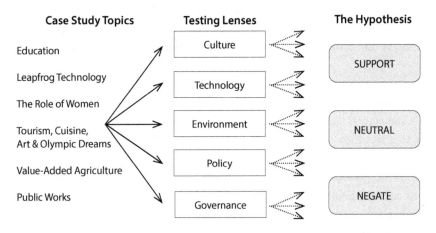

For example, does what is happening within the education sector point Vietnam towards supporting the hypothesis or away from it when viewed through all five of the lenses? In the case of education, the culture, technology, and policy lenses might point to 'support' while the environment and governance lenses might point to 'neutral.' When it comes to education, none of the lenses arguably point to a negation of the hypothesis. However, in the case of public works, the governance lens might point to 'negate' due to corruption in the sector as would the environment lens considering the impact of climate change on infrastructure development. The answers to these questions are set out in the following six case studies.

Case Study 1: Education

Start With the Children
Planting the seeds for a bilingual nation

Tired, stressed, and bent over almost double because the backpacks they are carrying contain so many heavy books, they keep marching forward. They look like the soldiers their grandparents and great grandparents had once been in the country's fight for independence and freedom. But they are not soldiers. While some of their classmates are at home playing computer games, these children are yet again taking the 'extra classes' their parents have signed up for them. For a growing number of them, it starts early, as young as four or five years of age, and it never stops. There is always another test to get ready for, another extra class to take, or a new skill to learn, such as the piano, violin, or even tennis. It is all to help them stand out from their classmates and thereby find success.

Call it 'Tough Love,' life with a 'Vietnamese Tiger Mum,' or some other term, there is a significant trend among the current generation of Vietnamese parents who are firmly, lovingly no doubt, pushing their children to achieve academically. Many of them did not have that chance when they were young because Vietnam was too poor. Now that life is better, these parents are determined to make sure their children will succeed in ways they used to only dream about.

"I was born taking extra classes," says Nguyen Cuu Minh, a fourteen-year-old Vietnamese boy who has been studying English for as long as he can remember. He is currently enrolled in the German International School in Ho Chi Minh City. After attending an international kindergarten with Japanese and Korean classmates, he was enrolled in a Vietnamese primary school for his first two years of schooling before his parents transferred him to the German school. "I did not know a single word of German, but my English was pretty good," recalls Minh, who goes by the English name Harry and is currently in the ninth grade. The reason his parents chose the German school, which teaches in the German language, rather than one of the international English schools was a combination of cost, value for money, and the fact that they were already considering Germany as a potential destination for their son's university education. If he graduated from a German international high school abroad, his chances for entry into a university in Germany would be greater despite not being a German citizen. The fact that their son could not speak a word of German at the time did not enter their decision-making. They knew he would learn it. Harry is one of over three hundred thousand Vietnamese students enrolled outside of Vietnam's state-sanctioned school system.

Some children find themselves *way outside* the Vietnamese system. More and more families are sending their children abroad for university, but also to finish their last two years of high school in private schools in Australia, Canada, Europe, New Zealand, and the United States. Harry's older brother graduated from a private high school in New Mexico state in the United States before going to an American university. Completing high school abroad makes the step to university shorter and often easier to navigate. The fact that parents are putting their fifteen- and sixteen-year-old children on planes to go and live with host families or in boarding schools in foreign countries is part of the sacrifice that this generation of families is making in pursuit of a better life. The study abroad trend will not cease anytime soon. There will always be fifteen-, sixteen- and seventeen-year-old children, with parents and grandparents pushing them along, who are packing their bags to go and live and study in a foreign culture, language, and country. For those who can afford it, that is part of the deal in contemporary Vietnam. They must go.

While this is happening, something else is happening inside the country. Modern education is coming to Vietnam. It is bringing foreign curriculums and teachers. It is bringing new ways of looking at and solving problems. And it is doing so predominately in the English language. These moves are planting the seeds that will make Vietnam a bilingual nation more along the lines of Singapore and less along the lines of a monolingual nation like Thailand.

Mandarin Legacy vs. Project 2020

The sector of Vietnam's economy and society that receives the most criticism is education. This is not surprising considering the fervent belief in education. Parents consistently seek out the very best schools for their children and are highly critical of the conservative approach that many government officials have towards standardized education. This is changing for the better, but much too slowly for most Vietnamese families.

According to the Ministry of Education and Training (MOET), there are approximately fifteen million Vietnamese students in the country's K-12 education system, which is divided into four levels: preschool, primary school, secondary school, and high school. Beyond that, there is higher education at colleges and universities. Mandated formal education consists of twelve years of basic education (five years primary, four years middle school, and three years high school). The vast majority (97 percent) of students are enrolled in state-run public schools. The estimated 325,000 or so students who are not in public schools attend one of the growing numbers of international and bilingual private schools.

In the state schools, the education curriculum is set by the government and is based primarily on rote learning and memorization. It is essentially the same system that has been used in Northeast Asia for the past two thousand years. For Vietnamese students, there are three key exams that greatly impact their future and form the core of what teachers do—they teach to the test. Each exam builds upon the previous one, so getting it right from the start is what keeps parents up at night while simultaneously demanding their children study long hours into the night.

The first exam determines which middle school the student can attend upon completion of primary school. The higher the score, the higher the quality of the middle school they can get into. The second test determines which high school a student can attend. This is a very stressful and competitive time for young Vietnamese aged fourteen to fifteen. A high test score could mean admission into one of the high schools for the gifted or a gifted program within a high school. Parents and teachers increase the pressure on their children to do well at this stage because a top-tier high school paves the way for their next education step, the university entrance exam. Again, the higher the score, the higher the quality of the university, as well as the wider choice a student will have for university options and majors.

The examinations in Vietnam are like the standardized tests required in China, Japan, South Korea, and Taiwan, among other Asian nations. The stress on the eleven-year-old striving for a good middle school, the fifteen-year-old striving for a good high school, and the eighteen-year-old taking a test to determine his/her future is the same.

The government knows a change is needed but instigating change to a 2,000-year-old education model is not easy. Consider Project 2020. It was designed to change only one piece of the education system, the use of the English language. Signed by Prime Minister Nguyen Tan Dung on September 30, 2008, the National Foreign Language Project 2020 (Project 2020) was ambitious from the start.[1] The core idea was to improve the teaching and learning of foreign languages by reforming how languages are taught. All students from Grade 3 to Grade 12 would be enrolled in Project 2020 foreign-language programs within ten years. By the time students reached university level, it was expected that they would be able to use at least one foreign language at the B1 level.[2] The language was not specified but it was expected that English was the language most schools would choose to teach.

At the end of the first ten years of reform, how did Project 2020 score? One of Vietnam's most popular newspapers, *Tuoi Tre*, was not impressed: 'Vietnam's National Foreign Language Project Proves a flop.'[3] In a research paper presented at an academic forum in 2017, Thuong Nguyen from the National Chengchi University in Taiwan argued that the program failed for three reasons: a shortage of qualified teachers, the pedagogical methods used, and poor teaching materials.[4] It was back to the drawing board for the MOET and in a new, more realistic, plan it was mandated that all teachers of the English language in Hanoi must have an IELTS score of at least 6.5. Training and online learning would be provided[5] and the goal was to have half of Hanoi's English teachers qualified by 2025.

This approach is part of the pragmatic DNA that eventually rises to the surface in Vietnam. If something does not work, accept it was a mistake and try another approach to solve the problem. In this case, it was to start small—here the focus is only on Hanoi and on English teachers—and set a realistic goal that might work. If it does work, replicate that approach in other places. If

---

1. Decision No. 1400/QD-TTg, September 30, 2008.

2. A B1 level is defined by the International English Language Testing System (IELTS) as knowing simple greetings and conversations; able to read basic instructions; able to learn new vocabulary and phrases.

3. Education section, *Tuoi Tre*, January 2, 2018.

4. 'Vietnam's National Foreign Language 2020 Project after Nine Years: A Difficult State,' paper presented at the Asian Conference on Education and International Development, International Academic Forum, 2017.

5. Plan No. 28 KH-PCC, launched at the beginning of 2019.

all goes to plan, the goal will eventually be achieved even if it takes a bit longer than was originally hoped.

Another driver of change and the quest for alternatives in the education sector is the hope that some bad habits and customs can finally be dispensed with. One parent shared his frustration with the 'fiefdoms' that the better middle schools and high schools have become. An appropriately timed *li xi* envelope with financial gifts for administrators and teachers is part of the deal, despite the merit-based system for children to get into the school. Perhaps a more insidious issue is the problem of deliberate under-teaching and other methods used by teachers to drum up business for their personal home school classes and private tutoring sessions to supplement their incomes. Parents claim that teachers are often adept at convincing parents that their children need extra classes to keep up. Of course, these same teachers offer just such a class in their private home.

"My wife came home crying one day because our daughter's teacher says she's falling behind," lamented one father during an interview in Ho Chi Minh City. The teacher suggested extra classes so their daughter could 'keep up' with the other students. The father was frustrated with the teacher, did not know how to console his wife, and was not at all sure what to do about his daughter, an only child, for whom he felt it was his duty to get her ready for the next steps in her education. Their daughter is three years old.

Most observers agree that to do nothing and simply accept the education that the state provides is not an option. On its own, it is not good enough for the future. Vietnamese families consider education as an 'investment' rather than an 'expense.' There are plenty of examples of families buying real estate with the specific intention of selling it when their child/children is/are ready to study at a high-end school, whether it is a school that is inside or outside of Vietnam. There is a cultural and political element to this as well. Culturally, children take care of their parents when the parents are ready to retire. Investing in a child's education is, therefore, also an investment in a retirement plan. Politically, Western countries have more robust pension programs to care for the elderly, so children do not have to take care of their parents in the same way. In Vietnam, this is not the case, so there is a social contract that comes with paying a tuition bill. The authors learned of one story about a Vietnamese who had been accepted into an MBA program at Harvard University in the United States. The person did not have enough money to attend yet turned down an offer from a childless uncle who wanted to pay for everything because of the social obligations that would inevitably follow the person after graduation.

The Business of Education

Given the insatiable demand for education and the inability of the public sector to fully meet that demand, the great news for parents is the government is more than willing to let the private sector help fill the gap. This means that for those families with the financial means the private sector is bursting with education options for their children.

Increasingly large new campuses of international and bilingual private schools are appearing in the urban areas of the top tier cities. The top international schools teach the International Baccalaureate (IB), UK, or American curriculums on par with similar schools in other countries. In China and Taiwan as well as in many other countries, laws prevent local nationals from attending such schools. Only children of foreign diplomates and executives can be enrolled. But Vietnam is more open. There are no laws preventing Vietnamese citizens from attending international schools. The real determinants as to whether a child can attend an international school is if there is space for them and their families can afford the tuition fees, which can be up to US$45,000 per year.

This amount of tuition is challenging for many families so there is an increasing number of more affordable private schools available to children. Usually started by Vietnamese entrepreneurs, many are bilingual. "It's like there is a bilingual kindergarten on every corner," says Nam Hong Nguyen, the CEO of POLY English.

Nam's POLY English is a foreign-owned language center from South Korea which has several language centers in Hanoi and Ho Chi Minh City. It is just one of many English language training centers that provide English programs to thousands of students every month. Collectively, they are a third option for parents wanting their children to learn English, especially if they are enrolled in a state school.

The Singapore Model and the Seeds of a Bilingual Nation

In our interviews, we asked Vietnamese if the hypothesis proposed for the book was the right one to be pursuing. Was their country replicating or trying to replicate the Tiger Economy experience of South Korea and Taiwan? When we asked, "Can Vietnam do the same thing?" the response that often came back was "How about we follow Singapore instead?" The Vietnamese who admire what Singapore has accomplished understand why the island nation is not suitable for the hypothesis, nor as an economic model for their country. But, in terms of becoming a bilingual nation, a case can potentially be made for copying the city state.

When Singapore became an independent state in 1965, it had few natural resources and little agricultural land. It was considered a non-viable nation by many observers at the time. But under Lee Kuan Yew's leadership through the 1960s and 1970s, the government pursued a modernization program that focused on establishing a manufacturing industry and investing heavily in infrastructure and public education. An important part of this plan was the mandating of English as the main language of instruction. Mandating the use of English enhanced Singaporeans' ability to connect with the rest of the world, which helped Singapore become a regional economic hub and develop a highly skilled workforce. It is hardly surprising that Vietnam wants to pursue a similar path.

But it is not just the eventual development of a bilingual nation that Vietnam is seeking. The country's overall education network needs to be better developed to support a growing economy that has its eyes on escaping the Middle-Income Trap. This has started with a growing private sector of foreign and local institutions and numerous bilingual education programs. It has also begun due to a cultural mandate amongst parents who pursue every opportunity for their children as an investment rather than an expense.

Vietnam's universities are also improving and gaining recognition. The United Kingdom-based education organization Quacquarelli Symonds (QS) announced in November 2021 that twelve Vietnamese universities had made it onto its global rankings list of the best universities in Asia. On this same list, Indonesia had 34 institutions, Thailand 23, and the Philippines 15.[6] Singapore topped the list with the number one and three positions. Vietnam has a lot of ground to make up, but this has started. Can Vietnam do the same thing with a core of English-speaking Vietnamese in the 2020s and 2030s as Singapore did in the 1960s and 1970s? Can it continue to climb up the quality rankings for universities? We will see in the decades to come, but it is likely that it will.

---

6. QS World University Rankings 2021, London, UK.

Testing the Hypothesis

Using the five testing lenses given on pp. 5–8, our analysis reveals that the education sector is conducive to the hypothesis being correct. Currently, and on its own, the education sector is not conducive to a positive hypothesis. However, it is not static. It is growing and adjusting because of the culture and technology inputs that support the hypothesis. Vietnam's cultural affinity for education, a Confucian value shared by Northeast Asian nations, and the tools that technology provides for teaching blend well. The government's policy initiatives to allow investment in the sector and also to allow local Vietnamese to attend foreign-invested international schools usually reserved for foreigners is also a plus. The environment and governance lenses will not impact the hypothesis in any significant way. Vietnam may not be a fully bilingual nation by 2030, but it has a good chance at becoming one by 2050.

Figure 7. Hypothesis testing lenses for education

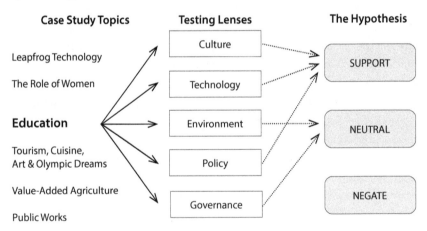

Case Study 2: Leapfrog Technology

Faster Than Google
Leapfrogging into the future at full speed

In 2018 car manufacturers doing online due diligence must have been confused to hear a rumor that somewhere in northern Vietnam, near the port city of Hai Phong, a Vietnamese businessman was building a multibillion-dollar state-of-the-art automobile plant. It was purported to be employing leapfrog technologies—the very latest machinery, technology, and robotics to manufacture products in hours rather than days. There was no easing in of older and cheaper technologies, and then transitioning to newer technology. True Leapfroggers *start with* the highest available technology. A billion dollar anything (high-tech or low-tech) must be big, especially if it is a manufacturing plant that makes cars, buses, and scooters. Something that big would show up. It could not be hidden. But when the company's reported address was keyed into the search bar for Google Earth, nothing showed up, just ocean.

Google can be forgiven for not having completely up-to-date satellite photos embedded in its databases. Google Earth relies on digitally stitching together snapshots from space satellites and aerial photos taken at different times. No one believed that so much of the ocean could be reclaimed and an automated car plant built on top, in just twenty-one months. The idea that a highly automated, billion-dollar car plant was being built in one of the world's remaining Communist-led countries was believed to be another internet myth. Except that in this case, the VinFast auto plant, a project of the Vingroup, was actually real.[7]

This 'Faster Than Google' anecdote is one of the favorite stories shared by senior Vietnamese staff and many foreign engineers and designers when they

---

7. Google Earth now shows the plant.

are asked to describe what exactly they are trying to do at VinFast. They were there to build cars, but there seemed to be something more. They wanted to be part of an 'aspirational journey' into the future. VinFast was offering an enormous example of what leapfrog technologies can accomplish when the right players show up at the right time and are ready to get to work.

Creative Destruction

The Austrian economist Joseph Schumpeter coined the term 'creative destruction' to describe the constant process of innovation and invention that occurs in capitalism. He argued that this process is essential to capitalism because it allows for new and better products and services to be developed, which in turn leads to economic growth. Schumpeter's theory of creative destruction can be seen in many examples throughout history. For example, the mass production of Henry Ford's Model T cars led to the decline of the niche artisan and mechanic as assembly line workers were able to produce cars much more quickly and efficiently. Similarly, the rise of the internet has led to the decline of physical stores as consumers are now able to shop online for a wider variety of products at lower prices.

Economists have also written about the resistance to new technologies for the simple reason that owners are not willing to give up the rents and fees they earn from the technologies that already exist. They do not want to disrupt the status quo. But what happens when an individual, company, or country has no such technologies to protect? They leap forward unencumbered. They do not have to creatively destroy anything and can immediately take advantage of technologies that already exist. This is what is happening in Vietnam today. Vietnamese companies are embracing new technologies to grow their businesses unimpeded by the barriers that can exist in other countries. VinFast is one such example of this.

The VinFast Story

The VinFast car company is one of the 'Vin' companies under the Vingroup, founded by Pham Nhat Vuong in 1993. Any time the idea of Vietnam following the South Korea *chaebol* model of development is brought up, the Vingroup is mentioned. Like a Korean *chaebol,* it is trying to provide goods or services for nearly everything a Vietnamese family needs, including housing (Vinhomes), shopping (Vinmart, although the chain store network was sold in 2019), education (Vinschools), tourism (Vinpearl), and healthcare (Vinmec).

Among its more recent investment projects is VinFast, a new and ambitious venture. A range of combustion and electric VinFast vehicles are already on the streets of Vietnam, including SUVs, luxury sedans, and several smaller cars. VinFast also has electronic scooters (with battery packs that can be easily charged at home or swapped out at a neighborhood Vinmart) available, and since October 2020 electric buses have been tested in Hanoi and Ho Chi Minh City's public bus network.

"It takes GM nine years to launch a new model while it took VinFast two years to build a car factory and then launch three models," says Jim Deluca, the CEO of VinFast.[8] He should know. Deluca is one of many foreigners who were recruited by VinFast to help build the company. Deluca had already retired from a 38-year career with General Motors, but the 58-year-old engineer and former GM executive recalls getting a phone call on a Friday from a woman in Vietnam inquiring about his interest in a new start-up auto company. The conversation was compelling enough for Deluca to say that he would think about it. He was being polite, because he had no intention of going back to work for a car company. However, the very next day the same woman, Le Thi Thu Thuy, a senior executive of the Vingroup and chairwoman of VinFast, called him back to get his answer. Two years later, in 2018, Deluca, Thuy, their team, and the football star David Beckham were presenting two new VinFast cars at the Paris Auto Show.

VinFast's ambitious plans have attracted a diverse team of global talent eager to be part of the company's aspirational journey. Vietnamese staff are excited about the challenge, while expatriate staff have left other car companies to join VinFast as it prepares to go head-to-head with Tesla in the American market. VinFast's state-of-the-art car plant uses the latest technology to produce vehicles at full speed. Visitors can see the company's 'how' strategy in action during a two-hour tour. From the Korean cold roll steel to the enormous stamping presses to the automated painting lines, the plant is a sight to behold. Deputy CEO Nguyen Thi Van Anh describes the plant as "an aspirational journey into the future."

Something to Emulate? The Hyundai Model

In the 1970s and 1980s, Japan was the dominant force in the global automobile industry. However, South Korea's Hyundai Motor Company was

---

8. Jim Deluca left VinFast in 2022 and was replaced by Le Thi Thu Thuy.

able to make significant gains in this period, and by the 2020s it had become one of the world's largest automakers. It rose to prominence by employing the right people, partnering with leading European and American companies for design and technology, and deploying the best leapfrog technologies in automated manufacturing.

Today VinFast is looking to emulate Hyundai's success. Although a relatively new company, it has ambitious plans to become a major player in the global automobile industry. The company has already made significant investments in new technologies and has partnered with foreign companies, such as BMW and Magna International. VinFast is also starting to export its electric vehicles to the United States. It remains to be seen whether VinFast is able to achieve its ambitious goals, but by aggressively adopting leapfrog technologies the company is taking the right steps to become a major player in the global automobile industry.

Intellectual Capital

Leapfrog technology is usually simple to use and deploy. However, it is essential that the country have the intellectual capital base and the people who can understand and implement these new technologies. This requires an education infrastructure to train the necessary workers and/or the ability to draw in workers with the necessary skills from other countries. It also needs an openness and adoption of open-source software platforms, the internet, global connections, online learning, and full engagement with free trade principles. While many people might reasonably question whether Vietnam has established the conditions needed to adopt new technologies successfully, companies like VinFast have proven it is possible and there is plenty of anecdotal evidence that Vietnam can continue to climb up the technology ladder.

Co-author Brook Taylor recalls a case study during his EMBA program. The class was studying the efficacy and value of outsourcing software programing and applications that are then incorporated into a larger project. A Silicon Valley start-up posted a job for software development on an international marketplace. All bids, except one, were US$5,000–30,000 and would take three months. A Vietnamese programmer bid US$55 and one week. The CEO took the risk and signed up the Vietnamese programmer. The software was delivered four days early and worked to the required specifications.

A better-known example comes from the gaming world. In 2013 Dong Nguyen, a 28-year-old Vietnamese game developer, created a simple game called Flappy Bird. He released it for free on the App Store and did not expect much to happen. But in February 2014 the game went viral and became a worldwide sensation. At its peak, Flappy Bird was earning Nguyen US$50,000 a day. As *Rolling Stone* wrote, "Not even Mark Zuckerberg became rich so fast."[9] It was a meteoric rise to fame, but Nguyen ultimately decided to take the game down, citing concerns about its addictive nature.

A newer story also originates from the gaming world, but it meshes with blockchain technology and has created one of Vietnam's unicorn companies.

Blockchain Games to Real World Challenges

What does FPT University, Forbes Vietnam, and the American entrepreneur Mark Cuban have in common? The common link is Nguyen Thanh Trung, the co-founder of the company Sky Mavis which created a game called *Axie Infinity* that uses blockchain technology and crypto currencies to allow gamers to create NFTs that battle against each other while also allowing the gamers to earn money by playing the game. When released it was one of the newest and most popular 'play to earn' games on the internet. Trung, a FPT University graduate, made Forbes Vietnam's 30 Under 30 list in 2022, and Mark Cuban is one of the investors in Sky Mavis.

The Sky Mavis story is all about the successful development and execution of blockchain technology. This development expertise and experience, not the game itself, is why Sky Mavis became a unicorn when it was able to raise US$152 million in venture capital funding at a US$3 billion valuation in October 2021.

The technical challenge is assembling enough software designers, coders, and engineers to build, maintain, expand, and troubleshoot the digital ledgers (the

9. Aside from its rapid and viral success, the Flappy Bird story resonated worldwide because no one knew who Dong was and then he abruptly pulled the game offline on February 10, 2014, after giving users just 22 hours of warning. He wrote that he was doing so because "I cannot take this anymore." Subsequent reporting revealed that he was worried about the unusual addictiveness of the game and how it was harming people's lives. The *Rolling Stone Magazine*'s piece, published on March 11, 2014, and still available online, focused on Dong who was hiding from international paparazzi but had agreed to talk with *Rolling Stone* about why he did what he did. It is a compelling read and worth searching for online.

blockchain) and related systems so transactions can occur seamlessly. When there are millions of users, this 'digital ledger' or blockchain becomes a very complex program and requires a tech-savvy group of workers to maintain the system. Sky Mavis has done this for its game *Axie Infinity*.

So why does a global leader like Sky Mavis suddenly appear in Vietnam and not in Silicon Valley or some other tech hotspot around the world? The obvious references to having a well-educated and motivated population that has online access to appropriate training tools and knowledge can be cited. However, there is another important factor not often stated. Developing countries like Vietnam have more problems and issues that can be solved using this kind of technology. There is more demand for blockchain technologies because there are clear and specific uses for it.

Blockchain technology can be used for the creation of national databanks for medical records, land registration deeds, household registrations, national identity cards, insurance policies, and other national-based products needed by the government and the private sector. These programs or 'digital ledgers' require multiple users and recipients to work seamlessly with each other. Developed countries have been building electronic systems to solve these problems since the invention of mainframe computers, while developing countries may still be using spreadsheets or manual filing systems. Blockchain technology allows countries like Vietnam to leapfrog into the future and quickly address national challenges that come with administering to the needs of a country with nearly one hundred million people.

This type and amount of evidence is not conclusive proof that Vietnam has what it takes to build a high-tech Tiger Economy success story. But scratch the surface in Vietnam and there are often some surprising findings. There is no shortage of intellectual talent in Vietnam. For example, there is Le Quang Liem, the current Asia chess champion who won the World Championship in Blitz Chess in 2013. He earned the title of Grand Master by the World Chess Federation (FIDE) in 2006. There is also Ngo Bao Chau who was born in Hanoi in 1972. After completing his high school education in Vietnam, Chau studied in France and in 1997 earned a Ph.D. in mathematics. In 2010 Chau won the Fields Medal, the highest academic honor awarded for the study of mathematics. Trung, Liem, Chau, and others like them are part of the intellectual capital base that exists in a country whose physical capital (infrastructure) is still being developed. In a leapfrog technology world, the former might be far more important than the latter.

Testing the Hypothesis

Using the five testing lenses proposed pp. 5–8, our analysis is that the technology sector is conducive to the hypothesis being correct. Vietnam does not need to create and build technology on its own. Instead, Vietnamese companies can collaborate on it, lease it, purchase it outright, and eventually develop their own based on their own designs and market needs. This is a classic example of the East Asian Development Model strategy, as well as evidence of the merits of leapfrog technologies. The cultural, policy, and technology attributes will sustain this trend. The environment and governance lenses will not have significant impacts. Arguably, the environment lens could point to support since the demand for non-carbon energy will increase in the coming decades. Vietnam is well situated to capitalize on all that leapfrog technologies have to offer, and it has few, if any, legacy rents to worry about. This will be one of the reasons that the country might replicate the success of South Korea and Taiwan.

Figure 8. Hypothesis testing lenses for leapfrog technology

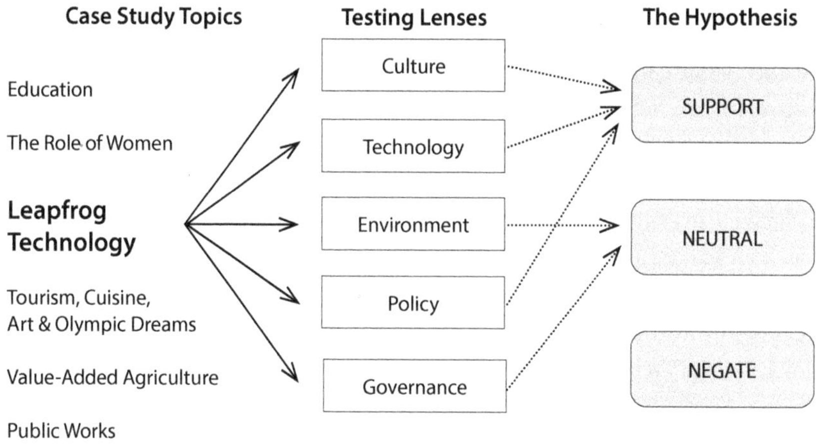

Case Study 3: The Role of Women

Holding Up Half the Sky
Vietnamese women's predominant and
culturally approved role in the economy

A little over two thousand years ago, two sisters with the family name Trung set the standard for what women could do for their country. As is learned by first graders in Vietnam and mentioned in the 'Immortalized on Maps' section of Chapter 2, the two Trung sisters (Hai Ba Trung) led Vietnam's first successful fight for independence and freedom from China. This was at the dawn of the first millennium. They ruled only briefly, but they made a stand for the Kinh people against the Han Chinese, and they are deeply revered and respected in Vietnam today for what they achieved.

The spirit of the Trung sisters is evident in more recent history. Numerous archives of print and film footage showcase Vietnam's wars against the French and the Americans. Although such images primarily served a propaganda purpose for the nationalist cause, they reveal something else—the indomitable spirit of a country, especially its women. This is most apparent in film footage from 1954 showcasing Vietnamese women carrying arms and pushing heavy artillery on overloaded bicycles up the 'inaccessible mountains' surrounding French military camps at Dien Bien Phu. Their efforts meant that on March 13 General Vo Nguyen Giap's troops could start raining shells onto the French forces below leading to the French surrender and ultimately the end of French colonialism in Vietnam. During the American War, women helped to maintain the Ho Chi Minh Trail which was the conduit for supplies from the north to Viet Cong and North Vietnamese Army units in the south. Vietnamese women have played enormously important roles in Vietnam's fight for independence and freedom. They held up their half of the sky and helped to win wars. Now they are contributing significantly to the development and growth of Vietnam.

Holding up Half the Sky

The phrase 'Women holding up half the sky' is attributed to Mao Tse Tung, but it has become more widely known because of a book written by New York Times journalist Nicolas Kristof and his wife Sheryl Wu Dunn. Their book, *Half the Sky: Turning Oppression into Opportunity Worldwide*, is about the oppression of women and girls in the developing world. It features several examples of women who have faced insurmountable odds yet succeeded. The authors core argument is how a little bit of help for girls and women can go a long way in the development of a country and that the key to economic development lies in the unleashing of women's potential. If, and when, they get this opportunity, they will hold up half the sky.

In many countries around the world, women are oppressed and not allowed to fulfil their potential. This same level of oppressiveness is not as apparent in Vietnam because there are very few cultural constraints that Vietnamese women have to face before they can move forward, join the labor force, or start a company. They just do it. After a history of moving forward and accomplishing numerous objectives during the war years, Vietnamese society has given them the freedom to do things that women in many other countries cannot do. In Vietnam there are few constraints due to religion, strict social mores, or male-dominated social role models. As noted in Chapter 9, The Cards It Holds, there are not many *shoulds* and *should nots* when it comes to roles that Vietnamese women can take on.

Women in the Labor Force

Among the numbers that often surprise new observers to Vietnam is the size of the labor force. According to most data sources, it is about sixty million people out of a total population of nearly one hundred million. With very little unemployment, the working-age population of Vietnam is larger than the entire population of South Korea and twice that of Taiwan, the two countries that form this book's case study comparatives. This is largely due to the high participation rate of Vietnamese women in the labor force, which is higher than in most other countries. According to World Bank data sourced from the International Labor Organization database (September 2020), (1) the labor force participation rate of women fifteen years and older is 47 percent worldwide (2020) and 68 percent in Vietnam, and (2) the ratio of female to males in the labor force is 67 percent worldwide and 88 percent in Vietnam.

Table 24. Female workers in the labor force, 2020

Country	Percentage of female worker in the labor force	Ratio of female workers per 100 male workers
Vietnam	68	88
Taiwan	52	88
China	59	83
Thailand	59	78
Japan	53	75
South Korea	53	74
Indonesia	53	66
Malaysia	52	66
Philippines	43	64

Source: World Bank; International Labor Organization database.

Vietnam has clearly taken a 'team approach' to its labor force and this has many benefits. The obvious increase in the number of workers leads to increased output and higher economic growth. The high rate of women in the labor force also reduces poverty because women are able to work to support themselves and their families. This also lowers the dependency ratio for families because there are more people working to support a household,[10] thus growing household wealth faster and making households more resilient to economic downturns and family crises.

The story does not end by accepting that Vietnam has high female labor force participation rates. Gender inequality still exists. Since 2018 McKinsey & Company have published at least three reports on women in Asia and their role in the economy. These reports and others like them consistently make the same argument which is that a lot of economic productivity is being lost because of gender inequality. In one of its reports, *The Power of Parity: Advancing Women's Equality in the Asia Pacific*, the researchers claim an additional US$40 billion could be added to the GDP of Vietnam by 2025 *if* women's equality was advanced over the current business-as-usual trajectory.[11] In a

---

10. The dependency ratio noted here is defined as the ratio between the number of citizens aged 0–14 plus the number of citizens over the age of 65 compared to those citizens aged 15–64. This latter group is the labor force to support the other two groups. It is the total number of working citizens who must support non-working citizens.

11. Jonathan Woetzel et al., *The Power of Parity: Advancing Women's Equality in the Asia Pacific*, McKinsey & Company, April 23, 2018.

McKinsey & Company video report about the future of Asian women in the workforce, the firm said that women in Asia contribute about a 36 percent share to Asia's GDP, about the same as the global average. Vietnam's average is also around 36 percent.[12] If women were doing the same jobs as men and being remunerated the same then this number should be closer to 47 percent.[13]

A key issue is the type of jobs Vietnamese women are typically involved in. A second, and more important issue over the long term, is how much women get paid compared to men for doing the same or a similar job. Agriculture still absorbs the major share of employment, but many factory jobs, especially in the off-season, are taken up by women. Service sector jobs in restaurants, stores, and other retail outlets are also predominantly held by women. Lower- to middle-level office work is primarily carried out by women. In this sense, the labor demographics in Vietnam in terms of gender and job roles are not too unusual for an Asian country. Whether this will change significantly in the years to come is uncertain, although it is unlikely to decline. The foundations of gender equality do exist in Vietnam. There is equal access to education and employment and a comprehensive legal framework that protects the rights of women, especially pertaining to matrimonial issues. But social and cultural traditions still exist and these ideas can take several generations to change.

Vietnam's Cultural Edge

Is Vietnam a matriarchal or patriarchal society? One viewpoint is that ancient Vietnam during the time of the Trung sisters was matriarchal, but it became patriarchal as China cemented its rule. For example, Vietnamese children are given their father's family name, but their mother keeps her own family name after marriage. Confucian patriarchal values from China were adopted by Vietnamese early on and continue today, but this is changing. It is particularly interesting that a range of socialist policies adopted since the mid-twentieth century have played an important role in moving society towards gender equality. As early as the 1930s, the Vietnamese Women's Union pushed for issues like paid parental leave and a right to be consulted on women's health issues. In the original constitution of the Democratic Republic of Vietnam in 1949, there was a clause that stated: 'Women are equal to men in all respects.'

---

12. 'The Future of Women in Asia's Workforce,' video interview with Anu Madgavkar, a partner with the McKinsey Global Institute, McKinsey & Company, August 2, 2019.

13. Using the ratio of female worker to male from Table 24 and assuming all other things being equal, the calculation is $88/(100+88)=46.8\%$.

When asked about Vietnam's gender roles, young people say it is a patriarchy, but an argument usually breaks out if there are both men and women in the group. Older women say it is a matriarchy while middle-aged men sigh and ignore the question. There is no easy answer, but when prompted most people tend to agree that Vietnam is a matriarchy within the family's walls and a patriarchy in public. In today's modern world of equality and inequality, it is not the most desirable place to be, but it does mean there is a degree of balance between the roles of men and women in society. It is undoubtably one of the reasons why the proportion of women to men in the labor force is so high. As Table 24 shows, Vietnamese women are more likely to be working than women in other Northeast and Southeast Asian countries, many of which are more traditional patriarchal societies.

During their Tiger Economy runs, South Korean and Taiwanese women did not have the same level of participation in the labor force and today both countries still have female labor participation rates at around 50 percent. South Korean and Taiwanese men made up the significant majority of the employed labor force growing their country's economies in the 1980s, 1990s, and early 2000s when their countries climbed out of the Middle-Income Trap to reach high-income status. Anecdotal discussions with Korean and Taiwanese revealed stories of how their fathers had two or three jobs while their mothers usually stayed home to take care of the children. This is very different to the situation in Vietnam today and is a very important driver of Vietnam's long-term growth.

More Opportunities

There is also a lot more that women can do in today's economy than what existed for South Korean and Taiwanese women thirty years ago. One McKinsey study revealed that the high-tech sector has been hugely impactful for women. In Indonesia, for example, the percentage share of women-owned businesses is 15 percent for offline businesses but 35 percent for online businesses. The study also reported that of the 150 self-made women billionaires in China, 114 of them earned their wealth through the high-tech sector.[14] Although there may not be too many high-tech millionaires or billionaires in Vietnam, there are plenty of women with compelling stories that reflect the spirit of a Tiger Economy.

---

14. 'The Future of Women in Asia's Workforce,' 2019.

Secret Weapons

Twenty years ago, life must have been a bit frustrating for Ha Vo. She had what could only be described as 'the perfect resume' for a young, twenty-something-year-old Hanoi woman. She had earned a banking and finance degree from the National Economics University in Hanoi. She had completed auditor training and then worked for the international auditing firm Arthur Andersen for three years. She then won a scholarship and earned a master's degree in development economics from The Hague University in the Netherlands. She had done everything right. Yet, when she put all that on a resume and started applying for jobs, there were no offers.

"I felt so ashamed. I have Arthur Andersen. I have a master's degree but cannot find a job or get a job offer. I'm always the second one [in line] to be chosen," Ha said noting that she looked for three months straight.

Whether it was an epiphany or desperation, the memory of a lunch during an Arthur Andersen factory audit sparked an idea in her mind. The audit team had been invited to have lunch at the workers' cafeteria. When a factory employs hundreds and often thousands of workers who have one hour to eat their lunch, the key culinary issues of cafeteria-style food are focused on volume, speed, and of course cost. Ha's lunch at the factory was not a case of unmet expectations. Instead, it was the source of that age-old spark of creativity common to all entrepreneurs—*I can do better than this.*

In this way, the seeds of the TriStar Company were planted. The initial goals were modest. Choose a factory, make a pitch for the catering contract, win it, and then focus on providing a quality product with more choices and at a price that allows for a decent profit margin.

Of course, focusing on quality, choice, and price is nothing new in business. Successful entrepreneurs need to develop more than these metrics, and Ha's business strategy was different from the start. The first step was to make direct sales calls on her own. The second step was to select Japanese companies as her first potential clients for those direct sales calls. This was based on a belief that Japanese factory managers would place a higher value on nutritious and high-quality food compared to managers from other countries and cultures. The Japanese, Ha believed, would be more receptive to the link between food quality and worker productivity. Ha wanted to focus on food quality and freshness, not just cost, but she needed clients with the same ethos. The Japanese were followed by the Koreans, who had large factories with hundreds and sometimes thousands of employees within a single factory.

Her strategy worked. She got her first Japanese and Korean clients. The client list grew through word-of-mouth marketing and continued direct sales calls by Ha and Ha alone. TriStar's combination of food quality, variety, service, and price resonated with large foreign-invested companies as well as other industrial-sized clients such as hospitals and schools. As the 2020s began, TriStar worked with more than two hundred carefully vetted food suppliers and served food in more than sixty locations where her team was dishing out over 250,000 meals a day.

Ha also has a secret weapon for her operations. This is to employ women who are all-rounders (i.e., those who can multitask and effectively balance multiple projects simultaneously) and put them in charge. The Tristar Company employs around three thousand people in its many operations in northern Vietnam. In the Hanoi home office, there are around one hundred staff, but Ha says she works most closely with around ten people, nearly all of whom are women.

"Before, we could be successful up to a certain level. People would say 'Okay, that's enough for you because you're a woman.' After a certain point, you must hide your success. They are jealous, and society doesn't want to have women be so successful," says Ha, noting that her female friends who are ten to fifteen years older than her and are like mentors have advised her to slow down. Ha is confident that her business will continue to grow, but she is looking at the future in a different light. This is by learning more empathy and finding the best ways to help other entrepreneurs like herself to succeed.

Ha is part of a growing group of women business owners and leaders. In March 2021 the accounting firm Grant Thornton published its annual *Women in Business* report.[15] Vietnam ranked third worldwide, together with Brazil and India, in terms of women in leadership roles, with 39 percent of women holding senior positions. This was behind the Philippines (48 percent) and South Africa (43 percent). This was based on surveys with more than ten thousand business leaders in twenty-nine countries, including over a hundred business leaders in Vietnam.

---

15. *Women in Business 2021: A Window of Opportunity*, Grant Thornton, March 2021.

Areas for Improvement

One difference between Vietnam and the case study comparatives of South Korea and Taiwan is leadership in politics. There are a lot of women in senior government posts and in the role of deputy ministers in Vietnam but not as many as in South Korea and Taiwan. The photos and names that appear in the state press of the Party leaders usually only feature one or two women. There has not yet been the equivalent of a female leader who has risen to the top like current President Tsai Ing-wen of Taiwan and several of her cabinet ministers, or former President Park Guen-hye and Prime Minister Han Myeong-sook in South Korea.

More importantly to the central thesis of this book, Vietnamese women are a crucially important part of the current growth trends occurring in Vietnam today, and they will be for the remainder of the 2020s and beyond. In its own Vietnamese way, the Party and government will likely include more women in the political sphere over time. Short of political participation, most Vietnamese women have not experienced the levels of oppression that Kristof and Wu Dunn wrote about in their book. For the most part, their playing field has been level to that of men and their participation has been near capacity in terms of taking part in the business of building the country. The unleashing of the potential of Vietnamese women has been going on for a long time, maybe for as long as two thousand years. For the 2020s, and with Doi Moi beginning its fourth decade, women are more than holding up their half of the sky.

Testing the Hypothesis

Using the five testing lenses detailed on page 5-8 our analysis is that the role of women in the economy and in society is conducive to the hypothesis being correct. There are simply too many women who are too active in the world of business and the economy, and who hold leadership positions, to negate the hypothesis. Culturally there are many examples of women's positive impacts for the country. Technology holds some strong potential as has been shown in China, Indonesia, and other countries. Policy also leans towards a fair and equitable deal for women. In cases of divorce, for example, women have equal rights to the assets of the family. A married man cannot sell a major asset without his wife's consent even if her name is not on the ownership papers. The environment and governance issues do not seem to add to the hypothesis, but these issues also do not negate it. Those two issues alone will not prevent Vietnam from replicating the success of South Korea and Taiwan. There is too much value being added by too many women to come to any other conclusion.

Figure 9. Hypothesis testing lenses for the role of women

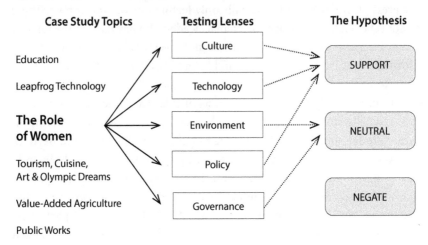

Case Study 4: Tourism, Cuisine, Art, and Olympic Dreams

Building a National Brand
Vietnamese tourism, cuisine, art, and sports
are branding 'Vietnam' to the world

Emerging countries with promise and ambition need more than just strong economic and business metrics. They also need to leverage their intangible assets, such as their history, culture, and quality of life, and share them with the rest of the world. The world is a diverse place, but global culture is largely dominated by wealthy nations, so emerging countries need to work hard to show the world why they deserve attention. They need to provide tangible reasons why they are worthy of increased engagement, tourism, investment, and the opportunity to host global events. They need to take their place on the global stage and show how they can contribute to a richer global community while at the same time protecting their unique cultures. This is all part of building a national brand. It takes time and effort, but there are increasing signs that Vietnam is succeeding in building a strong national brand through its tourism, food, art, and sporting achievements. This brand will contribute to the country's economic growth and may even position it to host a major international event one day.

Hot Travel Destinations

The tourism sector generates significant revenue worldwide. Travel and tourism accounted for one in five new jobs created around the world from 2014 to 2019 and 10.4 percent of global GDP (US$10 trillion).[16] Although COVID-19 disrupted tourism, the long-term outlook for the industry remains strong. This is promising news for countries that are looking to boost their economies through tourism. However, not all countries are created equal when it comes to attracting tourists. Countries that want to capitalize on this trend

---

16. World Travel and Tourism Council, *Travel and Tourism: Economic Impact 2023*.

need to recognize the opportunity that tourism presents and be proactive at attracting visitors. Vietnam is one country that recognizes this and since 2000 has been promoting its tourism assets to capitalize on this trend. In 2019 it received more than 18 million foreign visitors.[17] This was after a 16.5 percent compounding growth per year since 2010.[18]

Table 25. International tourist arrivals to Vietnam, 2010–2019

Year	2010	2011	2012	2013	2014	2015	2016	2017	2018	2019
Int'l Arrivals (millions)	5.0	6.0	6.8	7.6	8.0	7.9	10.0	12.9	15.5	18.0
Tourism Receipts (US$ billions)	4.5	5.7	6.9	7.3	7.4	7.4	8.5	8.9	10.1	11.8
Receipts per arrival (US$)	900.0	950.0	1,014.0	960.0	925.0	937.0	850.0	690.0	652.0	656.0

Source: United Nations World Tourism Organization.

Vietnam is a popular tourism destination for several reasons. There is a lot to do, it is fun, it is safe, the people are friendly, and the tourism offerings can accommodate all types of travelers. There are beach resorts for all income levels, the food is good, and there is free WIFI everywhere. The country is very suitable for backpackers (budget travelers can live on less than US$15–20 a day), cultural explorers (temples, churches, and world heritage sites), nature lovers (thirty national parks, mountains, and rainforests), athletes (organized marathons, ultras, trail runs, etc.), soldiers and veterans (war memorials and battle sites), and high-end travelers (five-star beach resorts all over the country). Tourism operators have expanded their programs to provide niche photography tours, caving, bicycle tours, motorcycle tours, kite surfing, diving, kayak trips, cooking classes, and most recently, multiday trekking expeditions into the mountains.

Even though much of Vietnam's travel infrastructure is being developed, it is still relatively easy to get around. The rail network is improving, and the North–South highway is in various stages of completion. There are also a lot of seats available on the four domestic airlines that serve the country.[19]

---

17. Vietnam National Administration of Tourism (VNAT).

18. United Nations World Tourism Organization.

19. According to OAG Aviation Worldwide Limited, an aggregator of travel data for the airline industry, the Ho Chi Minh City–Hanoi route in 2019 was the fourth busiest route in the world measured by the volume of scheduled seats available for passengers with more than 10.2 million seats.

The growth in international tourism shows that Vietnam is a popular destination. More foreigners want to visit to experience what is on offer. This trend has similarities with Thailand, which built a huge tourism industry by attracting a wide range of tourists in the 1990s and 2000s. It is more than likely that Vietnam's tourism sector will develop like Thailand's in the years to come.

Vietnamese Cuisine: A Window to Vietnam

The first exposure many foreigners have of Vietnam is through its food. This may be a US$8–10 bowl of Vietnam's national dish, *pho* (pronounced in English 'fuh'), or a US$6–8 *banh mi* (Vietnamese baguette) in a tiny restaurant or pushcart in metro cities around the world. It is being driven by the Vietnam diaspora (Viet Kieu) which is comprised of around five million people who have kept their cultural ties in their new homelands.[20] From the 1970s onwards, the bulk of their customers were other Vietnamese who missed the food from their homeland. Over the past 10–15 years, other non-Vietnamese patrons have been taking up table space. They do not speak Vietnamese and often mispronounce the names of the dishes, but they are becoming loyal customers and Vietnamese food connoisseurs in restaurants worldwide. Like Thai food before, Vietnamese food is becoming trendy and it is positioning Vietnam as a country to be added to everyone's travel list. Vietnamese food has become a global advertisement for Vietnam tourism.

And the food does not disappoint travelers when they arrive. Food options are available everywhere, from mobile food carts on three-wheel bicycles to streetside shops with tiny plastic chairs and tables, and from modest restaurants to upmarket places with linen and nicely dressed servers. There is also an incredible diversity in the offerings. It is not just about *pho* and *banh mi*. Vietnam's three distinct regions—Northern Vietnam, Central Vietnam, and Southern Vietnam—each have their own history, terrain, climate, accents, and food which has influenced their cuisines and created unique specialty dishes. There are literally hundreds of unique dishes served by the thousands of restaurants and street vendors across the country. For example, in Central Vietnam the food from Hue includes a special kind of soup called *bun bo hue*, which is the former imperial capital's version of the traditional Vietnamese *pho*. A popular Southern Vietnam dish is *banh xeo*, a Mekong Delta creation,

---

20. See Chapter 9, The Cards It Holds, pp. 123–38, for more data and analysis of the Vietnamese diaspora.

which is often translated as 'Vietnamese pancake' or 'Vietnamese crepe.' There is also *hu tieu nam vang*, a distinctive take on *pho* with Khmer influences (in the Vietnamese language Nam Vang is a traditional name for Phnom Penh). In the Old Quarter District of Hanoi, there are numerous small shops and restaurants serving various northern dishes. Many places have served just one dish for generations, such as *cha ca Hanoi* (a fish dish) or *bun cha* (rice vermicelli with grilled pork), which was made famous when United States President Barack Obama and Anthony Bourdain ordered the dish in a streetside café during Obama's state visit to Vietnam in 2016.

Perhaps the ultimate sign that Vietnamese cuisine has come of age, and is worthy of worldwide attention, is the arrival of Michelin Guides in June 2023. Thirty-three local restaurants received distinction awards, and four were awarded a Michelin Star.[21] For dedicated 'foodies,' there might not be a more interesting country in the world to explore than Vietnam today.

Vietnamese Art: Yet to Be Fully Appreciated

There is something interesting going on in the world of art. Vietnamese artists have traditionally been influenced by French artists. However, they have their own styles and employ their own materials, such as the use of silk canvases and lacquerware. One of the more famous artists whose work can fetch hundreds of thousands of dollars is Bui Xuan Phai (1920–1988) who painted scenes of Hanoi's Old Quarter. During the war years, he used local newspapers as his canvas. In the past ten years, Vietnamese art has begun to go global and record sales are being set.

Portrait de Mademoiselle Phuong by the Vietnamese artist Mai Trung Thu (1906–80) is an oil painting produced on traditional silk canvas over ninety years ago. At a Sotheby's Auction in Hong Kong in 2021, it sold for US$3.1 million, the highest price ever paid for a Vietnamese painting. The reserve price was US$500,000, although Sotheby dealers thought it might sell for as much as US$900,000–1.2 million. The previous highest price for a Vietnamese painting was US$1.4 million for *Nude (Nue)*, auctioned two years previously, by the artist Le Pho (1907–2001). The sale price was 2.5 times higher than what was anticipated.

---

21. The four restaurants awarded single Michelin Stars were Anan Saigon and Gia in Ho Chi Minh City, and Hibana by Koki and Tam Vi in Hanoi. In the same annual guide, Michelin spotlighted 103 other restaurants in the country. *MICHELIN Guide*, June 6, 2023.

Mai Trung Thu spent most of his life and professional career in France. *Portrait de Mademoiselle Phuong* was first displayed in Hanoi in 1930 at the Ecole des Beaux-Arts de l'Indochine, and again the following year at the Exposition Coloniale Internationale in Paris. The painting had another French-Vietnam connection when it appeared prominently in the Vietnamese language film *The Scent of Green Papaya*. Directed by the French-Vietnamese director Tran Anh Hung, the film was nominated for an Oscar by the Academy Awards for Best Foreign Language Film in 1994. The sale of Mai Trung Thu's painting is indicative of the growing demand for Vietnamese art. According to a report by the Fine Arts Association of Vietnam, the average price of Vietnamese paintings has increased by over 500 percent since 2013 due to a growing interest in Vietnamese art from both local and international collectors and the growing number of Vietnamese artists who are gaining international recognition. These trends, and the continued upward movement in prices, are sure to continue in the years to come.

A Sports Window to the World

Football is the most popular sport in Vietnam and the national team is gaining some success. When Vietnam's U23 team made it to the final of the 2018 AFC U23 Championship in China, the feat was nothing short of a miracle. It signaled to the world that Vietnam football was becoming a force to be reckoned with. The tournament was held in January, when the weather in China is typically cold and snowy. In the group stage Vietnam won just one match, a 1-0 victory over Australia, but it did well enough in the other games to make it to the quarterfinals. It won its quarterfinal and semifinal matches against Iraq and Qatar, respectively, in penalty shootouts to make to the final against Uzbekistan. The final was played in Changzhou city in a snowstorm with several inches of snow on the pitch. Uzbekistan scored in the 8th minute, but Vietnam equalised in the 41st minute. The match was tied at 1–1 after 90 minutes, but in the final minute of extra time Uzbekistan scored to win the match 2–1, breaking the hearts of the millions of people in Vietnam who had tuned in to watch the game.[22]

---

22. According to CSM Media Research and Kantar Media Vietnam, a historic record of 77 percent of the televisions in Vietnam that were turned on were tuned into this final championship match.

Despite the loss, Vietnam's performance in the 2018 AFC U23 Championship was a major achievement. Vietnam had never reached the final of such a major international tournament before, and they did it in only their second appearance at this event. The team's success inspired a sense of national pride in Vietnam that has had a lasting impact on the country's football culture. In 2020 and 2021 the men's team made its best ever run in the qualifying rounds for entry into the 2022 FIFA Men's World Cup in Qatar. It did not quite make it. However, in 2022 the Vietnamese women's team went one step further to qualify for the FIFA Women's World Cup in Australia and New Zealand in 2023.

The recent successes of football in Vietnam are not the only changes taking place in sports. Basketball has always been popular among Vietnamese youth with many fans closely following their favorite NBA teams from America. There is a professional league in Vietnam, the Vietnam Basketball Association (VBA), which started in 2016. It comprises seven teams who play around fifty games per season. The games are broadcast live online and on television. Vietnam has athletes at the elite international level in badminton, taekwondo, and shooting. There have also been several excellent chess players in international competitions.

Vietnam even has a Gold Medal Olympian. Hoang Xuan Vinh competed in the 2012 and 2016 Olympic Games. At the 2016 Games in Rio, Vinh dueled the local favorite in the 10-meter air pistol competition to win Vietnam's first ever Olympic Gold Medal and set an Olympic record for the event. He also won a Silver Medal in the 50-meter pistol competition. The local Vietnamese press were undoubtedly proud of Vinh's success and embellished it even more when it was learned that Vinh trained without using live ammunition due to lack of funding.

Vietnam began the 2020s with a U23 championship match under its belt, a professional basketball league, a two-decade old professional football league, and perhaps a legitimate claim to the title of 'ASEAN Football Powerhouse.' Sport (and watching sport) is becoming an increasingly large part of Vietnam life. These are small steps that developing countries need to take to achieve a viable level of global interest amongst their peers. As nations become wealthier, their sports teams do better, their art is more valuable, the country is safer for travel, and the opportunity to host a global event becomes more realistic.[23]

---

23. As noted in Chapter 7 – Is Vietnam a Tiger and Can It Jump?, Vietnam won the right to host a Grand Prix Auto event in 2020. COVID-19 caused a delay and then a cancellation,

These were just some of the steps completed by two of Vietnam's neighbors who have been able to host a FIFA World Cup and multiple Olympic Games.

Olympic Gambits: Tokyo and Seoul

The first fourteen Summer Olympic Games were hosted by developed wealthy nations in Europe and North America. This changed in May 1959 when Japan was the first Asian nation to be awarded an Olympic Games (the 1964 Tokyo Games). This came just fourteen years after the atomic bombs were dropped on Hiroshima and Nagasaki. Next came South Korea in September 1981, when it was awarded the 1988 Seoul Games. In both countries, the planning and final decision to pursue such an audacious goal would have begun at least five years before these announcements (i.e., the planning work began around 1956 or 1957 for Japan and the late 1970s for South Korea). In the mid-1950s Japan was still recovering from the aftermath of World War II. In the 1970s and early 1980s South Korea was very much a developing country and often considered on the same level as North Korea in terms of development. The fact that the leaders of these two countries had the foresight and ambition to one day host the world's largest sporting event is a testament to the belief in their country and the value of hosting such events as part of their country's development.[24]

By the early 1980s, South Korea had not only successfully won the right to host an Olympic Games but it was catching up in terms of economic development. The Koreans revealed to the world something that was intangible, but also showed that they were 'ready' to host such an important event. Therein lies the lesson for emerging countries like Vietnam that are constantly looking to the future. No one can legitimately argue that Vietnam is ready to host an Olympic Games. But the point is that both Japan and South Korea emerged from the devastation of war to pitch successful proposals to host the Olympic Games within approximately one generation of the end of their wars. Hosting an Olympic Games or Football World Cup Finals is a marker of a mature and secure nation that had organized itself sufficiently to pull off something significant on a global scale when it was still a developing country.

---

but its initial acceptance as a host nation for such an event is significant. There are just 23 host cities/nations in the world for Grand Prix Formula 1 racing.

24. China's decision to host the 2008 Summer Olympics would have also followed a similar line of thinking.

We have argued that Vietnam's starting point was in 2007 when the country joined the World Trade Organization. That was a mere sixteen years ago. That is when Vietnam's developments began in earnest. In terms of hosting an Olympic Games, is such a goal even possible for Vietnam? Could it feasibly prepare a proposal in 2042, for example, to win the right to host the 2052 Olympic Games? If it can achieve high-income status, it probably is.

For more than 130 years (and much longer if the conflict with China is included), Vietnam was focused on a single goal—to gain independence and freedom. With that in place by 1990, the country's next step was to reach out to the world and begin inviting people into the country. This started in 1990 when Vietnam officially declared its first ever 'Year of Tourism.' Since then, the country's food, art, and sports teams have been increasingly projecting the 'Vietnam' brand around the world. Whether it is buying 'Made in Vietnam' products, trying Vietnamese cuisine, traveling to the country, or simply learning about its unique history and culture, Vietnam is moving onto the world's stage and capturing the world's attention.

Testing the Hypothesis

Using the five testing lenses proposed on pp. 5–8, our analysis is that the tourism, cuisine, arts, and sports sectors lends to an affirmation of the hypothesis. This does not mean that Vietnam will one day host an Olympic Games like South Korea and Japan did, but it will become a nation of consequence and will increasingly draw attention on the world stage. In some cases, it may host international events, but in nearly all cases Vietnam will participate in them. The culture, technology, and policy will all lend to this trend. The culture is the spirit that enabled the U23 football team to do so well in 2018 and the richness and sophistication of Vietnamese art and cuisine. Technology is the means to spread the 'Vietnam' brand. Policy allowed for an annual growth of international tourism arrivals to get close to 20 percent per year prior to COVID and this will almost certainly return. We argue that the environment and governance index play non-specific roles in either sports, tourism, art or cuisine.

Figure 10. Hypothesis testing lenses for tourism, cuisine, art, and Olympic dreams

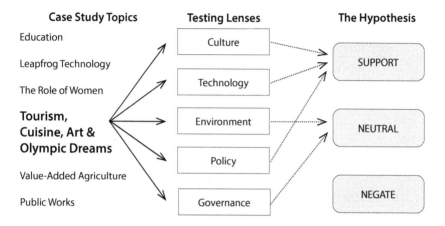

Case Study 5: Value-added Agriculture

How Vietnamese Coffee Farmers Disrupted an Industry
*And farmers of beans, grains, fruits, and other products
are preparing to disrupt even more*

The red, basaltic soil started the disruption. In the highland provinces of Vietnam, the red soil has the right texture, color, and especially the right amount of organic matter, with high levels of potassium, which is evenly spread throughout the ground. Because the soil cannot retain water well, it is not particularly good for some agricultural crops. However, the soil of the Vietnamese mountain provinces of Dak Lak, Lam Dong, Dak Nong, Gia Lai, and Kon Tum is ideal for growing coffee, especially the robusta coffee plant (*Coffea robusta*). Around 600,000 hectares of land have been planted with coffee. The plants grow quickly from grafting to bearing fruit within twenty-four months and can then produce coffee beans for up to thirty years.

In the late 1970s and early 1980s, displaced farmers and former military personnel arriving in the Central Highlands after the American War were eager to accept the government's offer of agricultural land. They worked the red basaltic soil and became skilled at growing coffee. Within a generation they had disrupted the global coffee market by flooding it with robusta beans. Coffee is one of the most highly traded commodities in the world and Vietnam has made its presence known for several decades. Every year Vietnamese coffee farmers export around 1.4–1.5 million tons of coffee beans while retaining around 350,000 tons for local production and consumption. The global coffee export market is worth about US$30 billion. For Vietnam, coffee exports earn the country around US$4 billion in foreign currency every year. In terms of volume, Vietnam is the second largest exporter after Brazil. In the 1990s coffee was earning significant foreign exchange for the country when Vietnam did not have much else to sell on global markets. This has continued, but the 2020s and 2030s is going to be all about value-added agriculture and not just with coffee.

'Miracle Rice'

Rice production is another commodity where Vietnam has excelled. It is the fifth largest overall producer of rice in terms of volume, and its 6.4 million tons of rice exports in 2019 ranked behind only India and Thailand. Some 90 percent of rice exports were from the Mekong Delta and earned the country US$1.4 billion. The story behind Mekong Delta rice is relatively new, interesting, and some might even say *miraculous*.

In the late 1960s Vietnamese rice farmers in the Mekong Delta began to experience a 'miracle.' It was due to the introduction of a new variety of rice called IR8, which had been developed by the International Rice Research Institute (IRRI) in the Philippines. IR8 had a shorter stalk, which allowed for more efficient use of sunlight and prevented the plants from toppling over in storms, and its larger heads contained more grains. But even more important was that it had a shorter maturation time, which allowed for two crops to be planted per year, hence doubling production.

The government also encouraged the development of rice production in the Mekong Delta by improving the dike network and empowering scientists at Can Tho University to take the lead in developing the 'miracle rice.' But this was not without issues. In 1975 the government also tried to collectivize agriculture in the delta. This erased many of the gains that might have been made by IR8 because farmers had no incentive to increase production or become efficient since they were tied to agriculture collectives that shared all the output. The net result was famine in the cities in the early 1980s.

Fortunately, common sense prevailed in 1986 and Doi Moi changed the dynamic. The collectives were abandoned, farmers were given the right to sell their rice on the open market, and Vietnam transitioned from importing rice in 1988 to being the world's third largest rice exporter by 1991. The variant IR8 strain was part of this success. Among Mekong Delta rice farmers, the rice strain earned the nickname 'Honda Rice' because one good rice crop of IR8 earned enough money to buy a Honda motorcycle. Ultimately, the real success of the 'miracle rice' was allowing farmers to be farmers. Doi Moi was responsible for that.

What Comes Next?

It is not just about rice and coffee. For the 2020s and beyond, Vietnam is likely to be one of the world's biggest food exporters. The agricultural products detailed in Table 26 below earned Vietnam US$41 billion of foreign exchange in 2019. At the end of 2020, the Ministry of Agriculture and Rural Development submitted a plan to increase agricultural exports with the goal of earning US$50 billion by 2025 and US$60 billion by 2030. If successful, Vietnam will be the leading food exporter in ASEAN and within the top ten in the world. Much depends on the ability of Vietnamese farmers to grow crops. They can, but for the 2020s and beyond, growing crops is just the first half of the challenge.

Table 26. Vietnam's Agricultural Output World Ranking

Commodity	Rank	Volume in tons (million)
Cashews	1	2.6
Coffee	2	1.8
Rice exports	3	6.4
Natural rubber	3	1.1
Rice production	5	44.0
Coconut	6	1.5
Tea	6	0.3
Cassava	7	9.8
Sweat potatoes	9	1.3
Pineapple	12	0.7
Sugar cane	16	17.9
Oranges	18	0.9
Bananas	20	2.0

Source: Food and Agriculture Organization.

The Need for Transition

"It is all about value added. That's the future," says Jonathon Clark from ED&F Man Commodities. For more than twenty years, Clark has been working with the coffee industry to buy raw beans for export worldwide. In 1995 his firm invested in a joint venture with Simexco to form the Dakman Joint Venture Company. The joint venture supplies coffee roasters with the raw materials needed to sell to local and export markets. It also works with local farmers on good agricultural practices (GAP) that lead to certification from organizations like the Rainforest Alliance, Fair Trade, and others.

Due to modern communications, agricultural commodity markets are highly transparent in terms of price and production. Most informed observers know or can quickly find out the production output and market dynamics of different countries. For example, the moment the Brazilian Real moves either up or down against the United States Dollar and the Euro, Vietnamese coffee farmers and traders can immediately adjust their plans for the sale of beans, plans for their upcoming crops, and potentially any plans for new crops and new acreage. A drought or bumper crop in one part of the world can impact the agricultural planning of farmers for a non-drought region on the opposite side of the world. This is the nature of the commodity market. Everyone is connected and cannot fully control their own outcomes. This is the case for coffee, rice, cashews, pepper, and other agricultural products. Commodity brokers and the big traders who buy from the farmers and sell to food processers do not really care too much about who is growing the products so long as they get the supply they need loaded onto ships bound for their designated export markets. The system works well for the commodity traders and buyers, but less so for the farmers and local traders, whose financial well-being is dependent on events beyond their control. A bumper harvest elsewhere in the world can depress prices and cause financial ruin.

When farmers can escape the commodity market cycle, however, the story is different. They are no longer slaves to global prices but rather price setters and marketers of their produce to local, regional, and sometimes global markets. To do this, they need to invest in processing techniques that can range from adding simple value (such as new drying or curing methods) to some preproduction (such as roasting and sorting) to full-scale production that involves packaging and branding a finished product. The relatively low extra cost of undertaking these activities, at least in the early stages, generates incrementally higher prices and thus higher profits.

Fine Foods of the Earth

Dan On, the founder of Dan-D Foods Limited and a fourth-generation Vietnamese Chinese, who was born in Vietnam and is now a Canadian citizen, learned the back story of Vietnamese cashews in the late 1980s. It was one of his first introductions to the agricultural wealth of Vietnam.

According to On, Vietnamese cashew farmers and those who love to eat cashews are indebted to Mahatma Gandhi of India. In the 1970s, when Vietnam was trying to recover from decades of war, a group of government officials made the rounds of friendly countries to seek ODA to invest in Vietnam. When they arrived in India, the government told the group that they were too poor to have much of an ODA program. However, they did have something to give in the spirit of Mahatma Gandhi, the father of their country. This was to offer high-yielding red cashew seeds for Vietnamese farmers to grow. Instead of returning home with an ODA loan or grant, the Vietnamese team returned to Vietnam with cashew seeds and instructions on how to grow the trees, harvest the nuts, and ship them to commodity markets.

The timing was right. In the late 1970s the government had just launched its New Economic Zone program, whereby land was provided to people displaced by the American War. They were given land and expected to put it into production. Coffee and cashews were two of the agricultural products first tested and both were a success. As noted earlier, Vietnam became the world's second largest producer of coffee. As for cashews, the red cashews from India combined with the yellow cashews that were already grown by Vietnamese farmers, proved to be a winner. Today Vietnam is the largest producer of cashews in the world.

The On family started Dan-D Foods in British Columbia in 1989. They imported commodity agricultural products into Canada, added value, and then exported packaged food products to markets abroad and within Canada. Encouraged by his father, Dan On visited Vietnam in 1991 and noticed large quantities of cashews spread out on the ground for drying. He learned the story of cashews in Vietnam, recognized the volumes that local farmers could produce, and then got to work. One year later, he sent his first container of raw cashew nuts to the United States. Ten years later, in 1999, he launched the first of four manufacturing plants in Binh Duong Province. He had a single goal in mind: Value Add.

"We have to create a consumer brand," he told us in an interview. On had already learned the futility of sticking with the commodity industry as a means of getting rich. It would not happen. He also learned the merits of mechanizing and automating as many of his food-processing factory lines as possible. As of 2022, the company had operations in six countries, including four factories in Binh Duong, two in Canada (Vancouver and Toronto), and one in the United States (California). They have moved well beyond cashews into dried bananas, mangos, beets, yams, almonds (imported from the United States, processed in Vietnam, and exported to Asian markets), snacks, and granola. In some cases, a raw agricultural commodity is imported and mixed with some local products to make a finished product. For example, oats from Canada are imported and mixed with various nuts and fruits grown in Vietnam to make and package granola for export to Asian markets. In other cases, the company's food processing adds not just value but extensive shelf life to the product. Raw bananas, for example, need to be sold and consumed within seven to ten days from harvest, which limits their export potential. Dried, processed, and packaged banana chips, on the other hand, remain fresh for eighteen months. Dan-D has more than two thousand SKUs (stock-keeping units or different packaged products) under the company's umbrella which are sold in numerous markets around the world.

"Vietnam needs to learn from Taiwan. They grow the best pineapples and papayas in the world and have mastered the food-processing industry," says On, noting that Taiwan used to grow mainly sweet potatoes prior to the arrival of Chiang Kai Shek in 1949. Chiang instituted land reform and encouraged farmers to grow enough food for the country to be self-sufficient and then to begin exporting. It is yet another Taiwanese success story that Vietnam can learn from. It is all about value add. On has told the government and industry groups repeatedly, "Don't play the commodity game. You'll never be rich."

The good news is that this value-added trend is happening for Vietnamese farmers. With time, investment, technology, and a strong and patient work ethic (i.e., to try and replicate the Taiwan agricultural model), this trend for value-added agricultural can succeed in Vietnam. The bad news, however, is what is coming next. This is something that no farmer in the world has ever really had to deal with on a scale that is on everyone's horizon. Vietnam is particularly vulnerable.

The Climate Change Challenge

Miracles with rice strains, progressive politics, and advancements in value-added technology are great. They have helped transition Vietnam from a food importer to a food exporter, as well as ensuring its people will always have enough to eat while raising their standard of living. Mother Nature helped by placing Vietnam in an enviable position on the globe with good soil, rainfall, two large river deltas that bring nutrients to the soil, and a geography that allows for agricultural products to easily reach international ports. This is all good, but Mother Nature is not yet done. There is a piece of the future that looks grim, and to date there are no new IR8 strains, new Doi Moi policies, or new equipment that can solve the coming problems caused by climate change.

In October 2019 the *New York Times* published a story about rising sea levels that should have concerned everyone who lives near the ocean. The story specifically mentioned Vietnam. In fact, it led with an example and a map of the Mekong Delta. It reported on a newly published scientific paper from Climate Central, a science organization based in the United States that monitors sea-level rise in locations around the world.[25] The *New York Times* article reported that new technologies had been employed to better measure the landscapes of the world's coastlines.

Previous forecasts predicted that the world's low-lying coastal areas like sections of Vietnam would not be under water until well after 2050. However, when more accurate measurements were incorporated into the model, the story was dramatically different. At high tide the sea would overwhelm coastal areas much earlier than had been predicted. In the case of Vietnam, the new scenario was significantly different to what had been thought previously, and thus it became the lead to the *New York Times* story. The report stated that by the year 2050 "Southern Vietnam could all but disappear." It reported that at high tide the rising seas would completely cover the delta and encroach on much of Ho Chi Minh City.[26] While coffee in the Vietnamese Highlands might be spared the high tide impacts of climate change, farmers who grow rice, shrimp, cashews, pepper, and many other crops are not going to be so lucky. Assuming the forecasts are correct, if a solution does not reveal itself soon, they will need a new miracle, which has yet to appear.

A Competitive Advantage in Agriculture

South Korea and Taiwan were productive societies in the 1980s and 1990s. This led them out of the Middle-Income Trap and into the group of high-income countries. In terms of agricultural resources, however, they did not have enough resources to build large industries focused on processing and exporting food. By contrast Vietnam has been a net food exporter for thirty years. Vietnam has considerable arable land and Vietnamese farmers have shown how productive they can be at growing agricultural products. Entrepreneurs who seek opportunities to add value to Vietnam's agricultural

---

25. 'Flooded Future: Global vulnerability to sea level rise worse than previously understood,' Climate Central, October 29, 2019.

26. 'Rising Seas Will Erase More Cities by 2050, New Research Shows,' *New York Times*, October 29, 2019.

wealth have also shown their productivity. They are taking coffee beans, rice, cashew kernels, shrimp, fruit, and other products and converting them to higher-value, higher-margin finished products. This is the essence of the East Asian Development Model and why, climate issues aside, agriculture is likely to be another important driver of economic growth in Vietnam.

Testing the Hypothesis

Using the five testing lenses given on pp. 5–8, our analysis is that the hypothesis has slightly more evidence of being correct than incorrect. While there are two positive lenses (technology and policy) and two neutral lenses (culture and governance), the big issue will be climate change, which can easily overwhelm any positives that technology or policy provide, and thus we have pointed this lens to negate. Perhaps Vietnam has enough agricultural resources in enough locations to continue to produce the food it needs, or perhaps technology and infrastructure yet to be built, such as dikes and canals, will save the day. For these reasons, our analysis tips slightly into the affirmative column for the hypothesis despite the environmental lens.

Figure 11. Hypothesis testing lenses for value-added agriculture

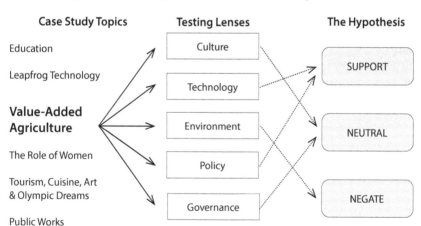

Case Study 6: Public Works

It's Just a Metro. How Hard Can It Be?
The first time is the hardest and then everything grows

In the annals of city metro systems, it was the running joke of Asia. The design phase took forever. Finding the money took even longer. Then the work began for an underground metro system only to learn that the groundwater was higher than expected in some neighborhoods so they had to change the design and erect large concrete pylons to carry the trains above ground. Then they ran out of money, so the pylons just stood there like abandoned giants. Meanwhile, the city streets remained clogged with crowded buses that belched smoke while thousands of motorcycles buzzed around the metro city of a few million residents. The place was desperate for its own metro system, but the country's leaders could not deliver. Who would have thought that life in Taipei City in the 1980s was so chaotic?

Taipei City, like Bangkok whose traffic jams were the stuff of legends and many cities in countries around the world, eventually figured things out. They got their metro systems up and running as well as their airports, water systems, sewage, highways, bridges, and other major infrastructure. Most citizens seem to have collective amnesia about these kinds of projects. They forget how long it took to get the first set of trains running. They forget the traffic jams caused by the construction project. They forget about the project going over budget and the missed deadlines. Instead, they quickly become used to having an operating metro network and a new round of complaining begins: The stations are too far from their homes! The trains are too crowded! Why did they increase ticket prices?

Big infrastructure invariably means big headaches. To make these projects happen, the local government has a long list of items to check off. Original landowners must be compensated, designs must be approved, tariffs must be agreed upon, routes must be created based on population centers and trends, construction contracts must be tendered, and capital must be raised (and eventually be repaid). Because local and central governments often cannot afford these projects, they need to engage with foreign governments who have the capital and the willingness to help. It is frustrating, lengthy, costly, inefficient, and ripe for corruption, and many countries lose their way.

The running joke of a city's metro system is not funny for the people who live there, and it is a joke that sometimes keeps running without an end in sight. Not for all though. Taipei City, Seoul, and Bangkok, among other Asian cities, managed to figure it out. Is there any reason to believe that Hanoi and Ho Chi Minh City cannot do the same thing? Late *is* better than never. Going over budget *is* better than never having a budget to begin with.

Where Is the Money Coming From?

Since the 1990s Vietnam has been popular in ODA circles. The OECD reports that from 2004 to 2018, over US$43.4 billion was pledged to the country during that sixteen-year time frame.

Table 27. ODA funding commitments for Vietnam: Fifteen-year snapshot, 2004–2018 (in US$ billion)

2004	2005	2006	2007	2008	2009	2010	2011	2012	2013	2014	2015	2016	2017	2018
1.83	1.91	1.85	2.51	2.54	3.73	2.94	3.61	4.11	4.08	4.21	3.15	2.89	2.36	1.63

Source: OECD

But when it comes to ODA funding, there are two specific numbers to consider. The US$43.4 billion of ODA funding from 2004 to 2018 is *pledged* investments or loans. It represents the capital that will be made available if various conditions are met. The more important number is *disbursed* investments, which is capital that comes out of a project bank account to purchase supplies, pay equipment invoices, and remit wages to workers because the various conditions have been met. As Table 27 shows, there is a lot of ODA capital coming into Vietnam, which is indicative of how well Vietnam uses the funds pledged to it. According to a 2018 country report by Development Aid, an organization that collects and collates aid information for the international development sector, the amount of *disbursed* ODA funding to Vietnam from 2007 to 2016 was US$38.5 billion. This made

Vietnam one of the leading countries for the receipt of and then the successful disbursement of ODA funding. In 2016 it ranked sixth worldwide in terms of ODA disbursements.[27] In terms of donor countries, the support is widespread and disbursed among several key sectors.

Table 28. The top five ODA countries to Vietnam, 2018 (in US$ billion)

Country	Total aid	Main sectors
Japan	14.06	Transportation 6.6 billion; Energy 2.7 billion; General Budget Support 1.0 billion; Water Supply and Sanitation 958 million
France	2.11	Education 397 million; Agriculture 279 million; Transportation 270 million; Environmental Protection: 266 million; Energy 194 million; General Budget Support 143 million
South Korea	1.44	Transportation 754 million; Health 163 million; Water Supply and Sanitation 129 million; Education 127 million; Environmental Protection 69 million
Germany	1.38	Education 346 million; Energy 297 million; Water Supply and Sanitation 199 million; Environmental Protection 82 million; Forestry 61 million
Australia	1.04	Education 245 m million; Transportation 225 million; Water Supply and Sanitation 136 million; Government and Civil Society 92 million; Agriculture 57 million

Source: *Country Report Vietnam*, Development Aid, 2018.

What motivates donor countries to give ODA funding to other countries? First there is the sense of philanthropy and partnership building. For example, at the entrance to the Saigon River Tunnel in Ho Chi Minh City, there is a plaque with the Japanese and Vietnamese flags embedded into it and information about the project which recognizes it as an ODA project between Japan and Vietnam. A similar sign appears at Ho Chi Minh City's Tan Son Nhat Airport to ensure that visitors know Japan funded the terminal's construction.

For many projects, there is also a compelling economic reason—general contractors from the donor country are awarded design and construction contracts. This means that at least some of the ODA money disbursed in Vietnam returns to the donor country. This was also the case with the construction of the Saigon River Tunnel. The general contractor was the Obayashi Corporation which led a consortium of Japanese contractors to build the tunnel.

There are further benefits as well. When Obayashi Corporation and its partners took on the tunnel project, they were probably looking at it as an entry into the Vietnam market. The experience, capabilities, and reputation

---

27. *Country Report Vietnam*, Development Aid, 2018.

generated from building the tunnel would help them win future construction contracts from the private sector as well as major infrastructure works from the government.

Corruption Hurdles

Major infrastructure projects invariably face numerous challenges, and corruption tops most people's list. Among foreigners who specialize in managing ODA-funded projects, there is a joke. It is not so funny, but it is worth sharing to make an important point. It is about a foreign development official who visits two countries to inspect bridge construction projects funded by multilateral money. The projects need more money so the official is doing his due diligence on its status and the officials involved.

> *In the first country, he arrives at the government official's home and is astonished by its beauty. He's never seen such an opulent home. The house sits on the bank of a wide river with a large terrace overlooking the river. He asks the government official how he could afford such a beautiful home. The man escorts him out to the terrace and points to a huge bridge. It is busy with cars that are rushing back and forth across the river. "10 percent!" the man says with a proud smile.*
>
> *In the second country, he arrives at the government official's home and is even more astonished because it's more beautiful than the home in the first country. It also sits on the banks of a river with a large terrace. When he asks this official how he could afford such a beautiful home, he is escorted to the terrace and the official points to a large and wide river where there are several cargo boats ploughing back and forth. In the middle of the river, there is a single concrete pylon sticking up above the water and nothing else. The government official points to the river and says with a proud smile, "90 percent!"*

The not so funny joke is about corruption. A bridge over any river is expensive. The first official might have stolen 10 percent of the project money to build his house, but in the end the bridge got built and the community benefited significantly from it. The official who stole 90 percent of the funding stole so much that nothing got built except for a single pylon halfway across the river. Each official was proud of his accomplishment, but the level of shame and the culture of impunity in each country was obviously quite different.

Corruption exists in every country to some degree. Transparency International's 2021 Corruption Perception Index determined that two-thirds of the 180 countries that were surveyed were closer to 'highly corrupt' than 'very clean.'[28] In some countries some of the money vanishes from the books but the bridge gets built. In other countries the bridge never gets built. Corruption starts because of a weak legal infrastructure, conflicting and negative bureaucratic decision-making, turf wars, and a lax legal environment. All these negatives exist in Vietnam, but Vietnam also has a lot of functional roads and bridges that have been funded by ODA capital.

The real challenge for many developing countries remains getting infrastructure built and working even with the existence of corruption. This, it would seem, is happening in Vietnam because the country continues to attract ODA financing. In fact, the success of earlier ODA-funded projects can be seen as having an even wider impact today. Once the first bridge is completed, the second bridge (or road, tunnel, water system, etc.) is much easier. It is better designed and completed more quickly and there is a likelihood that it will be locally funded. The suspension bridge over the Mekong River near Can Tho is a good example. It was an Australian ODA-funded project in the 1990s. Prior to the bridge being built, the only way across the Mekong was by ferry. The river was too wide for a standard pylon bridge, so a suspension bridge was needed, which is far more technically challenging in terms of engineering and construction. But with the help of Australian engineers and construction companies, the bridge was built and the Vietnamese contractors on the job learned a lot. Those same contractors went on to build suspension bridges in numerous locations throughout Vietnam.

To return to the earlier point in this case study: 'Late *is* better than never.' Vietnam gets a passing grade for infrastructure development for one reason only. The projects are getting done despite being rarely on time, sometimes poorly constructed, often over budget, and maybe with a portion of the funds being diverted. Eventually the projects become operational, and in many developing countries such projects do not get that far.

---

28. Corruption Perceptions Index 2021, Transparency International, the global coalition against corruption.

Developing Ho Chi Minh City's First New Residential Area and Beyond

In the 1990s Ho Chi Minh City was bursting at the seams. It was becoming the business and economic capital of the country. There were jobs, a better standard of living, and foreign investment was starting to flow in. But there was no room for it to grow as a modern metropolitan city.

From the center of Ho Chi Minh City, residents could look to the east and see a huge expanse of open land called Thu Thiem. It was undeveloped except for a few vegetable gardens. The area was ripe for development, but it was separated from the city by the Saigon River. To the west there were miles of homes stretching almost to the border with Cambodia. To the north the Saigon River once again blocked the way. There was only one bridge, the Saigon Bridge, which took commuters to destinations to the north and east of the city. The city was thus surrounded on two sides by a river and on a third side by its six million residents. The only way out was to the south, but there was nothing there but swampland and no roads. The best option seemed to be to wait for a new bridge to be built across the Saigon River, but a Taiwanese group thought otherwise.

To embark on the challenge, Central Trading and Development Group, a Taiwanese corporation, entered a joint venture with the Tan Thuan Industrial Promotion Company of Vietnam to form the Phu My Hung Corporation to develop the swampland, better known in the early days as Saigon South. The first phase was to build an 18-kilometer-long road from central Ho Chi Minh City through the swampland to the highway leading to the Mekong Delta. The first two lanes were completed in 1998, the second four to six lanes in 2003, and the full ten-lane highway by the end of 2007. It was appropriately named the Nguyen Van Linh Parkway after the former general secretary of the Vietnamese Communist Party, who was the instigator of the Doi Moi reforms in the mid-1980s.

Saigon South won numerous local and international awards for its foresight, vision, and especially for the design and master planning of an entirely new city. Within District 7 alone—the closest in terms of boundaries to the original footprint of Saigon South—there are more than 350,000 residents living on what was swampland twenty-five years ago. There are several hospitals, including the 220-bed Franco Viet hospital, an international standard medical center with 150 full-time physicians and over 1,000 staff. The area is also home to the Royal Melbourne Institute of Technology (RMIT) from Australia, the first full campus foreign university in Vietnam, and there are a number of international high schools as well as primary and middle schools.

Similar urban developments are now being seen in other areas of the city. Today in 2023 the views from the center of Ho Chi Minh City are very different to those of the 1990s. The Thu Thiem area is beginning to host large property developments with residential housing, office space, and modern community spaces now that the Saigon Bridge has been expanded to ten lanes and there are two additional bridges and a tunnel crossing the river. Looking to the west there are more people, homes, and businesses because the roads have been improved. Improved bridge access to the north of the city has advanced the development of industrial parks and factories on what used to be rice fields. In turn, this has led to the expansion of neighboring towns like Thu Dau Mot, Thu Duc City, and other 'satellite cities' to support the foreign and locally invested factories churning out goods for export.[29]

Forty kilometers to the east, the international airport at Long Thanh is under construction and will eventually lessen the pressure on Tan Son Nhat Airport. The first phase of the Long Thanh International Airport project, which is expected to be completed in 2026, will handle twenty-five million passengers per year. By 2040 the airport is expected to be able to handle one hundred million passengers per year and will be one of the most advanced and modern airports in the region, if not the world.

There are also administrative changes underway to facilitate the city's growth. In January 2021, Thu Duc City, a city within a city, was created.

Thu Duc City

A city within Vietnam's largest city

On January 1, 2021, an idea that the *Tuoi Tre* newspaper called a 'creative urban area' came into existence. Other newspapers called it an innovation hub and some even claimed it was the beginnings of what might become the Silicon Valley of Vietnam. The idea was a city within a city and its name was Thu Duc City. It is a combination of District 2, District 9, and Thu Duc District, all located east of the Saigon River. The core idea was to develop a strategy that best manages the strengths and opportunities that each district had on its own and pull them into

---

29. See the profile of Thu Duc City in this case study.

a single entity. For example, the key feature of District 2 is Thu Thiem, which for years has been labeled the future financial district of Ho Chi Minh City. District 9 is home to several industrial parks and hi-tech centers for manufacturing. Thu Duc District is like a university town with around seventy thousand students living and studying there. Vietnam National University of Ho Chi Minh City is there along with several other universities.

In 2019 these three districts alone contributed one-third of Ho Chi Minh City's GDP, according to government statisticians. This total was more than what Binh Duong and Dong Nai provinces produced. It equates to a 7 percent contribution to the country's GDP. Government planners say this share will grow if the key strengths of each district are better aligned and connected.

Learning from Pudong

The creation of Thu Duc City has obvious similarities to the earlier development of the Pudong area east of Shanghai. In the 1980s Pudong had an image problem. Although the area was directly across the river from the infamous Bund, it had nothing to show for itself but a handful of vegetable gardens. Older Shanghainese recall and repeat the phrase, "A bed is Shanghai is better than a room in Pudong." No one wanted to live in Pudong.

That changed in 1993 when the Shanghai government created a Special Economic Zone and the New Pudong Area was established. Most importantly, it installed an administrative structure that enabled the local authorities to govern the area directly. The leader of Pudong had the same power as the vice mayor of Shanghai and as a result the area flourished. Pudong is now China's main financial center and is host to high-tech industries such as semiconductors, artificial intelligence, biotechnology, and aviation.

For the past thirty years, foreign investors, urban planners, politicians, and travelers have been extolling the Pudong-Thu Thiem dynamic. The two locations are patently similar in geography. The Saigon and Huangpu rivers have the same bend that forms a similar oval-shaped peninsula. The width of the two rivers is nearly the same. But thirty years later, only Pudong has developed. The creation of Thu Duc City is a step in the right direction, just as the creation of the New Pudong Area was for Shanghai. There are other similarities between Ho Chi Minh City and Shanghai that could offer a blueprint for Vietnam.

The Bund in Shanghai is an inspiring place. Every day, and especially at night, thousands of Shanghainese and visitors to Shanghai stroll along The Bund to chat, take selfies, buy drinks, and otherwise enjoy each other's company. When the strollers look out onto the river, the history of China, the grand nineteenth- and early twentieth-century buildings that were built by bankers and traders stand behind them. In front, a couple of hundred meters across the Huangpu River, are the dominant skyscrapers of Pudong, the twenty-first-century future of Shanghai and the future of all of China.

Ho Chi Minh City is still working on its 'Bund-like' promenade so that Saigonese can take a pleasant stroll that offers views with history at the back and the future to the front. On the District 1 side, there is room for only a short stroll compared to The Bund in Shanghai, but one day the experience may be just as inspiring. The comparison is apt and the model of what can happen in Ho Chi Minh City has been defined by Shanghai.

The Shanghai Metro offers another model to learn from. It is a model of what happens after the first metro line gets built. The second line arrives more quickly, more easily, and on time. The third line is even faster. The fourth, fifth, and sixth lines are faster still. Today the Shanghai Metro has sixteen lines. The first line started operations in May 1993. Line two started in September 1999. Things really took off after the millennium. A more relevant comparison for this book is the earlier mentioned Taipei City subway. It was approved in 1986, started construction in 1988, and began operations in March 1996. Today in 2023 the daily ridership is 2.2 million in a city with a total population of 2.6 million.[30]

In Hanoi and Ho Chi Minh City, urban transport networks are also being rolled out. The Hanoi metro will be an eight-line underground and elevated network of trains capable of carrying 200,000 passengers a day. It is being financed in part by Chinese ODA. The first line began operating in November 2021. The Ho Chi Minh City metro will have nine lines (a metro system, light rail, and monorails). Line One is currently under construction with Line Two in the planning stage. It is being financed in part by German and Japanese ODA. Saigon commuters are scheduled to board Line One trains (labeled the 'Red Line') in 2024.

Both metros will be late by several years, but is that really a cause for concern? By then collective amnesia will have settled into the minds of

---

30. Metro Taipei Website.

Hanoians and Saigonese. They will have forgotten how long it took to get their Line One trains in operation while they are waiting to board the trains on Line Two. The amnesia will be the same for the next lines as well as airport expansions, new bridges, wider roads, and other essential infrastructure. Vietnamese are being asked to wait for infrastructure to be built, but in the overall scheme of things that is not such a bad place to be. At least they are waiting for something that is in the process of being built and, as history has shown, it will be finished.

Testing the Hypothesis

Using the five testing lenses detailed on pp. 5–8, our analysis is that there is a draw on how well public works and infrastructure point to the hypothesis being correct or incorrect. Certainly, policy has been helpful, as can be witnessed by the enormous amount of ODA funding the country has received. Technology is positive since infrastructure builders can employ leapfrog technology solutions that were not around when South Korea and Taiwan were building their infrastructure. We list culture as having a neutral impact because it does not play a significant role like it does with education or the role of women. Although we would argue that corruption in general in Vietnam is more of the '10 percent' variety than the '90 percent' as described in the not so funny joke in this case study, we point the governance arrow to negate because of the inefficiencies that can occur on large infrastructure projects. This loses money and time even if not all the money is stolen. Lastly, the impact of climate change will be felt first by the infrastructure of a country. It is simply too unknown to place a neutral bet on this issue and it certainly cannot lead to a positive impact.

Figure 12. Hypothesis testing lenses for public works

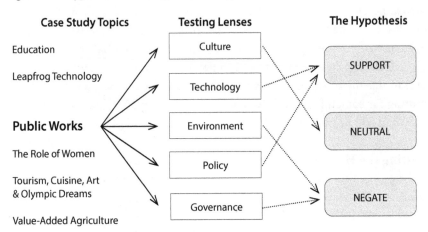

Chapter 11

THE RISKS AHEAD

At the beginning of 2020, we decided to focus on the future of Vietnam from 2020 to 2050 by testing a hypothesis based on South Korean and Taiwanese economic growth models from the 1980s and 1990s. If Vietnam could replicate the South Korea and Taiwan experience, it would mean that Vietnam would be a high-income country within the next thirty years. To better understand this potential, we researched and analyzed the comparative advantages that South Korea and Taiwan had in the 1980s and 1990s and contrasted those with the comparative advantages Vietnam has for the 2020s and 2030s.

South Korea and Taiwan did not have all the key ingredients that experts would argue a country should have (e.g., energy independence, agricultural wealth, large demographics, and foreign investment,), but they still became wealthy. We detailed the advantages the two countries had to help explain or, at least, to begin to understand how they did it.[1] Despite all these advantages and adoption of strategies like the East Asian Development Model, humans and governments are not infallible. We have an immense appreciation and respect for what South Korea and Taiwan accomplished from their poverty years of the 1950s and 1960s through to the 1980s and 1990s when they were considered Asian Tigers, then their escape from the Middle-Income Trap around the year 2000. They accomplished something that is incredibly hard for most countries – they became rich.

The central thesis of this book is whether Vietnam can do the same thing. The country has many comparative advantages that often must be balanced with extreme precision (e.g., trade agreements, financial policy, FDI, and

---

1. See Chapter 8: What the Asian Tigers Had, pp. 107–22.

ODA) if it wants to become rich.[2] When Vietnam joined the World Trade Organization in 2007, it made clear its intention to pursue free trade as one of the central themes of its journey to wealth. But it is not only free trade policies that have to be executed well. There are many more issues and challenges to overcome.

In the previous chapters we have presented a mostly positive perspective of this challenge. Over the next few decades, Vietnamese leaders will have to skillfully manage anything untoward that arises, from a new pandemic to environmental threats to security to financial policy and diplomacy. Falling short on any of these issues could disrupt Vietnam's journey to becoming a rich nation. The sections below describe some of the most important challenges and risks that Vietnam must pay close attention to and deal with as it continues its current growth path.

The Wealth Gap

As discussed in earlier chapters, disparity in wealth and income is an issue for many developing countries. The rich get richer, and the poor get poorer. Moreover, the rich not only get richer but they also do whatever they can to make sure they stay rich. The poor are usually powerless to change the dynamic or their situation. When the poor or disenfranchised do organize themselves, they are frequently called 'agitators,' 'terrorists,' or some other negative label to marginalize them and prevent their concerns from being addressed. In these environments aristocracies and autocracies form while meritocracies fade. Regardless of their political agendas, the power structures of governments are made up of the 'aristocracy' (i.e., politically elite families). There is little or no merit-based system for advancement, thus nepotism takes over.

Such rhetoric and use of '-isms' and '-ocracies' have been around for centuries. The problems that wealth inequality has caused in countries are also not new. Hong Kong, for example, is one of the most unequal countries in the world in terms of wealth. It has a Gini-coefficient of 0.54, the highest or near the highest in Asia depending on the data source. This level of inequality has consequences. Both Hong Kong citizens and foreign journalists and analysts have referred to the wealth gap as one of the key reasons for the political

---

2. See Chapter 9: The Cards It Holds, pp. 123–38.

turmoil in Hong Kong over the past few years. It is particularly apparent in the property market, where young Hong Kongers continue to live with their parents and often do not get married because they cannot afford to buy their own house or apartment. Link this trend with the belief, real or imagined, that it is 'the Mainlanders' who have caused property prices to spike so severely, and the result is social unrest. Another manifestation of such trends is a culture of impunity among the elite. The sense that they can 'get away with anything' is often apparent as is the creation of policies that protect certain industries and companies which they own and control. In such an environment, powerful business groups and monopolies are formed and exploit the working classes.

Vietnam's Gini-coefficient is around 0.35 (much like that of South Korea and Taiwan), which makes it a relatively equitable environment compared to other Asian nations as well as the rest of the world. While there are well-connected families, it cannot be claimed that these same families are aristocrats, or at least the kind of aristocrats that exist in some other Asian countries. Vietnam is too young in terms of its economic development for such families to have established themselves as aristocracies. There is also reason for optimism because of Vietnam's socialist roots. If at least part of the country's socialist ideology is maintained, it should be sufficient to fend off the most severe threats from wealth inequality over the long term.

Systemic Corruption

Systemic corruption is when corruption has become the norm and is so established that organizations, society, and/or the culture it is linked to cannot function without it. Pinpointing systemic corruption is not easy, but for the authors one of the more obvious indicators is when the people benefiting from such deeds are admired by others for their cleverness and achievements, rather than be reviled as criminals.

When we asked our interviewees about the future of Vietnam, the most frequent response was the word 'corruption.' "It is just so corrupt. You can't get anything done," or something similar was frequently stated. In most cases interviewees could not provide any evidence, first-hand or otherwise, of an actual case of corruption that prevented something from happening. Still, it would be naive to claim corruption does not exist and that it is not an important issue. The daily media reports evidence that it exists. It is most definitely a challenge that must be addressed.

The point of the not very funny joke on infrastructure in Case Study 6 is that there is one kind of corruption that makes infrastructure and investment more costly than it should be, i.e., the 90-10 approach, whereby 90 percent of the funds are invested in a project and 10 percent is graft to ensure a project gets started and will be completed, and another where the corruption is so severe that good projects never get implemented.[3] While life is rarely 100 percent of anything, the most important point of the 'joke' and our discussion of corruption in the public works case study was that, in the end, public infrastructure using ODA money *is* getting built in Vietnam.

Vietnam is also getting better at managing this issue. In 2022, Transparency International rated Vietnam in the top half of countries at 77th out of 180 countries, up ten places from the year before and a significant improvement from 2011 when it was rated 112th.[4] These improvements are due to several factors, including an increased political will to fight corruption, improved transparency and accountability, and the strengthened enforcement of anti-corruption laws. The Vietnamese government is now going beyond jailing high-level government officials who have been caught stealing and extending this to the replacement of officials that have failed to prevent such activities happening within the ministries and portfolios they are responsible for.

Although Vietnam has already made significant progress towards reducing the impact of corruption, two primary concerns remain. First is the risk that anticorruption campaigns are abandoned or slowed down and low- to middle-level corruption is ignored. Without controls and a conscious effort to eliminate it, corruption can become systemic as it has in several other Southeast Asian countries. Second, corruption could become so entrenched that the moral and nationalist imperative that served Vietnam so well during the war years and the early days of poverty, begins to dissipate. It becomes an 'every man for himself' environment rather than one in which people agree to collectively do something for the sake of the country. If a collective national imperative to become rich breaks down and is replaced by self-interest, the country will not move forward or grow at the same rate, and economic and

---

3. See Chapter 10, Case Study 6: Public Works, pp. 184–94.
4. Transparency International, Corruptions Perception Index, 2022

political instability will prevail. There are many countries in the world that demonstrate how this can happen and how difficult it is to reverse.

State Capacity

One of the reasons that *former* 'Tiger Economy' Singapore has been successful is its government and civil society infrastructure. This includes the ability, education level, and professionalism of its civil servants who are well paid and well organized. Civil society organizations also work on a range of issues that impact the lives of Singaporeans, which the government does not fully address.

Vietnam is still in the process of developing public institutions that will properly support the nation's growth. It has launched numerous anticorruption campaigns to demand more accountability from its bureaucrats. But accountability is only one aspect of building a state capacity along the lines of Singapore. There also needs to be more organization, training and empowerment of highly skilled and educated bureaucrats which, in turn, will create higher quality institutions. This also needs to extend to the courts and other regulators which also need to be independent of interference and corruption.

The risk is that these objectives will not receive adequate attention, although this effort does seem to have begun. Over the last twenty years, there has been a steady improvement in the caliber of government officials. They are better educated, come from relevant backgrounds, know English well, and have a good understanding of their roles and objectives. The high-profile firing and disciplinary action taken against the CEO of the Ho Chi Minh City Stock Exchange and the Chair of the State Securities Commission in May 2022 is another sign that the Communist Party understands this issue. Local news reports stated the two were dismissed for 'very serious shortcomings,' and the quality of their respective replacements would indicate they were appointed based on merit. The resignations of the president and two deputy prime ministers in early 2023 for failing to detect and respond to corruption scandals relating to the COVID-19 pandemic is also evidence that government officials will be held accountable for failings that occur under their watch, even if they are not directly involved. These are the types of progressive actions that are needed to build state capacity over the next decade.

Free Trade Reversal

Vietnam's decision to allow free trade to flourish was a key turning point for the country and a key driver of economic growth. Free trade was no longer solely about the free flow of goods in and out of the country's airports and seaports, but included a free flow of people, investment capital, technology, and ideas, as well as allowing foreign participation in industries that many countries consider off limits to foreigners, and freedom to access internet portals. Access was given to anything and everything. The government did this knowing that some of what came in could be culturally inappropriate, politically risky, or put Vietnamese companies at a disadvantage economically. But it went ahead regardless because of a belief in free trade.

The result so far has been more than two decades of a growing economy and double-digit trade growth. Foreign direct investment is flourishing as so many areas of the economy are now open to it. Social media is booming and there is a vibrant venture capital environment. Vietnamese are studying in countries all over the world, not only in American universities, which was the primary destination for South Korean and Taiwanese students. The country's free trade philosophy has also resulted in a budding tourism economy that is expected to grow to at least 12 percent of GDP, much like the tourism industry's share of GDP in Thailand.[5]

These are all positive trends that should persist if Vietnamese leaders continue to believe in the merits of free trade. The caveat is that leaders could change their minds under the influence of individuals who mount nationalist-style campaigns to 'take back Vietnam' for the Vietnamese, which would inevitably result in a slowdown in economic growth. This would be like what we see happening in China today where the government is asserting control over all areas of society and business in ways that are unlikely to result in positive outcomes for many of its citizens.

A more threatening aspect of this issue is that Vietnam may have only a limited ability to manage this problem because of the behavior of other countries. There are current and future leaders of many countries in the world today who are questioning the merits of globalization. These aspiring leaders are touting anti-trade, anti-immigration, and other nationalistic policies that play to the sentiments of people who feel they are losing job opportunities

---

5. See Chapter 10, Case Study 4: Tourism, Cuisine, Art, and Olympic Dreams, pp. 167–75.

and having their wealth eroded due to the impact of globalization. These citizens are demanding action to prevent this from happening. How this pans out, nobody really knows, but it is likely to get worse before it gets better. The degree to which it gets worse will have a direct bearing on Vietnam which has staked its future on a free, open, and globalized world.

The Environment Rules

For liberal democratic nations around the world, the challenges posed by climate change and its effect on the environment must be one of the largest headaches facing leaders. This is especially the case in countries that have well-established businesses in carbon energy generation and mass-production techniques that use a lot of natural resources. Despite the calamities that climate change might wreak on their nation, these leaders of such countries have no short- or medium-term incentive to change the status quo. A commonly stated argument against change or reform concerns a country's readiness for the adjustments needed to provide a clean environment. The core argument is that too many jobs will be lost and that providing jobs should take precedence over the environment. The notion of creating 'green jobs' is still a relatively new phenomenon.

In the case of Vietnam, an additional issue is that many of the environmental challenges are not of Vietnam's making, such as rising sea levels or decreasing water levels in the Mekong River due to upstream dams. However, this does not mean that these issues can be ignored, especially in the rural areas of the country. The ultimate risk is that the negative impacts of climate change and an unhealthy environment becomes so large that policymakers eventually become irrelevant because they did too little or nothing for too long. By signing up to COP26, Vietnam has already made a significant international commitment to do what it can to address climate change. However, more needs to be done before it is too late. Vietnam's COP26 initiatives will not, by themselves, address the flooding of the Mekong Delta, where millions of people live. More effort needs to be put into understanding where the country is at the greatest risk from environmental factors and then adopt strategies that respond to those specific challenges.

Cultural Shifts

In the 1990s Lee Kuan Yew and Dr Mahathir Mohamad, the prime ministers of Singapore and Malaysia, respectively, spoke frequently about 'Asian Values' as the reason for their successful nation states. In general, they were talking about the values of filial piety, diligence, education, family, and obedience to authority, among other cultural traits. It was these values that helped two quite small and poor former colonial outposts become high-income countries.

Throughout this book we have referred to culture as one of the key drivers for what Vietnam has accomplished so far. We argued that Vietnam is more like and more attuned to Northeast Asian culture than Southeast Asian culture. We frequently cite the role of women as a key reason for Vietnam's success because its culture did not prevent their participation in the labor force. Vietnamese are also very accepting of new fashions, styles, religions, and other social issues which more conservative countries have difficulty accepting. Part of the reason for this is Vietnam's colonial past which forced people to adapt to new norms and social influences ranging from Catholicism to education to a Romanized alphabet for the Vietnamese language.

While it might be impossible to change the traditional culture of Vietnam, its leaders can change its laws in ways that challenge cultural norms and hinder the development of a progressive society. For example, it could alter divorce laws to favor men in the division of assets, child support, and child custody. It could join the culture wars that are active in several countries on gender issues, LGBT issues, and family planning. Abortion, for example, is a legal right for Vietnamese women and Vietnam has one of the most open policies for the procedure. The point here is that laws and cultures do change over time. Vietnam's culture and its free trade laws have been integral components of the country's success so far. If these were to change to a more conservative and closed approach to the outside world, it would make Vietnam's journey from a middle-income country to a high-income country all that more difficult.

Geopolitical Risks

One of the most uncomfortable global questions that Vietnamese political leaders will have to answer over the next several years will involve China and the United States, two countries seemingly destined to be engaged in a new

Cold War. The blunt version of the question posed in Chapter 9 is: 'Whose side are you on?' Currently, and going forward, the answer will be 'We are on Vietnam's side, and we want to be friends with both China and the United States.'

Vietnam's senior leaders and diplomats will almost certainly seek a path of neutrality, but they will still face many questions. The questions will be more nuanced and diplomatic, and therefore more difficult to answer in a normal exchange between leaders. The more diplomatic questions will be along the lines of trade and military alignments, regional balance, preservation of global shipping routes, and the overall security of Asia. Whether Vietnam likes it or not, the country's location as a border country of China, its long coastline, its military infrastructure (e.g., seaports like Cam Ranh Bay), and its long history of war has thrust it onto the global stage. The East Sea/South China Sea could become a global flashpoint like the Taiwan Straits, Kashmir, the Middle East, the Korean DMZ, and other conflict zones where there is constant tension on all sides of their borders. Vietnam must decide how it will respond to these issues.

Like any political challenge, it will be a balancing act. So far Vietnam has been able to maintain an optimal status quo. It is unlikely to make a blunt choice. But it does have to take care of its interests, and this will be a challenge. China *may have* the largest economy in the world within the next few years and Vietnam *will be* on its southern border. Vietnam will also be one of China's most important trading partners, and millions of Chinese tourists will visit Vietnam every year. Finding the right balance will not be easy, but it is something Vietnam will have to do well to continue its current growth trends. The status quo is working for Vietnam and leaders will seek to continue that status.

What happens if Vietnam loses its balance due to one or more of the issues described above will depend very much on the issue; especially as multiple entities are actively trying to maintain the balance. The Communist Party and the government are in the best position to influence outcomes, but not entirely on their own and not in every case. Business leaders within large local companies like PetroVietnam, Vietcombank, and Vingroup will play a role, as will outside influences such as regional organizations like ASEAN, global institutions like the World Bank, and NGOs, foreign governments, and large investors like Samsung.

Vietnam has several challenges to overcome if it is to achieve high-income status. Some like the Middle-Income Trap are already known, while others like COVID-19 are not. In a best-case scenario, the organizations noted above work together to address whatever challenges arise. As in the past, there will be some successes and some failures. But to enhance the chances of success, Vietnamese leaders can draw on the experience of Singapore, South Korea, Taiwan, and other countries on how they handled such missteps. Vietnam has the benefit of learning from others who have gone first.

Chapter 12

VIETNAM IN 2050

Vietnam is the next Tiger Economy of Asia, and it will grow and develop in a similar way to how South Korea and Taiwan grew as Tiger Economies of Asia.

Conclusions of the Hypothesis

In this book we have noted that Vietnam passed the 'point of no return' when it decided to pursue free trade as the means to develop its economy. The origin of this phrase is reportedly from bomber pilots during World War II, and it describes the point in time that pilots had to continue their mission because they no longer had enough fuel to return to their original base because trying to return would be too dangerous. We have argued that Vietnam's full embrace of free trade on January 1, 2007, when Vietnam joined the World Trade Organization, was its 'point of no return' moment. Thereafter, Vietnam had no choice but to continue to use free trade as the key means to develop its economy and country. It had to keep moving forward despite the risks. There were no options for a direct abort on free trade because doing so would be even more risky.

For three years we researched, interviewed, discussed, and mused on a hypothesis about Vietnam's future. The hypothesis had two parts. First, it asked whether Vietnam was a 'Tiger Economy.' Second, it asked whether Vietnam could replicate the growth and development of South Korea and Taiwan when they were tiger economies in the 1980s and 1990s. The first question could be answered with evidence and data. The second question has been addressed through anecdotal observations in the case studies and comparisons with other countries.

In the 1960s, 1970s and 1980s, the South Koreans and Taiwanese were like the World War II pilots. They ventured forth despite the risks. They did not necessarily know where they were going or what would happen, but they knew it was the right choice to make. They had the power of intention. The term 'Tiger Economy' did not even exist then, but they put their heads down and with grit and courage they outworked everyone else in the world. They became Tiger Economies and, eventually, high-income countries. They chose to go, they went, and they were successful. Can Vietnam replicate this feat?

Part 1 of the Hypothesis: Is Vietnam a Tiger Economy?

Ultimately, this is a 'yes' or 'no' question. We believe the answer is 'yes' because of the relatively simple definition that we used to qualify a Tiger Economy. We proposed that 'A Tiger Economy is the economy of a country which undergoes rapid economic growth, usually accompanied by an increase in the standard of living.' We added to this definition by identifying six specific metrics that had to be met to qualify Vietnam as a Tiger Economy.[1] These metrics are: (1) Numbers; (2) Exports; (3) Industrialization; (4) Expertise; (5) Markets; and (6) Leaders.

Throughout this book, but particularly in Chapter 7 (pp. 107–22), these six criteria were analyzed with evidence and examples. The Numbers, Exports, and Market issues have been documented by many observers. All these indicators are positive and lend credence to a 'Yes' answer for the Tiger Economy question. The Expertise issue is a work in progress, but positively so. The experts are being nurtured and should increasingly assume positions of influence within the next decade. The Industrialization metric is a soft 'No' because Vietnam is still in the early stages of any type of serious industrial development. We also qualified this metric with two components—policy and infrastructure—both of which are still in development, but positively, like the expertise metric. The Leadership issue is potentially the outlier because of the opaqueness of the political process and the persistent consensual decision-making that is used by the government and the Communist Party.

---

1. This is discussed in Chapter 1: The Hypothesis, pp. 1–12, and Chapter 9: The Cards It Holds, pp. 123–38.

While not all the factors point in the positive direction, we believe there is enough evidence to confirm that 'Yes, Vietnam is a Tiger Economy today.' Since at least 2000, Vietnam has undergone rapid economic growth accompanied by an increase in the standard of living for most Vietnamese. The economic and business growth has been going on too long and is too widespread and equitable to draw any contrary conclusion. The fact is the lives of virtually all Vietnamese people have improved over the past thirty years.

But there are other countries in the world, for example, Argentina, Indonesia, Poland, and Thailand, who can use similar metrics and credibly call themselves Tigers. Those countries have also had positive economic growth for many years and have improved the lives of their citizens. For this reason, the second half of our hypothesis is critical to determining our conclusion.

Part 2 of the Hypothesis: Will Vietnam replicate the South Korea and Taiwan experience?

This is a much harder question to answer 'yes,' 'no,' or 'maybe.' But we have concluded that the answer to this question is none of these. The best answer, an admittedly non-scientific one, is 'probably.' At the same time, it is also not a 'maybe.' We believe it is going to take more time to answer this question with any authority.

As a Tiger Economy, Vietnam has many of the features and advantages that South Korea and Taiwan enjoyed in the 1980s and 1990s when they were Tiger Economies. Like South Korea and Taiwan, Vietnam can use these advantages in the 2020s and 2030s. Moreover, Vietnam has comparative advantages that South Korea and Taiwan lacked during their Tiger Economy growth decades. In Chapter 8 (pp. 107–122), we noted the shared and semi-shared comparative advantages of South Korea and Taiwan, namely (1) The Priority of Education— fully shared; (2) Investment in High Tech—partially shared with room to grow; (3) Postwar Grit: The Greatest Generation—fully shared; (4) Most Coveted Nation Status—potentially shared in the future; (5) Commitment to Global Trade and Integration—fully shared; (6) Geography—shared, but Vietnam has more advantages; (7) Culture—fully shared; (8) Wealth Disparity—partially/ fully shared; and, additionally (9) Political Stability and Intent—partially/fully shared especially regarding intent.

In Chapter 9 (pp. 123–138), we discussed the comparative advantages unique to Vietnam, namely (1) Global Manufacturing: China + 1; (2) Mass Mobilization; (3) Demographics and Urbanization; (4) The Role of Women;

(5) Natural Resources and Agricultural Wealth; (6) The Vietnamese Diaspora; and (7) Digitalization and the Internet; and (8) A Leverage Point.

Based on these factors, we are ready to argue that over the next thirty years it is *probable* that Vietnam will replicate the South Korea and Taiwan Tiger Economy experience. In the previous eleven chapters, we have presented evidence to show that our analysis is accurate, and that Vietnam probably will replicate the economic success of South Korea and Taiwan.

In Chapter 11, we discussed some of the challenges and remaining risk issues that could derail Vietnam from replicating the South Korea and Taiwan experience. We summarize in this final chapter the reasons for our 'probable' forecast for replication of the South Korea and Taiwan model.

Free Trade

Vietnam is wagering that its free trade philosophy will lead to something beyond just being a Tiger Economy. The country's globalization rate is well beyond anything that the world has seen in recent history. It is an anomaly for countries of Vietnam's population size. Vietnam has also signed numerous free trade agreements. Even if this free trade plan slows down, Vietnam is already committed to too many free trade programs to back away from this strategy.[2]

Free trade is more than about imports and exports. It is also a philosophy and attitude that Vietnam can compete with the world. Thus, it can confidently invite in foreign investors and manufacturers. Government leaders are also comfortable telling their large SOEs that they must compete with foreign multinational corporations rather than be protected. For a developing country, this is remarkable, especially when considering how countries like China and the United States (America First) are doing the opposite with nationalist, inward-looking campaigns. As noted in Chapter 5, free trade for Vietnam not only works better for them, but it also must work. So far, it has, and we expect this will continue.

Cultural Traits

When technology, capital, progressive policies, and the many other features of a dynamic economy and country are available to all, why are some countries so much better at development than others? When everyone in the world agrees that education can lift people out of poverty, why are some countries

---

2. See Chapter 5, Free Trade Better Work, pp. 53–74.

better at educating their citizens than others? These 'Why …?' types of sentences all point to the same core question: Why are some countries better off than others? Throughout this book, we have tried to answer this question as it pertains to Vietnam. We used the case studies of South Korea and Taiwan to help guide the discussion because South Korea and Taiwan *are better off* today than other countries who started out in similar circumstances (i.e., postwar, mired in poverty, weak, crumbling or no infrastructure, etc.). They made it work, and we believe Vietnam can as well.

What do these three countries have in common? They share cultural traits, such as a firm belief in the power of education. This belief is backed up by investment and a high household savings rate. There is also a strong work ethic and fiscal prudence and a strong environment of entrepreneurship. In the case of Vietnam, there is a cultural ethic for women to play a full role in the labor force and economy. There is also the power of intention, which also means the refusal to give up. There is grit and there is pragmatism when dealing with complicated issues. This power, the idea of just deciding to go, is not something that can be obtained via Google or learned at a university. It is something that is integral to the culture. In Vietnam, it is apparent that this *something* is in place and is working well for Vietnam's growth and development.

Social and Political Stability

In May 2014, Thailand experienced its thirteenth coup since 1932. In the same period, there were nine unsuccessful coup attempts. Many believe that Thailand has a 'coup culture'—that changing the government by means of a military coup has become the norm, not an aberration. No matter the definition, a country with so many coups might have a social stability problem. There are many countries in the world like Thailand.

Vietnam, in contrast, is a single-party state with the Communist Party of Vietnam in control. There is no opposition party to lobby for a new way of looking at issues, nor is there much public dissent against the government. Because of this, for better or worse, there is political stability. This helps in combatting issues like COVID-19 or keeping the currency stable and inflation under control. Although certain political and human rights may be lacking, these factors are not of concern to many people. There is no pent-up demand for political and social change among the population.

Commentators will always find ways to criticize the one-party system, but to claim that democracy is an essential element for a nation to become a high-income country is incorrect. It could equally be claimed that democracy has been a barrier to many countries achieving high-income status. What is needed is good government where there is accountability to the people, and in Vietnam's case we believe this exists. Vietnam has stability, and we believe that this is what is needed right now rather than a multiparty democracy. There is also a level of accountability in Vietnam that is absent in many countries that promote themselves as democracies. This accountability reveals itself with new leaders coming into important government positions because of their skill sets and educational background, as well as the prosecution and expulsion of government leaders who break the law or are ineffective.

A final note about democracy and single-party rule. The most successful country in Southeast Asia, as well as the most successful Tiger Economy country, is Singapore. It has been ruled by a single political party—the People's Action Party—since Singapore became a nation state in 1965. In this time, there have been only three prime ministers—Lee Kuan Yew, Goh Chok Tong, and Lee Hsien Loong (Lee Kuan Yew's son)—in fifty-seven years. Since 1975 Vietnam has had eight different prime ministers. Singapore is, by definition, a democracy and Vietnam is communist, but do such labels really matter?

Demographics

Data on the demographics of Vietnam appear several times in this book. To reiterate, Vietnam will soon have one hundred million citizens. An estimated 60 percent of these people will be part of the country's labor force. To put this in perspective again, Vietnam's labor force is larger than the entire population of South Korea and two times larger than the population of Taiwan.

Also as noted throughout this book, the average age of a Vietnamese citizen is around thirty-two. They are also quite healthy compared to many countries. The country implemented a two-child policy in the 1980s, which has meant that household economics are likely an easier chore to manage than in countries with booming child populations (e.g., Ethiopia, Nigeria, Pakistan, and the Philippines). The most telling aspect of Vietnam's demographics is that its sixty million-strong labor force will eventually become part of the consumer middle class of the country. This will make Vietnam an attractive destination for consumer goods companies, education, leisure, travel, and other industries that are built on a healthy, educated, and populous middle class, which in time will create an economy based more on domestic consumption rather than export manufacturing.

2020s Technology

In the 1980s and 1990s, South Korea and Taiwan took advantage of their generation's newest technologies. For Taiwan, the computer chip, and especially the production of laptop computers, was a huge leap forward. This technology was technically available to all countries, but the Taiwanese mastered mass-production methods. South Korea's Samsung is doing the same thing with the production of smartphones. Hyundai is finding similar success with automobiles. South Korea and Taiwan demonstrate that while all countries might have technology made available to them, not all countries are able to use it effectively. With the passing of each generation, societies keep on moving up the technology ladder, but they do not move up at the same pace. Some are better at adapting to new tech than others.

Technology is in a constant process of change. However, the technology of the 2020s and 2030s that Vietnam will be using compared to the technology of the 1980s and 1990s that helped South Korea and Taiwan grow has at least one key difference. The new technologies of the 2020s and 2030s will be built and distributed on global digital platforms that reach every corner of the world. There is already evidence that the Vietnamese tech sector is well advanced in its application of blockchain technologies and exploration of the metaverse. Moreover, it is not just technology, but also capital. Vietnam's decision to fully open its doors to trade has also meant the doors are open to technology and capital coming in and going out of the country. Vietnam will be able to do all this at a much faster pace than South Korea and Taiwan. This will be part of its Tiger Economy strategy to become a high-income country.

Geography and Land

Throughout this book, we have detailed Vietnam's geographical advantages. This includes the country's shape (long and skinny with no deep interior regions) and the location of its many seaports and their proximity to international shipping routes. This means the country's agricultural wealth is close to local and international markets. Though the transportation infrastructure is still undeveloped, this matters less than in other countries because the distances are not too great. When the transportation infrastructure is fully developed, agricultural and manufactured goods can be shipped abroad more quickly and cheaply compared to other countries. This also ensures that the wealth is spread to the rural communities. This is one of the reasons that Vietnam's Gini Co-Efficient of 0.35 is on par with South Korea, Taiwan, and several other equitable nations. The country's geography means the most far-flung communities still have access to the country's urban centers for work.

The country's geography and land are also good for tourism. There are thousands of kilometers of beachfront property for tourism development. The geography also means that building infrastructure for all sectors of the economy (i.e., tourism, manufacturing, agriculture, etc.) is cheaper because access is much easier.

Finally, compared to South Korea and Taiwan, Vietnam is much bigger in terms of size. There is also no winter weather like in South Korea and Taiwan. Vietnam will have to deal with the impacts of climate change. This will be a big challenge. Yet, it is a challenge that other countries without Vietnam's geographical and land advantages would likely be willing to swap.

Predicting the Future

"A radio, refrigerator, and a television for every family within 10 years' time."

Vietnamese Communist Party Second Five-Year Plan (1976–1980).[3]

After thirty years of war against the French and the Americans that cost three million Vietnamese lives, optimism about the future was inevitable. The future had to be better than the past. Le Duan, the general secretary of the Communist Party from 1960 to 1986, had a two-pronged plan for the development of a unified Vietnam in 1976. It combined the industrial strength of the North with the agriculture base and light industry of the South. The planned result—in addition to radios, refrigerators, and televisions for every family—was annual GDP growth of 15 percent, agricultural growth of 10 percent, and industrial growth of 17 percent.

Those forecasts did not materialize, but they revealed a hopeful optimism about the postwar environment. They show even more clearly the futility of forecasting economic growth and development. Even forty-eight years later, and with many models to observe and emulate, it is still not easy to forecast economic growth and development. However, that is the purpose of this book

---

3. 'Vietnam's Economy: Paying for peace when it comes,' *The Economist*, October 13, 1984.

and what we have tried to do. With the previous eleven chapters as evidence, we are ready to offer our conclusions and a look into the future of Vietnam from 2023 to 2050.

Our methodology to forecast Vietnam's economic future is simple. Rather than select several metrics (e.g., trade, FDI, industrial growth, worker productivity, power generation, and foreign currency reserves) and make a range of assumptions to produce a forecast, we have selected just one metric: GDP per capita, which is calculated by dividing the forecast total GDP value by the forecast total population. It is a critical metric because, as we have previously discussed, GDP per capita is used to determine whether a country is high, middle, or low income. In current United States dollars, high-income status is achieved with a GDP per capita of over US$12,695.

To forecast Vietnam's future GDP per capita and, therefore, if it will become a high-income nation before 2050, we must start with its current GDP per capita level and project it forward using a constant compounding rate. At the end of 2022, Vietnam's GDP per capita was US$4,121[4] and from 2003 to 2022 Vietnam's economy grew at an annual compounded rate of 6.23 percent. This rate is based on a twenty-year period that included both good and bad economic periods, including several financial crises and the impact of COVID-19. While it is impossible to know for certain, it is reasonable to assume that similar periods of good and bad economic activity will continue to occur at a similar frequency in the future. Therefore, this rate seems reasonable to use for forecasting future GDP per capita in Vietnam.

By comparison, in the 1980s and 1990s, when South Korea and Taiwan were Tiger Economies working to grow their economies to achieve high-income status, their average annual GDP growth rates were more than two percentage points higher than Vietnam is growing today. In the five years prior to both countries achieving high-income status in the late 1990s, South Korea's average annual GDP growth rate was 10.89 percent and Taiwan's was 8.04 percent.

Why South Korea and Taiwan's economies grew faster than Vietnam's is growing today is due to a range of factors, many of which are stated in this book. There is also a plausible argument that Vietnam's economy could have grown equally fast if the government was less involved in managing

---

4. This GDP per capita data and the forecasts to follow are based on the research and analysis of data from the International Monetary Fund and the World Economic Outlook Database of April 2022.

the economy to ensure that it did not become overheated.[5] Irrespective of whether or not this is correct, projecting the growth of a Tiger Economy at the compounding rate of 6.23 percent per annum would seem conservative based upon what has happened in South Korea and Taiwan before.

Table 29. GDP and population historical growth rates, 2003–2022

Year	Unit	2003	2004	2005	2006	2007	2008	2009	2010
GDP constant prices	% change	7.34	7.79	7.55	6.98	7.13	5.66	5.40	6.42
GDP current prices	US$ billion	50.2	62.8	73.2	84.3	98.4	124.8	129.0	143.2
GDP per capita current prices	US$	610	757	873	996	1,152	1,447	1,481	1,628
Population	million	82.3	83.0	83.8	84.6	85.4	86.2	87.0	88.0

Year	Unit	2011	2012	2013	2014	2015	2016	2017	2018
GDP constant prices	% change	6.41	5.51	5.55	6.42	6.99	6.69	6.94	7.20
GDP current prices	US$ billion	171.3	195.2	212.7	232.9	236.8	252.1	277.1	303.1
GDP per capita current prices	US$	1,950	2,198	2,370	2,567	2,582	2,720	2,958	3,202
Population	million	87.9	88.9	89.8	90.7	91.7	92.7	93.7	94.7

Year	Unit	2019	2020	2021	2022
GDP constant prices	% change	7.15	2.94	2.58	6.05
GDP current prices	US$ billion	327.9	342.9	366.2	408.9
GDP per capita current prices	US$	3,398	3,521	3,725	4,121
Population	million	96.5	97.4	98.3	99.2

Source: International Monetary Fund and the World Economic Outlook Database, April 2022.

Although this rate is also less than the 7.00 percent GDP per capita growth rate that the Vietnam government has announced it was targeting to 2030,[6] we remain comfortable that 6.23 percent annual growth is reasonable for the purposes of our analysis. However, to allow for some variation in the long-term average growth rates, we propose three slightly different growth scenarios to 2050. These are:

---

5. For example, controlling commercial bank lending through new loan quotas and imposing lending limits on sectors deemed to be higher risk.

6. 'Vietnam government announces annual 7% GDP growth target by 2030,' *Tuoi Tre*, April 21, 2023.

1. **The Base Case.** Over the next twenty-seven years, the economy will grow at the same rate as the previous twenty years (i.e., 6.23 percent per annum).
2. **The Conservative Case.** Over the next twenty-seven years, the economy will grow 1.0 percent slower than the base case (i.e., 5.23 percent per annum).
3. **The Aggressive Case.** Over the next twenty-seven years, the economy will grow 1.0 percent faster than the base case (i.e., 7.23 percent per annum).

We considered whether it would be appropriate to assume Vietnam's GDP growth rate in the 2030s and 2040s would slow on the basis that the economy would be much larger. However, after analysis of our case study comparatives, we found that this did not happen in South Korea and Taiwan. The growth rates in both countries did not begin to decline until well *after* each country had achieved high-income status. Hence it is reasonable to assume the growth rates in the three scenarios above can be applied on a constant basis until Vietnam surpasses the high-income threshold.

It took South Korea and Taiwan eight and nine years, respectively, to reach high-income status after each country had a GDP per capita of around US$4,100, which approximates the current GDP per capita of Vietnam. It would be very bold to claim that Vietnam can achieve the same status in a similar period, as Vietnam is unlikely to achieve the high growth rates that South Korea and Taiwan experienced before. We believe it will take longer, but what is important is it will get there. Vietnam has already demonstrated that it can achieve sustainable economic growth over several decades and the resources and comparative advantages that have contributed to this growth remain in place for the future. By our analysis, Vietnam will reach high-income status between 2035 (aggressive case) and 2045 (conservative case). Certainly, achieving high-income status by around the year 2040 (base case) will be a tremendous accomplishment.

Figure 13. Vietnam GDP per capita, 2001–2050 (in US$)

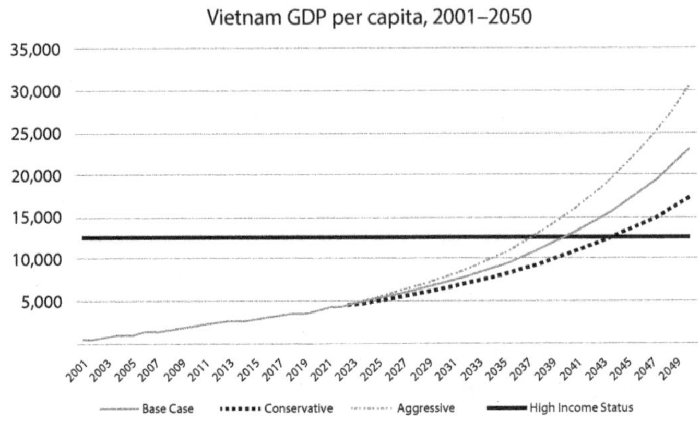

Vietnam GDP per capita, 2001–2050

——— Base Case   •••••• Conservative   ········· Aggressive   ▬▬▬ High Income Status

Source: The historical data for this chart was sourced from the International Monetary Fund, World Economic Outlook Database of April 2022, Vietnam GSO, and CEIC. The forecast data 2023–50 is from the authors' analysis.

Conclusion

Accept, Get over It, Reinvent

If the hypothesis holds true, Vietnam will be a high-income country by around the year 2040. Vietnam will be a success story that shows how a country can grow and develop from a war-torn state into one that thrives and offers its citizens the prospects for a good life. It will be healthy, engaged, and strong. Vietnam will be a fun place to visit, a great place to find smart and driven students, a profitable and safe place to do business, and a country that others want to trade with because it has a lot to offer. There will always be issues of disparity, roadblocks, environmental hurdles, corruption, and unclear policies, but the big picture will be positive.

The key reason for writing this book is to explain how Vietnam is becoming rich. By understanding the factors that are driving Vietnam's success, more people will be able to take advantage of the opportunities that are being created. This will help to ensure that the benefits are generated more quickly and shared more widely.

The world is full of countries that struggle to accept their place in the world. This could be because of their geography, history, relationships with border nations, and relations with other countries in the world. It could also be the work ethic, religion, and culture of their citizens. They want to find scapegoats rather than keep what they have and make the best of the hand they have been dealt.

The world is also full of countries that simply never get over a transgression from the past. This could be a border dispute due to a war long ago. It could be a war of words or a battle over history. Sometimes there is a cultural rift that gets wider over time because the rift becomes a central part of the country's character. Or more pervasively, the leaders of the country manipulate this rift to keep themselves in power while keeping their people in a place where they cannot grow and move forward.

The world is full of countries that cannot reinvent themselves for the reasons mentioned above and so they are stuck with the status quo. Reinvention is necessary for growth and development, but it takes courage, resolve, and more hard work and intention than some leaders and citizens are willing to put in. In these countries, there are enough people satisfied with the status quo to maintain it. There is no compelling reason to change or to do something new because it might put their position at risk and push the country into totally new, unpredictable, and potentially dangerous, territory.

Throughout its history, Vietnam has had to accept many things, ranging from its geographical location bordering China to its selection by European and North American powers as a location for a colonial outpost. These influences have impacted the country and could not be removed, so adaptation was needed. Vietnam has also had to get over the 'anticolonial-nationalist-communist' labels that were placed on it and hampered it from finding its own way. Starting on May 1, 1975, it had to deal with a post-civil war environment and bring two parts of the country together to create a single nation that could move forward. Rather than become mired in the past with a historical problem, it moved forward.

South Korea and Taiwan know what that is like because both have complicated unification issues, but they managed this issue well and simultaneously grew their economies. They learned how to maintain peace and move forward. Vietnam has too. Finally, and most importantly, the leaders of Vietnam had to accept that their efforts to build a healthy and prosperous country from 1975 to 1985 was a failure. It did not work. The country was moving backwards rather than forwards. They chose to wipe the slate clean and start over with Doi Moi. They had to reinvent themselves, and they did.

Whether Vietnam in 2050 will be a high-income country or not is an interesting question, but it is not the only question. The country's ability to accept, get over, and reinvent itself is part of the reason it might be destined to make it as a healthy and prosperous nation no matter the size of its economy or its GDP per capita by 2050.

For the readers of this book who have not yet visited Vietnam, we hope we have convinced you to come and see for yourselves this exciting nation. For readers who have a history with Vietnam as native Vietnamese or foreigners who have lived, worked, or visited the country, we hope this book has further convinced you of the need to stay or return to join in the building of this nation and sharing in its success.

ABBREVIATIONS AND ACRONYMS

AI	Artificial Intelligence
ARVN	Army of the Republic of Vietnam (South Vietnam)
ASEAN	Association of Southeast Asian Nations
BRICS	Brazil, Russia, India, China, and South Africa
BTA	Bilateral Trade Agreement
COP26	Conference of the Parties to the 26th meeting of the United Nations Climate Convention
COVAX	Covid-19 Vaccines Global Access
CPTPP	Comprehensive and Progressive Agreement for Trans-Pacific Partnership
DPP	Democratic Progressive Party (Taiwan)
EADM	East Asian Development Model
ESG	Environmental Social Governance
EU	European Union
FDI	Foreign Direct Investment
FII	Foreign Indirect Investment
FMCG	Fast Moving Consumer Goods
GDP	Gross Domestic Product
IFRS	International Financial Reporting Standards
IRRI	International Rice Research Institute (Philippines)
KMT	Kuomintang (Taiwan)
LSE	London Stock Exchange
MA	Master of Arts
MCN	Most Coveted Nation
MFN	Most Favored Nation

MOET	Ministry of Education and Training
MOU	Memorandum of Understanding
NGO	Non-Governmental Organization
NVL	Nguyen Van Linh and '*noi va lam*' [Vietnamese for 'speak and do']
NYSE	New York Stock Exchange
ODA	Official Development Aid
OECD	Organization for Economic Cooperation and Development
PISA	Program for International Student Assessment
PNTR	Permanent Normal Trade Relations
PPP	Purchasing Power Parity
QS	Quacquarelli Symonds (university education standard and listing)
RMIT	Royal Melbourne Institute of Technology
SCOV	State Commission for Overseas Vietnamese Affairs
SME	Small and Medium-sized Enterprise
SOE	State Owned Enterprise
TPP	Trans-Pacific Partnership
TSMC	Taiwan Semiconductor Manufacturing Company
VAS	Vietnam Accounting Standards
VAT	Value-Added Tax
VCP	Vietnam Community Party
WHO	World Health Organization
WTO	World Trade Organization

INDEX

Printed in the USA
CPSIA information can be obtained
at www.ICGtesting.com
LVHW041005010524
779021LV00014B/115